The Professional Practice of Design

To the memory of
Misha Black 1910–1977
who did so much
to establish and enhance
the design profession

Dorothy Goslett

The Professional Practice of Design

B T Batsford Limited London

Designed by Dieter Heil late of Design Research Unit
Photoset by Deltatype, Ellesmere Port
Printed in Great Britain by
Dotesios Ltd, Trowbridge, Wilts
for the Publishers
B T Batsford Limited
4 Fitzhardinge Street, London W1H 0AH

Contents

Acknowledgment   **9**

Foreword to the 1971 edition   **10**
Foreword to the 1978 edition   **11**
Foreword to the 1983 edition   **12**

Part One   **13**
Introduction   **14**

Chapter One   **Writing business letters**   **16**

Letterheads—Preliminaries—Dear Sir?—Drafting—A personal introduction—Layout—Lettering and numbering—Indenting—Style—Clichés—Polite conclusion—Ending the letter—The signature—Fastenings—Carrying on a correspondence—Our ref—Your ref—Content headings—Copies circulated—Continuity—Summing up

Chapter Two   **Being briefed**   **29**

Competitive clients—The contractual aspect of a brief—Asking questions at a briefing—How does your client brief?—The Professional Code again—Displacing another designer—Working for nothing—Diary notes

Chapter Three   **Writing letters about fees**   **36**

Finished working drawings—Adaptations etc.—Obtaining tenders and estimates—Supervising production and maintenance—Checking final accounts—Fees—Special clauses—Copyright—Breaking clauses and fees for abandoned work—Permitted modications—Free specimens—Signed work and design credits—Late information—Additional fees—Extra visits—Changes to brief—Extra work—Travelling time—Fee instalments—Special costs—Expenses and production costs—Request for written acceptance and conclusion—Special research, surveys and reports—Royalties

Chapter Four   **Estimating fees**   **63**

Fee categories—Lump sum or fixed fees—The time it will
take—Hourly rate fees—Fees at daily rates—Fees based on a
percentage of costs—A client's own materials and labour—Fees
for book illustration—Fees for textile design—Fees for dress and
fashion design—Fees according to circulation—Repetitive work
and multiple displays—Fees for contracting—Fees for attendance
at committees and panels—Fees for special research, surveys and
reports—Fees as royalties—Consultancy and retaining fees—
Sprats to catch mackerel—Reducing fees—Introductory commissions

Chapter Five   **Progressing work**   **76**

Job numbers—Progress charts—Date schedules—Time sheets—
Job sheets—Order books—Job files—Identification of drawings—Secrecy—Submitting preliminary designs—Approval of
designs—Verbal instructions and decisions—Diary notes—Development work—Submissions of finished work—Delivering
finished work—Checking proofs and prototypes

Chapter Six   **Simple report writing**   **87**

Design notes—A design report—First draft of the framework—
Second draft of the framework

Chapter Seven   **Contracting for a client**   **91**

Contracting procedure—The specification—A print specification—A display unit specification—Inviting tenders—Single tenders—Collating tenders and estimates—The covering letter—
Financial DANGER POINT—Your client's acceptance—Paying
bills for your client—Handling charges—Final accounts from
contractors and suppliers

Chapter Eight   **Invoicing**   **104**

When to invoice—Setting out an invoice—Invoicing lump-sum
fees—Invoicing hourly rates—Invoicing percentage fees—Other
invoicing and payment problems

Chapter Nine   **Finished work**   **110**

'Before and after' stories—Specimens of work in production—
Record photography—Your client's permission—Your press

list—Writing captions—Writing editorial notes—Sending material to the press—Press cuttings—Your slide and photo files—Work finished—Job histories

Part Two   **121**

Introduction   **122**

Chapter Ten   **Setting up a design office**   **123**

Position—Requirements—The lease—Your professional advisers—Getting a telephone installed—Registering a name—Nameplate and letterheading—Decorations—Light fittings—Furniture and fittings—Office and studio equipment—Floor covering and curtains—Filing—Cleaning—Amenities for your staff—A sole trader—A partnership—A limited company

Chapter Eleven   **A budget for the first year**   **135**

Your personal budget—Your capital outlay—Your overheads—Expenditure—Expenditure and revenue

Chapter Twelve   **Finding clients**   **145**

Action—The SIAD—The Design Council—Other organizations concerned with design—Promoting your services—The direct approach—Introductions—Following up—Artists' agents—Textile design—Working 'on spec'—Advertising—The third course of action—Local activities—Other designers and architects—Competitions—Publicizing your appointments—Finished jobs—Printed literature—Entertaining—Summary

Chapter Thirteen   **Running the office**   **159**

Bank accounts—Petty cash—Postages—Filing—Retention of letters and drawings—Paying bills—Book-keeping and accounts—Revenue and expenditure budget—Staff—Disabled staff—National Insurance—Maintenance

Chapter Fourteen   **Fee problems**   **170**

The cost of your time—The cost of time off—The overhead percentage—The profit margin—Work out your own—Retaining fees—Exclusive services—The value of your reputation—Consultancy fees—Fees for special meetings—Travelling time

Chapter Fifteen   **Survey reports 179**

The survey programme—Conclusions—Recommendations—A contents
page—Illustrations—Production and quantities—Strictly confidential

Chapter Sixteen   **Interior design and exhibition contracting 186
for a client**

Exhibition specifications—Interior design specifications—Tenders—Competitive and single—The quantity surveyor—Firm estimates and guess estimates—Collating tenders and estimates—Agent or Principal?—Interim payments—Final accounts and the QS—Defects liability period

Chapter Seventeen   **More about invoicing and getting paid 200**

Regularity of invoicing—Extra fees—Invoicing retainers and consultancies—
Renewals—Invoicing for interiors—A client's own materials and labour—
Invoicing for exhibitions—Records are vital—Statements—Credit notes—
Receipts—Debtors—References

Chapter Eighteen   **Estimating production costs 216**

Print—Price lists, catalogues and samples—Costs per square metre—Wage
awards and price increases—The quantity surveyor again—'. . . result happiness'

Chapter Nineteen   **Design and the law 220**

Safety regulations—Planning approvals—Patent agents—Types of industrial
property—New legislation—Patents—Registered designs—Trade marks—
Copyright—The copyright of photographs—Plagiarism—Arbitration—Summary

Bibliography 229

Appendix   **Some organizations concerned with design 231**

The Royal Society of Arts—The Design and Industries Association—The
Society of Industrial Artists and Designers—The Design Council—The
Institute of Contemporary Arts—The International Council of Societies of
Industrial Designers—The International Council of Graphic Design Associa-
tions—The Bureau of European Designers Associations—The International
Federation of Interior Designers

Index **255**

Acknowledgment

My grateful thanks are due first to the Society of Industrial Artists and Designers for being able to make such liberal use of all their available material; to Stanley Dehn and Mary Oliver MSIA for invaluable technical information; to the RSA, the DIA, the SIAD, the Design Council, the ICA, ICSID, ICOGRADA, and now BEDA and IFI, for allowing me to include them in the Appendix; to my many colleagues in Design Research Unit who, throughout twenty-five years of working with them, taught me so much of what is in this book, and finally to Michael Sadler-Forster BA, present Director of the SIAD for invaluable advice and help in connection with this 1983 edition.

Foreword to the 1971 edition

When I wrote the first version of this book in 1960 (then called *Professional Practice for Designers*) I did so in the hope that it would be of some use to freelance designers, except those old hands who had come up the hard way and had learnt it all by experience. There was little sign then that anyone had begun to realize that it was a subject which students needed to know about too.

But in ten years there has been a marked change. Great efforts are now being made to give students some knowledge of professional practice and design administration before they qualify as designers and I hope that the time is not far off when a professional practice examination may become obligatory.

To me, the most surprising and pleasurable aspect of the change has been to discover, during the lectures I have been privileged to give on the subject during the past decade, that students themselves seem eager for it, particularly those in their final year when the hard cold world is just round the corner.

When I was given the opportunity of revising the original book before it was republished, I decided therefore to take it to pieces and put it together again in two parts—the first mainly for students and the second for the practising freelance designer. At the same time I have brought up-to-date a lot of the original contents and added much new material to both parts. But there is a good deal of overlap between the two parts and for this I make no apology. The student who is interested and has time may find in Part Two more detailed information applicable to what he is studying in Part One. The practising designer who may have missed the opportunity of studying the subject at all during his period of training might consider reading Part One before Part Two since he will find that much of the former is a basis for the latter. Wherever possible I have cross-referenced the related information.

Foreword to the 1978 edition

Many changes in the seven years since the previous edition of this book was written have made revisions necessary. The most important were the significant changes made by the SIAD to its Code of Professional Conduct whereby designers were given much greater freedom to promote their services, even to the point of advertising them. This is reflected in a longer Chapter Twelve—'Finding Clients' where I have tried to suggest to the young free-lance designer how to make the best of his new-found freedoms and therefore, hopefully, to find clients more easily.

Changes in government have also brought changes in the names and sometimes the functions of government departments and official bodies referred to. Purchase Tax and Selective Employment Tax have gone, VAT is with us and metrication is imminent. As for inflation, it makes nonsense of any attempt on my part to suggest the sort of cost to put in a budget or the price of a useful book or advisory service. 'Probably not more than a few £'s' is the rather apologetic phrase I have often had to fall back on, knowing that if I had quoted an actual figure it might have increased even before this edition was in print. But if we are presently experiencing rapid changes, some of which we may not like, it may be comforting to look back to 1960, when the first version of this book was written and to realize the overwhelming changes and progress the design profession has made in those seventeen years. It is now an acknowledged and respected body, the SIAD has received its Royal Charter, the Design Council goes from strength to strength, the design schools and polytechnics are turning out well-trained intelligent designers in every field and the Royal College of Art in London is rated one of the best in the world. It would be hard these days to find an industrialist like the one I encountered all those years back who, when I mentioned that I was writing a text book for designers, asked me in all sincerity 'What *is* a designer? What does he *do*?'

Foreword to 1984 edition

Over the past few years further changes have been made by SIAD and other organizations with regard to professional practice, and new names concerned with design have come into being.

This 1984 edition includes material which is as up to date as possible to help the practising designer and the student alike.

Foreword to 1987 reprint

Please note that as from February 1987 the name of The Society of Industrial Artists and Designers (SIAD) has been changed to **The Chartered Society of Designers** so throughout the text for SIAD please read The Chartered Society of Designers and for MSIAD read MCSD.

Copies of their updated *Code of Professional Conduct* are obtainable from their new address: 29 Bedford Square, London WC1B 3EG.

Telephone: 01–631 1510.

Part One

Introduction

This part of the book is meant primarily for students, tutors and lecturers. It aims to give basic facts and advice about the administration of design jobs and the Clauses, as and when they apply, of the Code of Professional Conduct of the Society of Industrial Artists and Designers (SIAD), the designer's professional Society. The full Code will be found in the Appendix, page 238, together with a lot more information about the Society and about other organizations concerned with design.

Every job of designing something by a designer for a client goes through three phases in the designer's office and each of these three phases again divides into three. This invariable sequence of events can be set out as a simple pattern or chart which could provide a framework for a basic course of study. This is particularly useful as the pattern is one which must be constantly kept in mind by the practising designer as well, whether the job he is working through is interior design with a five-figure fee or a letter-heading for a few pounds, an egg-cup or an aeroplane, a pack or a power station.

The pattern may change a little according to the job but the sequence of the phases will never change. Each phase should start as the previous one is completed, in logical order. For a small quick job, it may be possible to work through the phases in a matter of weeks. For a very big complex interior design job, it may take several years to get from the beginning of Phase One to the end of Phase Three.

However short or however long the time span, the successful administration of a design job according to the pattern should make a considerable contribution to the success of the design work itself. It should provide you, the designer, with an orderly framework in which to do your creative best; which you will seldom if ever be able to do in a chaos.

Many designers, though admitting its necessity, think that design administration is boring, a tiresome chore always to be put aside for doing second if something more exciting crops up to be done first. But good design + good administration = good fees well-earned.

That equation provides yet another threesome, the components of which all emerge at the appropriate points in the pattern to remind you how and when to act in order to achieve the equation.

It can also provide what management consultants' jargon calls 'job satisfaction' and it will undoubtedly collect for you an increasing number of satisfied clients as well.

Here then is the pattern set out as a chart. A blow-up of it might be a useful visual aid for a course of lectures.

The anatomy of design administration

Phase One The fee contract	(a) Being briefed
	(b) Writing the fee letter
	(c) After any intermediate negotiations, receiving the written acceptance of it
Phase Two Progressing the job	(a) Setting up the job, research, preparation and submission of preliminary designs, followed by first invoice
	(b) Design development followed by subsequent invoice/s
	(c) Finished working drawings, supervision of production, followed by subsequent invoice/s
Phase Three Winding up	(a) Publicizing the job
	(b) Final invoice
	(c) Filing essential records

Each phase on the chart will be referred to in the following chapters as it is reached and as it is completed. But Chapter One steps aside as a preliminary exercise on writing business letters. Few students are likely to have had much experience of this essential activity. They cannot therefore be expected to plunge into the considerable complexities of fee letter writing unless they have had some practice in writing business letters in general.

15

Every design career probably starts with writing a business letter—applying for a job, replying to an advertisement, writing a fee letter for a first free-lance commission.

Is it so different from writing to a relative or friend? Yes, essentially so. A personal letter can ramble on, jump from one snippet of news to another, express emotions, even be badly written and mis-spelt, because it is usually meant to be read only by one person who will probably forgive its shortcomings for the pleasure of receiving it.

But a business letter must above all things communicate. The way it looks must communicate your ability as a designer to design it and lay it out. What it says must communicate precisely who you are, the reason for writing and the information you are giving or for which you are asking.

Nowhere are first impressions more important than in respect of a first letter from a designer. A professionally-designed letterhead, a good typed lay-out and a concisely and logically worded text will always engender in the recipient even a faint feeling of respect and interest and your first important lines of communication will have been laid.

Letterheads

First your letter-head. If you are a graphic designer this will present no problem. But if you are not, get someone on the graphic side to rough something out for you and advise you how to get it printed. This is well worth doing as soon as you can possibly afford it and have got a reasonably permanent address from which to write.

But do aim first at a very simple almost conventional design. The gimmicky ones can be rather irritating to the conservative business man and in any case they quickly look dated and then rather tiresome. If you can't afford a printed letter-head at first then a well-typed one will serve and as a last resort a handwritten one.

Whether or not you start with a printed letter-head, try to have the letter itself typed. It will look much more professional and business-like, the problem of difficult-to-read handwriting will not arise and you will be able to keep a carbon copy which is essential when you write a contract letter of any kind—fees, placing or accepting an order, etc.

What are the essential ingredients of your letter-head?

Your first name and surname:	John Smith
Any professional letters after them:	MSIAD
What you do:	Furniture designer
Your address:	15 Main Street Westby Eastshire
Your phone number:	Westby 1234

Give the appropriate postal code after your address and STD (subscriber trunk dialling) number *between* the name of your exchange and your personal numbers. It is usually put in brackets to avoid confusing the two numbers, as you see below.

If your letter-head has to be a typed or handwritten one, then it could be something like this:

John Smith MSIAD Furniture Designer 15 Main Street
                                               Westby
                                               Eastshire AB2 CD3
                                               Westby (34567) 1234

Punctuation can be almost completely eliminated from your letter-head. It will look pleasantly uncluttered without it and is really quite unnecessary.

If a hand-written letter is the only course open to you, then you simply *must* make a copy if it is a letter about fees or a contract, however simple, or accepting a job. Later on in Chapter Three you will see why this is so important.

Preliminaries

Now for the letter itself but first the preliminaries—the date, the name and address of the person you are writing to and the way in which you address him. The date nowadays needs no punctuation and the th's and st's can be left out: simply 21 May 19xx. It is a good idea to put ιne month in the middle to separate visually the figures of the day and year.

You will be addressing your letter either to a firm or association or to a department of either; to someone whose function you know—the Managing Director, the Sales Manager, the Personnel Officer, but whose name you do not. Or to someone whose name you already know or partially know. It is discourteous not to bother to get such a name correctly at the head of your letter and it is quite in order to ring his office and ask his secretary for the correct rendering of his title if he has one, his name and how he spells it and any letters after it. The name of the firm must also be correctly set out and obviously the address. So these various alternatives might give you:

Midland Furniture Company Limited	Design Department
Westgate Works	Midland Furniture Company Limited
Westby, Eastshire	Westgate Works
	Westby, Eastshire

The Managing Director
Midland Furniture Company Limited
Westgate Works
Westby, Eastshire

Sir Thomas Jones, ABC, DEF, etc.
Midland Furniture Company Limited
Westgate Works
Westby, Eastshire

Thomas Jones Esq (or Mr Thomas Jones)
Midland Furniture Company Limited
Westgate Works
Westby, Eastshire

The old-fashioned 'Messrs' in front of a firm's name is usually left out nowadays and you can put Co. Ltd for Company Limited. But I personally think that abbreviations should be avoided as much as possible. They tend to make a letter look jerky and slovenly and spoil its style.

As you will see in the fifth alternative you can either address Thomas Jones as 'Esq' or 'Mr'. The former is traditional in this country and completely acceptable but the latter, which I think started in America, is becoming equally acceptable. So the choice is yours. Notice that again almost all punctuation can be left out to maintain the desirable uncluttered look.

Dear Sir?

The problem of how you start your letter is solved by following a more or less established drill.

If you are writing to a firm or association or Government Department or Local Authority: Dear Sirs. If you are writing to a functionary (Managing Director, Sales Manager, etc.): Dear Sir (or Dear Madam if it were a fashion buyer or suchlike).

If you are writing to someone whose name you know but whom you have never met: Dear Sir or Dear Madam.

If you are writing to someone you have not met but have spoken to on the telephone or to whom you have been given a personal introduction: Dear Sir Thomas or Dear Mr Jones or Dear Miss Jones. When you get to know your clients and contractors really well, then it can be Dear Tom. But not too soon. The thing about switching to Christian names in business relationships is very subtle. It must be mutually acceptable and appropriate. Sir Thomas Jones, an important businessman in his 60's might well start calling you John in easy friendly fashion soon after you start working for him. But for you to start calling him Tom to his face or in a letter might be tactless and resented. You have to learn to play it by ear.

Drafting

Now comes the content of the letter itself. Until you become an expert at this, *always* draft the letter first. Then you can make as many mistakes and corrections as you like and go on refining and polishing until you have got it to your liking. Even when you are quite an experienced letter writer there are some tricky letters which are much better drafted first particularly those about fees or applying for a job.

You will also find it a great help to jot down first the bare headings of what you want to say in the letter. This will enable you to juggle them round until you get them in the right logical sequence and will give you a useful framework for the letter. For instance if you are writing for a first interview, your framework might be:

Say who you are and what you do
Why you are writing—interview
Reasons for being interested in working for his firm
Age
Your education, training and qualifications
Jobs you have had, if any
Married or not, children (if applying for a staff job)
Your availability for interview
Polite conclusion

Or suppose you are writing to a firm or association for some information you need for a project you are working on:

Say who you are and what you do
Why you are writing—information for your project
Ask for catalogues, samples, literature
Offer to pay costs/postage (or not as the case may be)
Polite conclusion

A personal introduction

A letter taking up a personal introduction would be a useful one for you and it would be important to get the first paragraph right. If a friend of *yours*, say Bill Smith, had told you to get in touch with a friend of *his*, say John Brown, because he knew he was looking for a designer, the link between the three of you must be established to ensure that you get a positive response which means an interview. So your first paragraph might be:

'Our mutual friend, Bill Smith, has suggested that I should write to you as he knows that you are looking for a designer for etc. etc.'

There seems to be a pleasant unwritten law that a personal introduction of this kind from one friend to another implies an obligation on the recipient to grant the interview. And after all, why not? Each party to the operation hopes to be doing the other a service. Bill Smith knows you are a promising designer, would like to help you get a job and wants to get you in touch with his friend John Brown who needs one. John Brown is quite ready to do his friend Bill Smith a favour by interviewing you and will be glad if he fills a vacancy at the same time.

Incidentally it is wise never to take up such an introduction by phone, when you might catch John Brown or his secretary in too busy a moment for them to deal with you. A letter can wait on his desk until he has time to consider it and reply.

Having set out the framework of your letter and got it to your liking now you can draft it with confidence that the contents will be on the right lines. There remain the two important points of layout and style to be attended to.

Layout

As I said earlier the way a business letter looks is always important but particularly so when it comes from a designer who should demonstrate that he knows how to solve this simple problem of communication if he expects to be commissioned to solve much more complicated ones for his clients.

However short, however long, a letter should first look inviting to read and this means lots of air and space, wide margins on either side, space at the top, plenty of space at the bottom (don't finish up so near the bottom edge of the page that it looks as if you couldn't afford a continuation sheet or just couldn't be bothered).

There should be plenty of paragraphs, preferably short ones, and sub-paragraphs if necessary and the latter should be lettered and/or numbered.

Lettering and numbering

Why use lettered or numbered paragraphs in a business letter or for that matter in any business document? There are three reasons: first for cross-reference within the letter or document itself. It is much more concise to be able to say 'I do not advise this for the reasons given in Para. 5' instead of 'for the reasons given in the seventh paragraph from the top of page 3'. Second, for the similarly convenient use of the recipient who may want to reply by letter or telephone and say 'I agree with everything except your Para. 8 because etc.' Third, it helps to give your letter form and structure and almost disciplines you into a logical sequence and lay-out.

There are a number of permutations for lettering and numbering. You can use capital letters only, lower case letters only or both together. You can use Arabic numerals only—1, 2, 3, 4 and (1) (2) (3) (4) or Roman ones: I, II, III, IV and (i) (ii) (iii) and (iv) or any mixture of letters and numerals. But the more the mixture, the less the clarity. The one method which avoids the mixture problem is the increasingly used decimal system of numbering. More of this later but first one absolutely essential rule. You must never repeat in its entirety any single letter or number or combination of both. For instance, a letter might read

My fees for this work would be
1 £xx for preliminary designs
2 £xx for development work
3 £xx for finished working drawings

My costs and expenses chargeable would be

1 Making a scale model £xx
2 Travelling expenses £xx
3 Long distance phone calls £xx

By using 1, 2 and 3 twice, both you and the recipient of your letter would be unable to refer to the correct paragraph if this were necessary. But now let's try again:

1 My fees for this work would be
   (1) £xx for preliminary designs
   (2) £xx for development work
   (3) £xx for finished working drawings

2 My costs and expenses chargeable would be
   (1) Making a scale model £xx
   (2) Travelling expenses £xx
   (3) Long distance phone calls £xx

But, you will say, we've still got two sets of the same numbers (1) (2) and (3). Yes but each set is what is called 'mastered' by its own different number, in this case 1 and 2. So that it is quite clear and easy to refer to Para. 1 (1) or Para. 1 (2) and so on. It is obvious that the brackets are necessary when you use numerals only. Without them Para. 11 would read as Para. eleven. With letters only it is not so necessary since Aa, Bb are quite clear; so is 1a, 1b, 2c and so on.
In a short letter with paragraphs only and no sub-paragraphs numbering is usually unnecessary. If you need only one set of sub-paragraphs in any letter the sub-paragraphs only could be numbered, the rest left un-numbered. But as soon as you need more than one set of sub-paragraphs, then the governing paragraphs must be given a mastering number or letter, as we saw above. In this case it might look better to number all the paragraphs right through from first to last.
By the way, do not use capital letters for lettering which is going to run over eight items because then you will have to use a capital I which will be confused with the numeral one.
Here is a little chart to show you some alternative ways of numbering a letter with more than one set of sub-paragraphs, reading downwards:

Dear Mr XYZ

Heading

Paragraph	1	1	1	A	A
Paragraph	2	2	2	B	B
Paragraph	3	3	3	C	C
Sub-paragraph	(i)	(1)	(a)	(1)	(a)

21

	Col 1	Col 2	Col 3	Col 4	Col 5
Sub-paragraph	(ii)	(2)	(b)	(2)	(b)
Paragraph	4	4	4	D	D
Sub-paragraph	(i)	(1)	(a)	(1)	(a)
Sub-paragraph	(ii)	(2)	(b)	(2)	(b)
Sub-paragraph	(iii)	(3)	(c)	(3)	(c)
Sub-paragraph	(iv)	(4)	(d)	(4)	(d)
Paragraph	5	5	5	E	E
Yours etc.					

A very long letter, as some fee letters often are, should always have some sub-headings to break the visual monotony and give the reader a first quick grasp of the contents. The presence of these sub-headings in amongst the paragraphs and sub-paragraphs needs another look at the numbering/lettering methods. It is quite appropriate to number/letter only the sub-headings and their following paragraphs and sub-paragraphs on the assumption that the first and last paragraphs will be largely introductory and concluding. This method is shown in the first, second and third columns in the chart which follows. The fourth column shows what is probably the best way to number a sub-headed letter or document, that is by continuous numbering of all paragraphs, appropriate sub-numbering of all sub-paragraphs and leaving out numbers against sub-headings altogether. This may look odd in the diagram but works very well when applied to the actual text of a letter or report.

The fifth column gives you a first sight of decimal numbering which looks easy, is more complicated to use than it appears and can be rather too space-consuming in a letter. It is best kept for longer papers, reports and suchlike about which there is more in Chapters Six and Fifteen.

Dear Mr XYZ

Heading

	Col 1	Col 2	Col 3	Col 4	Col 5
Paragraph				1	1
Paragraph				2	2
Sub-heading	A	A	1	–	3
Paragraph	1	1	(a)	3	3.1
Sub-paragraph	(i)	(a)	(i)	(a)	3.1.0
Sub-paragraph	(ii)	(b)	(ii)	(b)	3.1.1
Paragraph	2	3	(b)	4	3.2
Sub-heading	B	B	2	–	4
Paragraph	1	1	(a)	5	4.1
Paragraph	2	2	(b)	6	4.2
Sub-paragraph	(i)	(a)	(i)	(a)	4.2.0
Sub-paragraph	(ii)	(b)	(ii)	(b)	4.2.1
Sub-paragraph	(iii)	(c)	(iii)	(c)	4.2.2
Sub-heading	C	C	3	–	5
Paragraph	1	1	(a)	7	5.1

Paragraph	2	2	(b)	8	5.2
Paragraph	3	3	(c)	9	5.3
Paragraph				10	6

It is very useful to master and learn to use the various ways of numbering/lettering I have outlined above. But when you have learnt them, use them with discretion. They can help to clarify the structure of a complicated letter or paper. Equally they can complicate a visually simple paper.

Indenting

The typing of business letters is now usually done without any indentations for paragraphs and this makes for a neat chunky lay-out which can look pleasing and readable particularly if the paragraphs are short. But if you prefer to be an 'indenter' at least be a consistent one and keep to the same degree of indentation throughout. Keep also the same visual vertical relationship between the main blocks of writing or typing—your address, the date, his address, the heading if any (more about this below), the 'yours truly' bit and your signature. Then it will have a coherent pattern as well as a coherence in the text.

Style

Now a pointer or two about style, which is all that there is room for because it is a big subject. You must obviously express yourself in your own personal way but there is one golden rule to follow which will always give style to your own way of writing a business letter and that is—short words, short sentences and no clichés.

Short words and sentences first. If you find yourself drafting 'and I could commence the work on . . .' cross out 'commence' and substitute 'start' or 'begin'. 'I am writing to you with reference to . . .' reads much better as 'I am writing to you about . . .'. 'Thank you for your letter of 1 June' is shorter than 'I am in receipt of your letter of 1 June' and much crisper.

Here is an unnecessarily long sentence: 'After two years I left my first job at John Brown and joined Smith & Jones as chief designer where there was already a small design department which needed building up because the firm was beginning to go into overseas markets and needed to have most of its specialized products specially designed for individual customers'.

Now let's do a bit of pruning and re-arranging and see what we get: 'After two years at John Brown I left to join Smith & Jones as chief designer. Their small design department needed building up to meet the increasing demands of overseas customers for whom most products had to be specially designed'.

Fifty-five words in the first paragraph and forty in the second which conveys exactly the same information as the first but in clearer crisper style. It isn't a trick, it merely means disciplining yourself in your business letter writing to take a long hard look at every word and every sentence you draft. The process of pruning and refining can fairly quickly become a useful habit.

Clichés

A cliché is the French word for a printing stereo, something which can be reproduced hundreds of times. This is presumably why it is also used in English to describe a hackneyed phrase, something which has been said and written so often that it has got worn at the edges and lost all its initial meaning and vigour. We all use clichés all of the time without realizing we have got the habit but they become horribly apparent in business letters and add nothing to one's style.

The sort of clichés to watch out for in a business letter would be:

in this day and age	Say instead	now or today
last but not least		finally
few and far between		rare or infrequent
I will endeavour to ascertain		I will try to find out
it is obvious that		obviously
a certain amount of		some
in the majority of instances		most
and so on		

There is a splendid paperback by Sir Ernest Gowers called 'The Complete Plain Words' which is not only very useful for the business letter and report writer but often very entertaining as well. Don't miss the child's written description of a cow on page 70.

Polite conclusion

I referred further back under 'Drafting' to 'polite conclusion'. Although when you have said what you have to say in a business letter there is no reason why you should not go straight to the appropriate ending: yours truly, yours sincerely, this can sometimes seem a little abrupt. A final paragraph of only a sentence or two can dispel this impression. According to the circumstances your polite conclusion could be on the following lines:

I look forward to hearing from you . . .

Please let me know if there is any more information you would like . . .

I look forward to meeting you next week . . .

and when you are getting to know your correspondent better

With kind regards . . .

With my best wishes . . .

Admittedly all these polite conclusions are getting perilously near to being clichés but this seems to be inevitable in this context. But one can easily slither right over the edge with such horrible phrases as

Assuring you of our best attention at all times . . .

We await the favour of your reply . . .

and so on.

Ending the letter

If you have started your letter Dear Sir or Sirs or Dear Madam, you should end it Yours faithfully or Yours truly. The former is the most impersonal of the two and is generally used when you are writing to a firm. The other can be used when you are writing to an individual by name or function but whom you do not know at all.

If you have started your letter Dear Mr Jones whom you may know slightly or through a personal introduction or to whom you have already spoken on the telephone, then end your letter Yours sincerely. These are curious and illogical conventions but at least they provide you with a pattern to follow without the need to make tortuous decisions every time you write a business letter.

The signature

Then comes your signature and you might think that that was the end of it, but no. *You* may assume that your signature is exquisitely legible but to everyone else who reads it for the first time it may be in Urdu or Sanscrit for all they know. This is a curious phenomenon but an actual one of which I have personal experience both as a writer and recipient of business letters.

The simple but *essential* solution, when you are writing to someone for the first time (and for two or three times more until visual familiarity is established) is to type your name beneath your signature or write it in capital letters if you are having to handwrite your letter. A woman should add Miss or Mrs in brackets after her signature for the first few times to save the recipient the embarrassment of not knowing how to address her in the reply.

So you would end thus:

Yours faithfully   Yours faithfully
(normal signature)   (normal signature)
John Jones   Mary Jones (Miss)

If you are in a staff job where you have an agreed status or job title then it helps the recipient to whom you are a stranger to know what this is and again it should be typed beneath your typed signature, so:

Yours faithfully   Yours faithfully
(normal signature)   (normal signature)
John Jones   Mary Jones (Miss)
Assistant designer   Production assistant

In the absence of any status or job title in a big organization, it helps to put your department beneath your typed signature: Design Department, Research Department, etc.

Fastenings

If your letter has run on to a second sheet, always fasten the two together, either with a pin, a paper clip or best of all with a stapler. If two pages of a letter once get separated in a pile of correspondence or in circulation from one department to another they may never come together again and then both are meaningless. Having fastened the letter together are you also going to enclose something with it? A copy of a reference, a letter of introduction, a press-cutting about yourself or what is known as s.a.e. (stamped addressed envelope) might have to go into the envelope and this should be paper-clipped to the letter so that it can be easily removed.

Now at last everything goes into the evelope which should carry the full name and address as already at the top of your letter and again with due regard to lay-out.

Don't   But
type it   like
like   this.
this!

Carrying on a correspondence

Everything I have explained so far applies to a first letter to anyone and indeed to all subsequent ones (except for the diminishing necessity for having to identify yourself beneath your signature).

But when you get a reply then you have to write again and a correspondence starts which may last for weeks and months. There are a few more useful things to know relevant to carrying on a correspondence.

Our ref, your ref

You will often see these mysterious words at the top of a printed letter-heading with space left for filling in alongside each 'ref.'. The minimum filling-in can be just two sets of initials, say RGB/IS. Quite meaningless to you on the face of it until you know the trick. The first initials are always those of the writer of the letter, the second those of the secretary who typed it. So if *you* get a letter with an illegible signature to it you can ring the firm and tell the telephonist that you have a letter from someone whose initials are RCB but you can't read his signature. Who is he, please? Oh, she will say right away, that's Mr Ronald Carter-Brown, I'll put you through to him.

Some 'our refs' can however be much more lengthy and quite incomprehensible, particularly from Government Departments and Local Authorities. They usually indicate the coding of the file which has been started to contain your first letter and all subsequent correspondence with you. It is therefore very important for you to quote this coding on all your replies so that the file, the department, the section, the man can be easily identified by the central registry and your letter get on to his desk as quickly as possible. This system is also used by some very large commercial and industrial firms with offices, departments, factories all over the place so again it will expedite your letter to use 'our ref' when you reply although in your letter it will go against 'your ref.' And what about your own 'our ref?' In a design office which gets itself organized as it grows, the most that might be necessary would be a job number (see Chapter Five) and the writer's and secretary's initials. This will always be useful even for the simplest filing system and if you want to cut a dash in the early days, can look impressively efficient.

Content headings

Another identification device when a correspondence gets going is to give your letter a subject heading which describes what the contents are about in the fewest possible words. Then the busy recipient can know at a glance which letters must be dealt with urgently and which can go on the 'slow' pile for later action. This is particularly useful when you are writing to big contractors and suppliers and very helpful for filing purposes. The heading goes after the 'Dear Sir' or 'Dear Mr Jones' part and is also usually underlined. For example:

Dear Sirs
Exhibit for Tropax Ltd at Ideal Home Exhibition
Thank you for your letter of 1 October about the above exhibition, etc.

Copies circulated
It is often necessary to send a copy of a letter you are writing to one or more people other than the recipient. Sometimes for political reasons you don't want the recipient to know about this but when you do you should either say in the body of the letter that you are sending a copy to so-and-so or you can put a footnote at the bottom of the letter:

Copies to: Mr J. Jones
         Miss G. Smith
         etc.

The word 'copies' is often abbreviated to cc in this context.

Continuity
A business correspondence on a given subject is, or should be, a continuous written record on the files at each end of it of who said what and who confirmed that this or that would be or had been done. Not only is this essential for current references while the situation is still live but very useful for subsequent records. It could be vital for legal purposes if something had gone wrong somewhere and an irate somebody was threatening to sue everybody in sight. For this reason I think it is useful to see that every letter you write maintains this continuity in its first and final paragraphs. In the first paragraph you refer *back* to the date of the last letter you received, to which you are now replying, or to the date of a meeting at which agreements were made which you are now confirming. Sometimes, alas, you may have to refer back to the date of the last letter you wrote and to which you still have had no reply after two or three weeks.
In the final paragraph you refer *forward* to the action you anticipate or which you yourself will take or the date by which you need a reply or a decision and so on.

Summing up
The writing of business letters may sound to be dauntingly complicated to the beginner but it is surprising how quickly you can acquire the facility by sticking

to the rules I have suggested. Then you can begin to ease the rules and relax into a more personal style.

The business letter which is easy, pleasant, concise, logical and written much as you would talk but minus the slang, clichés and most of the colloquialisms you would normally use in speech, will always be acceptable and impressive to receive particularly when its contents are enhanced by a designer's expertise in its visual presentation.

Let us assume that you suddenly get a firm enquiry for your design services. It may come by telephone or letter. In either case the enquirer may start by saying 'What would your fees be for designing our . . . ?' He may then give very sketchy details about the job or he may give none. Even if he gives what might appear to be adequate details it is a golden rule *never* to quote fees off the cuff however hard you may be pressed to do so. 'Just give us an idea' he will say. But you must not be tempted. If the job seems an exciting one and you want it badly you may panic and quote much too low a fee which will be your loss. Or much too high a fee which may mean the loss of the job. No design fee should ever be quoted until after a briefing meeting and then always in writing.

Competitive clients
When you have your first approach from a client this is also the first point at which you, as a present or future member of the SIAD, may have to consider Clause 8 of the Society's Code of Professional Conduct which says:

'No member may work simultaneously for more than one employer or client known to be in competition, without their knowledge and approval.'

Your enquirer will have made himself known to you as, say, a manufacturer of electrical appliances. And you are already working for another manufacturer in that field. So straight away you must make this known to your enquirer with discreet but sufficient information as to who you are working for, to enable him to judge whether there would be direct competition. If he thinks there is, then alas for you, the enquiry would end there. But he might be open-minded about it and think that a briefing meeting would be worth while. That would not let you out completely. Further on in this chapter I shall return to your responsibilities under this Clause of the Code and another which should be observed in this phase of operation.
So you will have replied to your written or telephoned enquiry by asking for a briefing meeting and preferably on your enquirer's home ground. As well as collecting your briefing information this will enable you to get some idea of the firm and its capacity and of the people with whom you might be working. If the meeting is arranged on the telephone and if there is time, there should be a note from you confirming the date, time and place. This is the beginning of Phase One (a) on the chart on page 15.

The contractual aspect of a brief

Now I am going to jump ahead a little in order to show why a briefing meeting is so important from a contractual and therefore almost legal point of view. You are briefed by a client. You quote a fee for doing what you have been briefed to do, at the same time summarizing the brief in writing. Your fee is accepted and you prepare the preliminary designs for the agreed preliminary fee and submit them to your client. If he likes them unreservedly he instructs you to go ahead to the next stage of the work, i.e. development drawings, prototypes or finished working drawings. There are then no complications about brief or fees. If he thinks your preliminary designs have fulfilled an admittedly difficult brief and he likes them he may ask you for reasons of his own to amend one or two aspects of them and show him revised preliminary designs before he decides to ask you to go ahead to the next stage. For this extra work you would be justified in charging an extra fee, if as I said, the reasons for the amendments were your client's own. If however he points out and your conscience agrees that you have gone enthusiastically but perhaps misguidedly well outside the agreed brief and your client wants amendments for that reason then you will have to make them free of any extra fee. Finally if your client unhappily does not like any of your preliminary designs but if he is honest and reasonable, he will either call it a day and pay you off with the agreed fee or give you another chance for further fees to be negotiated. If he is neither reasonable nor honest, he will just say that he does not like them, that you have not done what he asked, that he will not pay your fees or that you must start again for nothing.

'. . . that you have not done what he asked'. That brings us full circle to the original briefing again. If you have extracted all the information you can get out of him by asking the right questions and then confirmed the brief in writing when you quoted your fees; if he has accepted your fee letter in writing; if you have submitted to him preliminary designs which fulfil that brief to the very best of your ability, then you could take him to court for his refusal to pay your fees.

That sounds drastic and fortunately very seldom happens but there are manufacturers who can still act in that way, more from stupidity than dishonesty and usually those who have never before employed the services of a professional designer. Some clients may genuinely but mistakenly feel that a designer has not fulfilled a brief and then your only protection is the detailed notes you have taken *and confirmed* to him. It would be no use arguing the case without them.

There is one other thing that may happen. Your preliminary designs are approved and you are instructed to go ahead to the next stage. Suddenly the firm may have to change its policy and this may radically affect your designs. There may have been a merger which changes the company's title on your letter-heading layout. There may have been a hold-up in production which prevents a new product being displayed on the exhibition stand you have designed. Anything like this means that you may have to be briefed anew and perhaps begin your design work again from scratch. When you confirm your second briefing in writing to your client you must also indicate the extent to which it differs from the first and the further fee which may be payable.

I hope I have shown how important are your briefing meetings and notes. Once agreed in writing they protect both you and your client and form the basis of the whole contract between you. You are able to say, in effect, 'This is what you have asked me to do; therefore this is what my fees will be for doing it', and you can only properly make that statement in that order.

Asking questions at a briefing

If you feel that you are likely to be nervous at a briefing it is a good idea to try and think up in advance all the questions about the job to which you will want answers and to make a written list of them in your notebook or on your clipboard.

As this is not a book about design I am not going to suggest what detailed technical questions you should ask. You will know all about those. But here are some suggestions for more general questions under various headings.

. . . about product design

What class of purchaser is aimed at—low, middle or high income group? Is the product for home sale only or also for export? What is to be the maximum production cost or selling price? Who are the chief competitors, at home and overseas?

What is the latest date for the product to go into production?

Has the client any surveys, reports or advertising material which might be useful?

Is liaison with the client's advertising agents a good idea? Will the new product be launched with an advertising campaign?

How will the product be packed, displayed? Will it have any supporting graphic material—explanatory leaflet, swing ticket, instructions for use?

Is there a trade mark or symbol which must be incorporated within the design concept?

Are there any colour limitations? If for export, are there any special colour taboos? Are there any accessory limitations—knobs, handles, fastenings, etc.?

Is there to be a range of sizes? If for export, are there foreign sizes or dimensions to be observed?

If prototypes are required, will the client arrange for these to be made, or will you be required to get them made under your supervision?

If final engineering drawings are required, will these be done in the client's own drawing offices or by you?

. . . about graphic design

What is the impression to be conveyed—prestige, elegance, luxury, practicality?

Is the appeal to be to one sex more than the other? To a special age or income group? A special section of the community?

What are the titles and text likely to be? How long?
Is there an existing trade mark, symbol or logotype to be used?
Could they be re-designed, re-drawn?
Should layouts allow for over-printings, variations in size? What quality of paper? Card?
If a house style is being designed, to what things other than print may it eventually have to be adapted—transport fleet, outside signs, on an actual product, in glass, metal, plastics?
Must continuity with an existing style be maintained or can the new design break completely with tradition?
How many colours may be used? Can embossing be used?
What are the required dimensions? Range of sizes?
Has the client his own printer? If so, can he be approached for information about type faces, processes? Name, address, contact?
If a pack, where does it sell? Self-service shops? At home, abroad? Competitors?
Is more than one language to be allowed for?
Will absolutely final text be provided? By when?

. . . about exhibition and display design
Are the organizers' site plans and regulations available? If not, will the client, as exhibitor, obtain them or should you?
What is the main impression to be conveyed—prestige, hard-selling?
Is there a budget for design and production?
What of the client's own material is to be displayed—exhibits, models, charts, diagrams, photographs?
Are dimensions and weights of exhibits, models, etc. available? Are they to be working or static? If working, what are their power requirements? Can they be inspected or are photographs of them available?
Must the exhibit tell a 'story' with titles, and sub-titles, copy, captions? If so, to about what length and who will write it? Is more than one language required?
How many of the client's staff will be on the stand at any one time?
Is an interviewing area required? A separate office? Facilities for typing?
How many telephones? Is storage space required for samples, leaflets?
Are leaflets to be displayed—for selective give-away or help-yourself?
Are drinks or tea to be served on the stand? If so, does the client want full facilities for this purpose—sink, hot water, refrigerator, lock-up drink cupboard?

. . . about interior design
Are structural alterations envisaged?
Has the client a house architect?
What is the proposed budget?
Are survey drawings available?
How many people will use the space? What are their functions?
What are their operational requirements?

How much storage space is required?
How many telephones? Where?
Are there any 'musts' to be used or displayed?
If any existing furniture must be retained, can it be refurbished, re-sprayed, re-upholstered?
Are there any names, titles or text to appear anywhere—name of firm or product, directional signs?
Has the client a pet contractor who must be used?

How does your client brief?
There are broadly three different kinds of client you are likely to encounter at a briefing meeting. The first will know precisely what he wants and will brief you in clear-cut detail with every *t* crossed and *i* dotted. It seems as if he hardly needs a designer—he could do it himself and it may result in a rather dull assignment unless you are clever enough to wriggle out of the strait-jacket at the design stage without having appeared to do so. At the other extreme is the client who does not seem to have any ideas at all about the problem and blandly leaves it all to you—a wide-open brief. This sounds perfect and sometimes is. But he is a client to be treated with special caution at the briefing stage. He may not have faced up at all to the problem in question and be in a muddled indeterminate state of mind about it. When he sees your preliminary designs however, they may begin to crystallize his thoughts for him and he may say that that is what he does *not* want. Then you will be in trouble unless you have done your utmost to drag information out of him at the initial meeting and confirmed to him in writing such brief as there is, making it clear at the same time that you have been given a very free hand. Finally in the middle is the perfect briefer—one who states the problem clearly, indicates the essential limitations but makes you aware that within them your design ideas will be respected as coming from an experienced specialist.

The Professional Code again
During your briefing meeting it should have been established that your enquirer Mr A who makes electrical appliances would for his part have no objection to your working for him although you are currently working for competitor client Mr B who also makes electrical appliances. It may seem to Mr A that they are working for quite different markets. All well and good so far but you are not out of the wood yet. Your professional obligations are still to client Mr B who is already paying you to design for him and he must therefore have the last word.
So before you get too involved with Mr A, write to Mr B, tell him the exact circumstances and ask if he has any objections. You should make it clear to him that if he has, you will withdraw immediately from all negotiations with Mr A. And that is precisely what you should do, with polite regrets to Mr A, if Mr B does object. It is sad when it happens but you will certainly gain one thing to comfort you—the increased respect of your client Mr B for your strict professional integrity. You may also gain similar respect from Mr A for the

design profession as a whole. I have even known one such Mr A who was so impressed that he *waited* for the relevant designer to be quite clear of all commitments to the competitive firm (ie all design work and supervision finished, final fees paid and product in production) and then commissioned him to go ahead.

Two further points to note about the 'competitive clients' clause. One: if you are retained by your client Mr B with an exclusivity clause in your retainer contract then there can be no question of your negotiating with any other firm making competitive products in his field. (There is more about exclusive retainers on page 185.) Two: if your client Mr B does agree to your designing for Mr A, ask him to confirm that to you in writing or if that proves difficult, confirm his decision to him yourself in a letter. This could be useful if any misunderstandings or arguments arose later on.

To sum up, in the case of any or all situations where you even suspect the possibility of your existing and prospective clients' products or services being in competition, your main professional obligation is to *tell* both clients about the problem in order that they both have the opportunity to say yes or no. I feel pretty sure that if you persisted in the face of a client who said no, you would lose him anyway even if you kept the other one. But if you deliberately kept quiet about working for two competitive clients simultaneously and they found you out then you would almost certainly lose both of them and a regrettable portion of your reputation for professional integrity as well.

Displacing another designer

Now there is another Clause, Number 19, in the Code of Professional Conduct of the SIAD which may also have to be invoked during your first meeting with a possible client. This Clause reads:

'There are occasions when more than one designer may be engaged on the same project. Where, however, a member suspects that his engagement may *supplant rather than augment* (my italics) the service of another, he shall seek assurance from the client that any previous association with another designer has been terminated. Similarly, no member shall knowingly seek to supplant another designer currently working on a project whether satisfactorily or not.'

The mechanics of observing this Clause are always a bit tricky for a designer because they involve asking rather probing questions without appearing to be doing so. You have to find out if you can whether another designer has been used recently by the firm for the same sort of design work for which they are briefing you. If so, who he is, whether he is still so employed, whether he has finished all the work he was commissioned to do and whether his final fees have been paid. Unfortunately the situation often arises when there have been difficulties between the client and his previous designer. They may have been due to unreasonableness, inefficiency or inadequacy on either side or on both. If the collaboration has ended in an unresolved argument and the firm has refused to pay the designer's fees, you must reserve your judgment, get in touch with the other designer as quickly as possible and hear his side of the story. You may discover that he seems to have a perfectly good case and is about to sue the firm for his unpaid fees. Then you must write firmly but politely to the firm and say simply that your professional code prevents you from entering into any negotiation with them until their arrangements with their previous designer 'have been terminated'. Warning: do not *on any account* try to enter into the argument. Even if you think you can see the rights and wrongs of the situation it is nothing to do with you. It lies entirely between the firm and its former designer. You may hear nothing more from them but equally your letter may make them realize that they will be unable to negotiate with any professional designer until they have properly paid off the first. And may then do so promptly. You will then have done a considerable service to your fellow-member of the design profession by helping to get his rightful fees paid and so avoid the cost of a possible court case and legal fees.

If in spite of whatever difficulties he is in, the former designer agrees that you should go ahead with your own negotiations with the firm then you are completely in the clear to do so. If however he seems to you to have been rather shabbily treated you may think twice before committing yourself to working for such a firm. But that is for you to decide.

Working for nothing
You may get to the end of your briefing meeting and then find your would-be client inviting you to work for no fees at all or for a fee which he will pay only if he accepts your preliminary design proposal. The SIAD has strong views on this situation, which is dealt with in detail on page 161 under 'Working on spec'.

Diary notes
When you get back to your office after the briefing it is a good idea to deal with your notes as soon as possible while the whole thing is still fresh in your mind. Write them, dictate them or type them into the form of diary notes amplified as fully as you can with all possible names, addresses, dates and telephone numbers, also the facts, the information and above all your own personal impressions where these are relevant. It could be alas many months before the enquiry becomes a job and in the meantime many of the important things to remember may have faded from your memory unless you have recorded them. To set out your diary notes thus is also a great help in tidying up your own thoughts on the whole thing and provides an excellent basis from which to write your fee letter.

We have now got to the end of Phase One (a) of the chart on page 15.

Although this chapter is going to suggest how to set about writing a letter quoting your fees, it is not going to include anything about the actual fees at all. Chapter Four deals with those.

This is because you will find it easier to draft most fee quotation letters in detail, setting out the brief, the various stages of the job, any ancillary stages which might arise, any point at which costs or expenses might be incurred and so on, without thinking about fees as amounts of money while doing so, but leaving blanks for the figures to be put in later. By this means, you can think your way right through the whole 'structure' of the job from the administrative and financial angles. This may prevent you from overlooking some stage or aspect of it which should justifiably earn you an extra fee or a stage payment of the total fee. The latter is particularly important if for any reason the job is abandoned before it is finished.

A well-constructed fee quotation letter will always be impressive to a possible client since it will demonstrate your ability to think clearly and logically about the problem you have been set. Length need not matter provided you are not unnecessarily wordy but set out the facts in their proper sequence. Most important of all, the letter you write will eventually become, if you get the job, your side of the contract between you and your client and it is therefore virtually a legal document. It might have to stand on its own feet as such, in the unhappy event of any argument ensuing which brought it into a court of law. The other half of the contract is, of course, the letter you will get from your client accepting your terms. There is more about that at the end of this chapter. It is therefore worth spending a lot of time and trouble over every fee quotation letter you write. There are many possibilities to take into account, many different stages to consider, some of them common to all jobs, some applicable only to certain fields of design. Writing a fee letter is never easy since every job is different, every designer's reputation and experience vary.

The structure of the letter

However I have tried in the following pages to give you some basic fee letter structures for groups of design work having elements in common which tend to affect the form of the letter. Then I have enlarged on each item in the structures to help you to fill in and adapt them to the particular circumstances in which you are using them. The numbers in brackets key up with the numbers of the explanatory paragraphs which start on page 43. The groups of design work which I have used are based on the SIAD's Categories and Sections (see page 237). The only omissions are letter structures for retainers and consultancies which would be unlikely to fit any pre-conceived plan. These are dealt with on pages 174–176.

Fee letter structure A—for product design

This is the SIAD Category A and includes engineering-based products, furniture, craft-based products and automotive design. It is work almost invariably done for a client who is himself going to produce what you design for him. Here is the structure or skeleton of the letter:

Introduction (1)
Summary of the brief (2)

Services provided:

Stage One	Discussions with specialists and technicians (3) in agreed number of visits (4); preparation and submission of preliminary design proposals (5)
Stage Two	Development work; checking prototypes and samples (7)
Stage Three	Finished working drawings (8); adaptations for size and range (9); advice during production, and checking first batch (11)

Fees:	For Stage One	£ ....
	For Stage Two	£ ....
	For Stage Three	£ ....

Special clauses:	Ownership and conveyance of copyright (13)
	Breaking clauses and fees payable for abandoned work (14)
	Permitted modifications (15)
	Free specimens and design credits (16 and 17)

Additional fees:	For extra visits (19)
	For changes to brief (20)
	For travelling time (22)

Fee instalments (23)
Special costs chargeable (24)
Expenses chargeable (25)
Request for written acceptance of letter and conclusion (26)

For a one-off job, say a special boardroom table for a non-manufacturing client or a piece of commemorative glass, silver or jewellery, you would need to amend the 'Services provided' as follows:

Stage One	Discussions with specialists and technicians in agreed number of visits; preparation and submission of preliminary design proposals with approximate estimate of cost (6)
Stage Two	Development work
Stage Three	Finished working drawings and specification; obtaining firm estimate of cost (10); placing contract on the client's behalf; supervising production, completion and delivery (11) and checking final account (12)

If it has been agreed at a briefing meeting that special research or an initial survey and report are necessary before design fees are quoted, this should be done in a separate letter (27). If such a survey and report are to be included in Stage One of the 'Services provided' then the fee for that stage should be increased accordingly.

If you are proposing to negotiate a fees-as-royalties arrangement for any work in this group, see Para. (28) for special advice about this before drafting the first letter.

Fee letter Structure B—for fashion and textile design
This covers all of the SIAD Category B which includes fashion and clothing, surface pattern and textiles.

Introduction (1)
Summary of brief (2)

Services provided:

Stage One	Discussions with specialists and technicians (3) in agreed number of visits (4); preparation and submission of preliminary design proposals (5)
Stage Two	Development work and checking samples (7)
Stage Three	Finished artwork (8); putting the design into repeat, transferring the design to point paper (for woven textiles), alternative colourways; inspecting first strike-offs of colour and first production runs (9 and 11)

Fees:	For Stage One	£ ....
	For Stage Two	£ ....
	For Stage Three	£ ....

Special clauses:	Ownership and conveyance of copright (13)
	Breaking clauses and fees payable for abandoned work (14)
	Permitted modifications (15)

	Free specimens, signed work and design credits (16 and 17)
Additional fees:	For extra visits (19)
	For changes to brief (20)
	For travelling time (22)

Fee instalments (23)
Special costs chargeable (24)
Expenses chargeable (25)
Request for written acceptance of letter and conclusion (26)

Free-lance textile and fashion designers sometimes work in quite a different way to designers in other fields. As well as being commissioned by their clients, they can also prepare a number of designs on their own initiative and offer them as 'collections' to prospective buyers once or twice a year. There is more about this unusual but professionally acceptable way of finding clients in Chapter Twelve but when an interested client has been found, fees are then negotiated in the usual way and the fee letter structure above could be used. If you are going to negotiate a fees-as-royalties arrangement with your client in any fields of design in this group, turn to Para. (28) and study it carefully before you draft your letter.

Fee letter structure C(1)—for inscape design

These SIAD Categories are exhibitions and display, domestic, commercial and industrial interiors, television, film and theatre design. I am giving television, film and theatre design a letter structure of its own because it is to my knowledge the only field of design where fees are usually quoted on a day rate. But now for the structure of your percentage fee letter:

Introduction (1)
Summary of brief (2)

Services provided:

Stage One	Discussions with client's departments to amplify brief (3) in agreed number of visits (4); preparation and submission of sketch proposals (5) with guide as to probable cost (6)
Stage Two	Preparation and submission of final designs (5), including agreed amendments to preliminary designs, approximate estimate of costs and time-table (6). Negotiations with relevant Authorities for approvals. (See Chapter Sixteen).

Stage Three	Preparation of finished working drawings, fullsize details and specifications (8), ready for inviting tenders and including the obtaining of estimates from sub-contractors and suppliers.
Stage Four	Inviting competitive tenders and estimates for all work (10), submitting collated cost budget to the client, receiving his instructions and place contracts and orders on his behalf. (See Chapter Sixteen)
	Supervising work in workshops and studios and installation and completion on site (11).
	Supervising maintenance (during an exhibition) (11); checking contractors' work at end of defects liability period (for interiors). (See Chapter Sixteen)
	Checking all final accounts and certifying for payment (12).

(Note that the completion of Stage Two can sometimes take in the first paragraph of Stage Three above, in which case Stage Three moves down one paragraph to 'Inviting competitive tenders etc.' and Stage Four also moves down one paragraph to 'Supervising work etc.')

Fees:

For all work	A percentage of all final production costs and related to them on a sliding scale.
For Stage One	One-fifth of the estimated total fee
Included in 'all work'	The agreed value of client's own materials and labour, if any
Extra to 'all work'	A separate percentage fee on the value of furniture and furnishings selected from stock

Fee instalments (23)

Special clauses:	Ownership and conveyance of copyright (13)
	Breaking clauses and fees payable for abandoned work (14)
	Permitted modifications (15)
	Design credits (17)

Additional fees:	For measured survey (27)
	For extra visits (19)
	For changes to brief (20)
	For travelling time (22)

Special costs chargeable (24)
Expenses chargeable (25)

Request for written acceptance of letter and conclusion (26)

If it is agreed that you should make a feasibility study and submit a report on, say, the suitability of premises for conversion or sites for an exhibition, this would need to be covered by a separate fee letter written and accepted before the main fee letter as above. (See (27).

A royalty fee arrangement is very unlikely to arise in this category of design but if it should, there is advice about what to do at (28).

Fee letter structure C(2)—for TV, film and theatre setting design
As already mentioned, fees are usually quoted on a day rate for these fields of design, so you could use the following structure for your fee letter:

Introduction (1)
Summary of the brief (2)

Services provided:

Preparing and submitting sketch designs; discussing costs and collaborating with script writers and technicians (5)
Preparing property plots (7), obtaining and submitting tenders and estimates (if required) (10)
Preparing all working drawings, scale drawings, etc. (8), supervising construction and erection; advising if required on captions etc., and collaborating with producer at rehearsals (11)

| Fees: | For self | estimated x days at £.......... a day |
| | For assistant | estimated x days at £.......... a day |

Special clauses:	Late information (18)
	Abandoned work and fees payable (14)
	Ownership and conveyance of copyright (13)
	Permitted modifications (15)
	Credits (17)

| Additional fees: | For changes to brief (20) |
| | For travelling time (22) |

Expenses chargeable (25)
Request for written acceptance of letter and conclusion (26)

Fee letter structure D(1)—for graphic design
This covers all sections of the SIAD Category D: typography, lettering and calligraphy, design for advertising and for print, corporate identity and signing systems, photography, audio-visual and TV/film graphics. It is a big group and as well as single commissions, a design assignment could include a number of

the individual items. So the following fee structure letter could need quite a bit of adapting:

Introduction (1)
Summary of the brief (2)

Services provided:

Stage One	Discussions with clients' departments, printers, advertising and publicity agents, etc. (3), in agreed number of visits (4); preparation and submission of preliminary design proposals (5).
Stage Two	Development work (7)
Stage Three	Finished artwork, layouts, printers' and boxmakers' specifications (8) etc.; adaptations for size and for departmental uses (stationery); foreign language adaptations (9)
Stage Four	Advising on production, checking proofs and first runs (11)
Fees:	For Stage One £ ....
	For Stage Two £ ....
	For Stage Three £ ....
	For Stage Four £ ....

Fee instalments (23)

Special clauses:	Ownership and conveyance of copyright (13)
	Breaking clauses and fees payable for abandoned work (14)
	Permitted modifications (15)
	Free specimens, signed work and design credits (16) and (17)
Additional fees:	For extra visits (19)
	For extra work (21)
	For changes to brief (20)
	For travelling time (22)

Special costs chargeable (24)
Expenses chargeable (25)
Request for written acceptance of letter and conclusion (26)

If your client has asked you to be completely responsible for getting a graphic job produced, then your Stage Four paragraph here should be amended accordingly (see next Chapter under 'Fees for Contracting'). If it has been agreed that an initial survey and report on a graphic problem is necessary before you do any design work or even quote design fees, this situation would need a separate letter and there is advice about this in Chapter Fifteen. If your preliminary design proposals are to include a survey and report then this should be recorded at Stage One under 'Services provided' and the fee for this stage increased accordingly.

Fee letter structure D(2)—for illustration
This is an SIAD Category D Section on its own and covers fashion, general and technical illustration and cartoons.

Here is a fee letter structure which could be adapted to any of these sections

Introduction (1)
Summary of the brief (2)
Services provided:
(Possibly in the case of fashion and technical illustration)
Submission of rough sketch to show proposed treatment (5)
Finished artwork with any required notes to author/editor/printer (8)

Fees: At £xx per illustration for xx illustrations
Fees payable (23)
Special clauses: Ownership and conveyance of copyright (13)
                    Abandoned work (14)
                    Permitted modifications (15)
                    Free specimens, signed work and design credits (16) and (17)
Additional fees: For extra work (21)
                    For changes to brief (20)

Expenses chargeable (25)
Request for written acceptance of letter and conclusion (26)

So there are six skeleton structures for almost every kind of job; now to put sufficient meat on their various bones to show you how to build up the body of your own letters. But this does not aim to be a Designer's Compleat Letter-Writer. A separate book would be necessary for that and even then would not serve since, as I have said, almost every design job has some peculiar aspect of its own.

What follow therefore are only suggestions, pointers and occasional examples. For actual use, only you can tailor them to fit. The numbers in brackets after each sub-heading correspond with the numbers in the skeleton structures. Now you are going to start Phase One (b) of the chart on page 15.

The introduction (1)
It will be courteous to say thank-you for an interesting briefing meeting, lunch, visit; practical to refer to the date and place of it and to others who may have been present and pleasant to express your interest in the possible job. For instance:

Dear Mr A

It was very pleasant to meet you and Mr B at your office on (date) and I thank you also for the excellent lunch afterwards. I have considered the interesting project we discussed and I am now writing, as promised, to set out what my fees would be and the services which they would cover.

Summary of the brief (2)

We saw in the previous chapter what an important part of your letter this would be. At first, it will be better to err on the side of too much detail in your summary, rather than too little. In time, as you perfect the technique of asking all the essential questions at a briefing, and then compiling your diary notes from your rough notes, you will find it progressively easier to summarize them in your letters so as to stress all the policy points and omit the, for this purpose, irrelevant details. If the summary is a long one, set it out in short numbered paragraphs. If your client has been vague about production costs or budget this should be tactfully recorded ('you have not at this stage set any limit to the cost of producing this . . .'), in case he later complains that you have designed something too expensive for him.

Discussions with specialists and technicians (3)

This would be part of the services you give for your Stage One fee for preliminary designs. It might refer to visits to factories, showrooms, branch offices; or discussions with sales and production staff, advertising agents, house architects, printers, script writers, lighting specialists, exhibition organizers and the like, according to the job.

Visits (4)

The preliminary activities described in the previous paragraph are very necessary but very time-consuming and you should specify quite clearly in your Stage One formula how many of them you have allowed for. If you have been able to assess a fairly safe total at your briefing, it would be wise to allow for one or two more unforeseen ones as well. Some clients have a way of suddenly remembering a number of useful people you should meet after the original list has been drawn up and agreed. The alternative is to include them all in the 'Extra visits' clause in your fee letter. If you were charging hourly rate fees for all stages after Stage One, this would present no problem. Your formula for this clause would be 'Any extra visits above the number allowed for in my fees for Stage One, if requested by you, would be charged for extra at hourly rates'.

Preliminary designs (5)

In setting out your formula for the preparation and submission of preliminary designs, it is useful to try and state what you propose to give in terms of *quantity* for your fees, i.e. a design or designs. Misunderstandings sometimes arise on this score and can lead to bad relations between designer and client. The latter will usually expect, for what *he* may consider a fairly high fee if he is new to employing a designer, to see several alternative preliminary designs so that he can choose which he likes best and feel that he has had value for money. You will hope to find what you consider to be the best solution to the problem and persuade him to accept it with the full weight of your specialist training and experience to back up your arguments. Or you may consider that the job does not call for more than one preliminary design in any case particularly if the brief is a very tight one. On the other hand some kinds of work almost always result in providing several alternative suggestions—house marks and symbols, packs for a new product and particularly where the brief is wide and unrestricted. So give some thought to the way in which the work is likely to go at the preliminary design stage and try to decide whether you are going to provide 'a preliminary design' or 'two or three alternative preliminary designs'. The singular will not preclude you from deciding later of your own volition to submit alternatives. The plural may make it necessary for you to do so. If you do not, your client could quite justifiably demand to see further designs for no extra fee. The end of your Stage One formula should clarify this therefore and might read:

'. . . preparation and submission of a preliminary design (or two or three preliminary designs) in the form of a coloured perspective drawing (or general arrangement drawings or model or dummy)'.

In the paragraph of your letter about preliminary designs for a product, an interior or an exhibition, you should make it clear as to the form in which you will submit these—i.e. one or more black and white or coloured perspective sketches, general arrangement drawings or a scale model or all three. This is important because it could affect your fee. If you are not able to draw your own perspectives or make models you will have to pay someone else to do these for you. If on the other hand you only contract to provide perspective sketches and later the client asks to see a model, you could then justifiably ask for an extra fee or costs for the model.

It is even more important to record what you propose to provide for the Stage One fee in the case of house styles or corporate identity programmes. Stage One is almost certain to include the survey and report illustrated with your recommendations in visual form. But your preliminary proposals may be in two parts. First you may design the essential components of the house style— possibly a symbol, a logotype, a colour scheme, one or more letter forms. Then you will show them applied to various items—a letter-heading, a label, a pack, a van side, an exterior sign. It is advisable always to agree with your client before you start work, *and in writing*, precisely what these items should be. Without such an agreement, you may get involved in argument after you have presented your scheme, as to how many examples of its application you should have presented. I know of a case where, owing to a vaguely phrased letter, the client insisted on seeing the house style components applied as preliminary designs to some fifteen or more items without paying any extra fees. The fee quotation letter was not precise enough to protect the designer on this point and so the client had his pound of flesh.

It may not always be possible at a first briefing to agree as to exactly which of the client's various items the house style components should be applied but at least the number could be agreed, say 'any four or six', subject to final selection. It may be necessary to have further technical discussions, visit a factory, talk to the sales manager. Part of the initial work for a house style scheme may be to rationalize and condense in quantity existing ranges of packs, labels, stationery. However, when the way is clear and before drawing-board work begins, the proposed final list should be agreed in writing with your client.

Therefore your Stage One formula for a house style might read:

'Meetings with your technical and sales staff at your factory, studying the existing ranges of your packs, labels, stationery, etc. to see if these can be condensed in number; investigating the house styles of your two chief competitors and visiting six of your retailers (ten visits in all); preparing and submitting a report and recommendations illustrated with preliminary designs for the components of a new house style, and showing these components as applied to not less than four and not more than six items, yet to be selected and agreed, as coloured perspective sketches and full-scale dummy packs'.

And later:

'I am confirming our agreement at the meeting at your Factory on (date) that I shall show the components of my proposed house style applied to the following items:

Company letter-heading
Catalogue cover
Swing ticket
Cellophane bag
Van side

for the agreed fees as set out in my letter of (date)'.

In the case of interior design you will see in the structure that Stage One refers to preliminary designs and Stage Two to final designs. This is because it is usually necessary and advisable in the first place to submit plans, elevations and sketches to show only your proposals as to how the areas should be used. When this has been agreed (and it usually takes a lot of thrashing out) only then can you prepare firm proposals as to how the agreed area should look. But since these second proposals are based on an agreed plan, they can be considered as nearly final as you can get.

In the case of book typography, Stage One would probably cover an agreed number of typical pages and spreads as examples to establish the style you are proposing.

Illustrators are usually selected from published examples of their work, the style and treatment of which seems to provide the client with what he is looking for. But if there is any uncertainty at a briefing meeting, you could offer to provide say one rough sketch to show how you propose to illustrate the subject matter in question, particularly in the case of technical illustration. See next chapter, 'Fees for book illustration' on page 69.

Making an approximate estimate of cost (6)

For exhibition and interior design you are usually required to give a guide as to costs as part of your Stage One fee and an approximate estimate at Stage Two, the latter being a much firmer figure than the former. But if your client has more or less fixed a budget, the necessity for this advance estimating may not be necessary. It will be part of your brief to design to his budget. Other occasions when advance cost estimating may be necessary have been referred to in the fee letter structures. Chapter Eighteen gives you some advice about how to estimate production costs.

Development work (7)
When your preliminary designs have been submitted and discussed, your client will either approve them as they stand and instruct you to prepare the finished working drawings forthwith. Or he may discuss them not only with you but with his own staff, as a result of which you agree to amend the selected design to meet reasonable criticism; or to develop it from an outline idea to something more elaborate but still preliminary; or to show how it would look when adapted to different sizes or uses but still as preliminaries.
Any or all of these intermediate activities should earn you extra fees, a point which is very often overlooked by a designer, to his considerable loss. Therefore, the next paragraph of your letter should deal with these eventualities on these lines:
'On acceptance of my preliminary design proposals I would then develop them further in collaboration with you and your Production Department, making any agreed amendments to them, re-submit them to you as revised preliminary design, check samples etc'.
Development work on product and engineering design can go on for months, sometimes even for years. It covers the time spent in your client's factory, in preparing drawings for prototypes, conferring with his production people, checking a first prototype, amending your drawings as a consequence, checking a second prototype and so on.
Development work as such seldom arises in the case of interior design, displays or exhibitions.
In respect of all development work, the SIAD advises that 'a record should be kept of all modifications made or suggested during this work and copies retained by both parties'. This is an important activity, particularly in respect of engineering product design, in case of later technical difficulties or disappointing sales, which might give rise to disputes as to responsibilities.

Finished working drawings (8)
With everything at last agreed, you will be instructed to go ahead with the necessary finished working drawings (or artwork), and the necessary specifications, ready to go to the factory, printer, box-maker, bottle manufacturer, contractor, builder. This stage also includes all the work necessary on adaptations for size, range, colour and for advising during production and checking first production runs. It is the final stage, both of your work and your fees, in all work except that covered by the percentage fee structure letter.

In the case of engineering product design, shop drawings, as they are called, are often done by agreement in the client's own drawing office. If this has been settled in advance, it should be suitably referred to here. If you are not to do the final drawings, there is an important clause to note under 'Supervising production and maintenance' below.

Adaptations, etc. (9)
On some graphic and product design work you will have to produce adaptations of your finished working drawings. Designs for packs and labels may have to be adapted to larger and smaller sizes; printed matter may have to allow for departmental sub-headings or other languages; textiles, carpets, wallpapers may require a range of alternative colour ways. For finished artwork in colour, particularly for commercial and book illustration, the question of colour separations for the blockmaker must be considered. If it is agreed that you should do them instead of the blockmaker, it is reasonable that you should earn fees for this, instead of the charge which the blockmaker would make for doing it. Obviously too, the necessity for adaptations arises in many product design jobs—saucepans of different capacity, all the pieces in a dinner service and so on.

Obtaining tenders and estimates (10)
In graphic design your final responsibilities may be only to see and check the proofs or samples which your client should show you. But you are much more likely to be involved in getting your work priced for production and supervising it right through.
Your client may be dissatisfied with his own printer. He may then be grateful for your offer to recommend not less than three reputable printers and to obtain competitive estimates from them, place the contract on his behalf and supervise all stages of the work.
Chapter Seven deals with contracting for a client. It can take up a surprising amount of your time in discussions, telephoning, writing specifications and letters, possibly visiting the print works, blockmakers, etc. and chasing dilatory deliveries.
Only in exceptional cases would the designer of an exhibition or an interior not be required to obtain tenders and estimates and submit them as a collated budget to his client, with his recommendations, as part of his normal services. Chapter Sixteen deals with this particular kind of contracting.

Supervising production and maintenance (11)
You will always supervise the production, and installation, of your interior and exhibition designs. The only possible exception to the latter would be an exhibit to be installed on an overseas site where the client might have a local agent to do this for him and would therefore not be prepared to pay your travelling expenses. This will be sad for you since the only substitute you will get for an exciting trip abroad will probably be the harassing job of getting your exhibit into crates and on to a ship or plane. You will never see your brain-child

in being, except in the form of those curious and almost unrecognizable pictures which may eventually reach you from the local photographer.

Every designer wants to be concerned with the production of his work, to ensure that it reaches his own high standards and fortunately most clients prefer that he should be. In the case of graphic, product, textile designs which your client is producing himself, it is usual for this final supervision of production, checking of proofs or first run, to be considered, as we have seen, as part of your Stage Three services for the finished working drawings. Where this is applicable, therefore, a phrase to cover it should be inserted towards the end of your Stage Three paragraph:

'. . . and (my services) would also include liaison with your printer (or production staff) and the checking of proofs (or approval of first production batch)'.

If you have not done the final working drawings, then here you must add the following important rider to this paragraph which I mentioned on page 48. Something on these lines would cover you: 'Unless specially agreed I would not be responsible for general dimensional or specification checking.'

If you *have* been involved in getting estimates for the production of your job, we have seen how your Stage Three services would also include the supervision of the work.

In the case of an interior or an exhibition your supervisory work is likely to be very heavy. You will have to pay regular rounds of visits to your contractors and suppliers and check their progress; chase dilatory deliveries; deal with unforeseen crises on the site when something does not fit or has not arrived or looks awful and worst of all, cope with the client who wants to make changes at the eleventh hour.

All this anticipated turmoil will be dealt with in your fees letter by a brief calm paragraph on the following lines:

'With your approval of the estimates and the placing of contracts and orders (which I would do on your behalf if you wished), I should then supervise all production in workshops and studios, deliveries to site and final installation and completion'.

Maintenance in the case of a short term exhibition would be a service you would include in your overall fee, provided it did not involve you in lengthy journeys. You might be required to supervise the clearing away of the exhibit at the end of the exhibition and instruct the contractor about demolition, dispersal and any making good that might be necessary, again within your overall fee.

But for a long-term exhibition, running for several weeks or even months or for an exhibit abroad, you could reasonably negotiate with your client for some special arrangement regarding the supervision of maintenance and clearing away. This might take the form of an additional fee if you were prepared to give the time to it yourself, or instructing a reliable contractor to do it if you wanted to be absolved from it altogether.

For interior design, you will obviously not be involved in clearing away and demolition. But you will certainly decide with your client and contractors that there should be a six months defects liability period. This means that for six months after the completion of the work, the client retains 5% or 10% of the contractors' bills and of your fees. When the six months are up you and the contractors inspect the work and agree what the latter must remedy in the way of workmanship or materials which have proved defective. This work must be carried out at no extra cost to the client and when it has been done to your own and your client's approval, then the retained 10% is payable.

Therefore, according to the circumstances and for either interior or exhibition design, you might enlarge your Stage Four paragraph for an exhibition job:
'In addition, I would supervise maintenance during the run of the exhibition, and dispersal, demolition and the clearing of the site at its close'.

And for an interior design job:
'In addition, I would inspect the work after the usual six months' defects liability period, at the end of which I would instruct and supervise the contractors as to agreed remedial work to be carried out within their original contract'.

Incidentally there will be some clients with very large interior design jobs who will insist, quite reasonably, on a twelve months' defects liability period.

Checking final accounts (12)
This will be the last of your responsibilities and will only arise when you have placed contracts on your client's behalf. Then you will have to see that the final bill tallies with the estimate and order and that any extras charged are reasonable. If not, you will have to battle away by telephone, letter and discussion with the erring contractor until you reach agreement and can send the amended accounts on to your client, certified correct for payment by him. In respect of interior and exhibition work, the process can sometimes take months or even a year or more on a complicated expensive job. Until you have brought it to a satisfactory conclusion you cannot compute your total fee, since it is almost certain to be on a percentage basis and you cannot therefore invoice the final instalment of it. (See Chapter Seventeen.)

So your paragraph where relevant would probably say:
'Finally I would check and certify all final accounts from contractors, suppliers and specialists and send them to you for payment direct'.

Fees
As I said at the beginning of this chapter, these are dealt with quite separately and in detail in the next chapter. Therefore only note here the point at which they should occur in your fees letter and that they should always be given in stages, related to the stages of work which you will first have described under 'Services provided'.

Special clauses
Now we come to the special clauses part of your fee letters and the first two of these are vital to every design job.

Copyright (13)

This is a very complicated subject and particularly when applied to design. As an experienced textile designer once said to me 'One line of thread changed is not the same design'. There is as much general information as I can give about copyright and design registration in Chapter Nineteen so here I am only going to tell you what to include in a fee letter in order to protect yourself as much as you can.

The first thing to know is that a designer should always retain the copyright of his designs at the preliminary design stage and, if the job proceeds, normally throughout the development stages too.

Therefore your paragraph about copyright should start by saying 'Copyright in my preliminary designs would remain my property . . .'.

When the job is complete the final fees paid, then the designer can either
(a) still retain full copyright
(b) assign restricted copyright to his client
(c) assign full copyright to his client.

It is most unlikely that any client, save in exceptional circumstances, would accept alternative (a) so we can leave it out here. But restricted copyright often applies in sections of graphic and applied design. If you are going to design a poster you would agree to convey restricted copyright to your client which would mean that he could not use it for, say an advertisement or brochure cover without negotiating further fees with you for such extended repro-duction rights. A printed textile design might have restricted copyright to prevent it being used for a wallpaper without further fees for the designer.

Another form of restricted copyright is concerned not so much with usage as with circulation in the publication sense. If you are going to design editorial or advertisement material for newspapers or magazines you should find out at your briefing whether the particular publication in which your work will appear will circulate locally, nationally or internationally. If the first then your fee with restricted copyright would be negotiated accordingly. But if your client wants eventually to extend the use of your designs, he must come back to you to agree a further fee and extended or full copyright.

The same would apply to posters and in fact all commercial printed matter except book illustration. For that you can negotiate to convey first British reproduction rights only which leaves you free if you wish to sell the foreign rights wherever you want to.

The conveyance of full copyright gives your client not only the complete ownership of your designs but the right to use them or to change them in any way he wishes. It sounds harsh but it is a situation which must be faced in nearly all fields of design (except those I have referred to above) and particularly in product design. Few if any manufacturers would agree to restricted copyright conditions imposed on something they were going to make, finance and sell. If you tried this on I am sure you would not get the job.

In such cases therefore the second part of your copyright clause should read '. . . and on completion of the work and payment of my final fees full copyright in my designs would pass to your Company without restriction'.

Here are some special points to consider when you are drafting your copyright clause:

Exhibition and display design—The designer normally retains full copyright in his designs and drawings, conveying to his client one use only in the case of exhibitions and exhibitions stands and the first multiple use as originally agreed in respect of displays. Television scenery design—If the programme is to be transmitted as a series of repeats the fees agreed would normally include conveyance of full copyright. For a single transmission the fee agreement should include a copyright fee payable for repeats. This usually averages 20% of the original fee.

Royalties—If you are negotiating these instead of fees, the copyright position will be a very important clause in the legal agreement which will have to be drawn up between you and your client (see pages 73 and 225).

A final warning about the inclusion of the copyright clause in your fee letter. Watch out for the situation where you are going to be commissioned to *re-design* something which already exists or where you are going to work closely with a firm's own design office or production team. In such cases it might be quite inappropriate to make any mention at all of copyright.

Breaking clauses and fees for abandoned work (14)

I have already referred on page 35 to the fact that the SIAD has views which deter a designer from working for nothing (see page 152). Now you have to make it quite clear in your fee letter that if your client decides not to go on for any reason, you will expect to be paid nevertheless.

There are two main reasons why design jobs stop before they are complete and they both stem from the client. One is that he has internal policy problems which force him to call a halt—production difficulties, cuts in his budget, a sudden merger or take-over, a change of management and so on. The other reason is that when he sees your preliminary designs he just does not like them and cannot be convinced of their validity. He realizes that for his purpose (whatever that may be) he has chosen the wrong designer. So the point at which a job may be abandoned for this second reason is nearly always at the end of Stage One.

You must therefore include a breaking clause relevant to your Stage One fee to ensure that you get paid for what you have done and to enable your client to break the contract there and then without having to pay you further fees. This might read: 'If after the submission of my preliminary design proposals at Stage One you should decide for any reason not to proceed, my fees as quoted above for Stage One would be your only commitment'.

When work has got past Stage One and is then cancelled by the client it is much more likely to be for the sort of policy reasons I have referred to above. If you have quoted hourly rate fees for all work from Stage Two onwards you would charge for the number of hours worked up to the moment of cancellation by the client and your fees paragraph for these stages should include a suitable reference to this.

If you had quoted fixed fees for all stages you would be entitled to your full fee for each stage if cancellation came exactly at the completion of a stage. But if it came in the middle you would be entitled to full fees up to the end of the previous stage and what is called *quantum meruit* (ie, as much as it is worth) for the intermediate work. This means that you would suggest a reasonable halfway sort of fee for the work you had done, probably based on your hours of work.

Work being done for percentage fees is a little more complicated. You will see in the next chapter how these fees are on a sliding scale related to the final production costs. Your client will either have fixed a budget or you will have provided an approximate estimate of cost at Stage One. This will enable you to pick the relevant percentage and compute the estimated fee.

If work on a percentage fee job is abandoned after your design proposals have been submitted you are normally entitled to not less than one-fifth of your estimated fee. If it is abandoned after you have produced planning drawings for approvals, you should get one-third of your estimated fee and after detailed working drawings, another one-third. If abandonment comes in the middle of a stage you can then charge on *quantum meruit* as above.

If cancellation comes after you have obtained tenders and estimates and submitted them to your client, you can then claim your fees on the lowest tenders and estimates received instead of an estimated percentage fee based on estimated costs.

Should you by any chance have quoted a single lump-sum fee to cover all stages of a job and if it were abandoned or deferred after preliminary designs had been prepared, you would be entitled to not less than 70% of the total fee. Should the job be abandoned after development work had been completed, again for a fixed fee job, you would charge not less than 80% of the total fee; after working drawings, 90% and after the production of prototypes, 95%.

Permitted modifications (15)

The SIAD advises that 'the client may not make modifications or alterations to the designs without the consent of the designer'. This of course applies where you are retaining copyright until the completion of the job and payment of your final fees. If you are then conveying full copyright without restriction the client can do what he likes with your designs but he should certainly be asked to observe the clause during the period of the collaboration with you and thereafter if he only has restricted copyright. The clause does I think need to be worded rather tactfully '. . . I would wish to reserve the right to be consulted about any amendments you yourselves might wish to make to my designs as I would hope to be able to suggest alternative ways of making any such amendments which would not detract from the overall validity of the designs' or words to that effect.

Free specimens (16)

One actual specimen of finished work is worth a dozen photographs of it and in all reasonable cases you are entitled to receive such specimens. It would obviously be unreasonable to expect to receive a car, a refrigerator, a diamond necklace or a suite of furniture which you had designed. But there are clients who are good about specimens and those who are forgetful and difficult about them. You must therefore make a tactful claim to them in your fee letter. In the case of textile design, metre samples or small pieces should be politely asked for. The same would apply to wallpapers. In the case of printed publicity material, three to six copies would be reasonable. You would be entitled to receive three free copies of a book which you had designed or illustrated and also to buy further copies of it at trade prices.

Signed work and design credits (17)
If you want your published or publicised work to be signed or suitably credited to you, it is important to refer to this in your fee quotation letter. You may be unlucky enough to find a client who is churlish about signatures and credits (and a few unaccountably will be) and it may be too late to argue him out of it at the moment of production, if you had not got it settled in writing to begin with. If he is adamant in his refusals and if you are equally determined on a signature or credit, you could then only refuse the job altogether, which would be a pity. Better either to retreat gracefully from your insistence or try to compromise by suggesting, if you can afford it, a reduction in your fees in return for a credit. There are, of course, cases where a signature may not always be possible.
The SIAD advises that 'the designer is entitled to claim authorship of a design for which he has been responsible . . . his consent shall be obtained before his name or signature is reproduced on any finished product or otherwise published by the client'. Which implies that there are always some jobs, as we all know too well which, in spite of the designers' best endeavours, turn out in such a way that they would not wish to have their names associated with them, however generous the client.
So it is obviously a matter of discretion, humility, and negotiation according to circumstances and personalities. Unless you feel very strongly about it either way, and if you sense that your client is going to be a reasonable sort of person to work for, you could first refer to it in very general terms in your fee quotation letter, so as to open the door on the subject, and then come back to the details later, when the job is progressing satisfactorily. It is more important, however, to get it settled if your client is another designer who has invited your collaboration on a job or part of a job which he cannot tackle himself. You will want to be sure that you get your fair share of whatever design credits are going, assuming that your work will be a large enough part of the whole to warrant it. But equally there are cases where a designer who has been in employment decides to set up on his own and shows examples of his work to potential clients without revealing that such work was done while he was an employee; nor has he obtained his late employer's permission to use it in this way, which he certainly must do.

Late information (18)
This applies only to television scenery design and the SIAD advises that where information is given late to the designer, his day-rate fees are not to be reduced

54

although he has less time in which to do the job.

Additional fees
Few but the smallest simplest jobs go through without situations arising where you would be entitled to ask for additional fees. It is infinitely better to cover the possibility of these happenings in your first fee letter than to have to stop urgent work to negotiate such fees when the need for them arises.

Extra visits (19)   These have already been dealt with on page 44.

Changes to brief (20)
These can happen frequently during the course of almost any kind of design job and particularly in interior design. When they are rather major changes they are in a way easier to deal with but there can be a surprising number of small ones which creep insiduously in during friendly enthusiastic exchanges with your client. It is only when you get back to the drawing board that you realize just what they involve in scrapping work which you have done and starting again.

Your clause under this heading should therefore read something on these lines: 'Should there be any changes to the brief as summarized above involving me in extra work to make any such changes, this would be charged to you at hourly rate fees.'

Extra work (21)
This is very much the same problem as changes to brief but is more likely to crop up in big house style and corporate identity programmes where additional items keep on getting added to the agreed list. Again the problem is easily solved if you are charging hourly rate fees for all stages from Two onwards. Your clause might read 'Should extra work or items be added to the agreed programme for implementation, these would be charged at hourly rates as above'.

Travelling time (22)
As well as charging your travelling expenses, whether you are visiting your client or someone else on his behalf, there are circumstances where it is also appropriate to charge as extra fees the *time* spent in making such journeys. The SIAD advises that 'an additional charge may be made should the work be at such a distance as to lead to an exceptional expenditure of time in travelling'. What would be considered 'an exceptional expenditure of time'? There are no rules to define it, you have to decide almost by instinct and the 'feeling' of the job and the client, when to raise the issue. But it might be considered that any return journey which, without the visit itself between, took *more* than two days (ie a day to get there and a day to get back) would be an exceptional expenditure of time since it would involve you staying overnight.

If you decide to do so, it is essential to stake your claim for travelling time fees when writing your initial fee quotation letter and to receive your client's agreement to them. Your relevant paragraph therefore might read like this: 'As I shall need to make several visits to your offices at A during the course of this work, and probably also to your factories at B and C, I shall be involved in an exceptional expenditure of time in travelling, since each such return journey will take approximately x hours. May I therefore suggest that extra fees should be payable for this travelling time, at £xx for each journey (or at £xx per hour for all time spent in transit). Such fees would be additional to actual travelling and subsistence expenses'.

Fee instalments (23)
It is not usually necessary and generally not very tactful to refer in a fee letter as to when you will invoice your fees. But there are three situations when it is essential.

The first is when you are quoting hourly rate fees either throughout a whole job or from Stage Two onwards. As you will see in the next chapter it is important to reassure your client that he will get a monthly invoice from you for hourly rate fees so that he can have a fequent check on how the time is going. So a paragraph to cover this could read: 'From the beginning of Stage Two onwards my hourly rate fees and accrued chargeable expenses would be invoiced to you monthly'.

The second case is percentage fees and here the instalments (sometimes called progress or interim payments in this context) are due on an established pattern: on completion of Stage One, one-fifth of the estimated fee based on estimated costs; at the end of Stage Two, one-third of the estimated fee; at the end of Stage Three, another one-third; the final balance of the fee is chargeable when all final accounts are checked and certified less a retention (either 5% or 10%) until the completion of the remedial work by the contractor at the end of the defects liability period.

You will have seen the note in the middle of fee letter structure C(I) whereby the completion of Stages Two and Three can differ. The first alternative is more usual but it means that both Stages Two and Three of your fees must still be based on *estimated* costs. The second alternative, which is quite acceptable, means that your Stage Three fee can be based on the firm contract price of the job, or on the lowest tender received if the job should fold up at that point. There is more about how the two stages might vary in Chapter Seventeen.

A very large and very long interior job, say a new hotel or passenger ship or big suite of offices in a new building, can run for several years and the gaps between the stage payments outlined above would be unreasonably long for the designer to wait for his instalments. In such cases it is usual to negotiate interim payments. These could be flat-rate quarterly instalments or just reasonable amounts at ad hoc intervals. In either case the usual adjustments would be made as each of the more normal stages is completed. The same could apply to big long-term exhibition jobs such as a pavilion in an overseas exhibition.

The third case concerns the instalments of retaining and consultancy fees but these are also dealt with separately in Chapter Seventeen.

Special costs (24)

We have seen that, after the presentation of preliminary designs as perspectives, you may be asked to produce a model. Later you may be instructed to have a mock-up or prototype made or it may be agreed that you should commission a specialist artist or craftsman. The possibility of these eventualities arising should be covered:

'If development work or finished working drawings should call for further perspectives (or models) or the services of outside specialists, artists or craftsmen, these costs would be additional to my fees but would not be incurred without prior agreement with you'.

In the case of graphic design you might be more specific:

'If my selected preliminary design calls for an illustration by a specialist artist, such work would only be commissioned with your approval and for an agreed fee, which would be chargeable extra'.

This last paragraph is important. You are designing, say, a pack for a cat food and your preliminary design calls for a superbly drawn head of a cat. You may be anything but a cat artist and can only therefore indicate what the finished pack might look like in this respect. But with your client's approval of the idea, you can commission John Jones, the famous cat artist, to provide the necessary finished artwork, for a fee which will be extra to your own. *Your* fee will include the responsibility of recommending John Jones for the job, finding him, negotiating his fee, briefing him and supervising his work to see that he delivers it to you as you want it and on time.

If by chance you *can* draw cats, your own quoted fee for finished working drawings and illustration could be increased to reflect this additional skill.

Under the 'Special costs' heading would also come the agreement to commission on the client's behalf a quantity surveyor, lighting consultant, structural, heating or ventilating engineers according to the requirements of the job, usually a big interior.

There are occasions, increasingly nowadays, when big corporate identity schemes for big clients call for special presentations of the preliminary design proposals on a sequence of colour slides or even film, with in either case a spoken or recorded commentary. These can be very expensive to produce. I have known the costs run well into four figures particularly when the actual scheme itself is prefaced by a build-up of 'before' photographs of the client's current image compared with that of his competitors. On the other hand the impact of this kind of professionally-produced presentation is very strong. It is therefore very valuable to you and maybe to the client as well who will probably need himself to sell your proposals to his entire board of directors, his sales staff, even to all the widely dispersed member companies of a big group of companies.

If you are fully aware of this situation as a result of your briefing or if you sense that the situation may subsequently arise, then ideally it should be discussed during your meeting and agreement reached, at least in principle, as to whether you should allow for such production costs in your fee or charge them separately as costs. The second alternative would be the best for you as they would be very difficult to estimate before you had got the job and begun work on it. But even so you should undertake to submit as soon as possible a reasonably safe estimate to the client as otherwise he might be staggered when he saw his bill.

Expenses and production costs (25)
It might seem at first sight that expenses and costs are the same thing. They are, in fact, often used interchangeably but there is a difference. If they are amplified more correctly as 'out-of-pocket expenses' and 'production costs', the difference will become apparent.

Out-of-pocket expenses include fares and subsistence (hotel bills, meals, etc.) dyelines and photostats of designs; long distance phone calls; heavy postage on parcels; special delivery charges; in fact, any general petty cash type of expenditure.

Production costs are clearly part of the cost of producing the actual final job, usually fairly minor amounts which it is quicker and more convenient for you to order, pay for and recharge, as opposed to the larger contracts for printing, box-making, construction and so on. These, as we have already seen, usually have to be tendered for and discussed with your client. The production costs we are considering here would usually be in connection with a graphic design job, probably typesetting, copy negatives and photoprints, perhaps a block or die. You may incur quite a lot of similar costs in the preparation of your preliminary designs but at this stage they are not usually chargeable, being considered as costs against your fees. For instance, if you are working on a cover for a booklet you could either draw in by hand the type-faces you propose to use or you could decide to have them typeset for a more impressive effect. The cost of this would clearly not be chargeable. But when you are preparing final working drawings, adaptations for size, overlays, etc., then all such costs are justifiably recoverable extra to your fees.

These sort of production costs in the case of exhibition and interior design (for the latter they would probably be for lettering and signs) would not have to be referred to in this way in a fees letter, as they would be included in the whole production budget for the job (see Chapter Sixteen), nor would they be likely to arise in the case of product design unless it had been agreed that you should pay for and recharge special models or prototypes.

Out-of-pocket expenses are certain to be incurred for all jobs. So your relevant paragraph might be:

'All out-of-pocket expenses—travel, subsistence, dyelines, long distance phone calls, etc. incurred at all stages of the assignment, would be chargeable extra to the fees quoted above'.

Production costs should be referred to thus:

'Production costs—typesetting, copy negatives, photostats, etc., incurred in connection with the production of all finished working drawings would be charged extra to the fees quoted'.

Request for written acceptance and conclusion (26)

We have seen that your fee quotation letter is, in its final form, your contract to your client. But there are two parties to every contract and, on its own, your letter is not much use. You must get your client's *written* acceptance of it. That last sentence should be hung like a text over your drawing-board. All too often a designer will go ahead on the strength of verbal instructions and never give another thought to ensuring that he gets them confirmed in writing. Until some trouble arises, when it may be too late. If the client's acceptance comes to you in writing in the first place, all is well. File the letter safely after you have made certain that the acceptance is in accordance with the terms of your letter and contains no subtle qualification which might change your brief or your fees. If the acceptance is verbal, in a meeting or by telephone which it often is, ask politely but firmly for confirmation in writing 'for your records'. You will probably get it without any difficulty or delay but if it has not arrived after a reasonable interval you should ask for it again, this time by letter:

'I have started work on the design of your . . . as you instructed me at our meeting (or by telephone) on (date), in accordance with my letter to you of (date).

I should be grateful, however, to receive written confirmation of your instructions for my records'.

If that produces no response, then either your client's office is inefficient or dilatory or something is wrong. If you know him, or of him, well enough it is probably the first and you must go on asking till you get the letter. But if you suspect the second you should stop work (it would always be wise never to start until you have a written acceptance) and announce that you have done so. That something wrong might be a sudden internal crisis in your client's firm by which its whole policy had gone into the melting pot—a take-over, resignations, production difficulties, and the whole arrangement with you cancelled thereby. If you had done much work on the strength of only verbal instructions you would be unlikely, under such circumstances, to get any fees for it.

From very large organizations and from most advertising agencies, written acceptance of your fees often comes from their buying departments as printed orders for 'artwork' or 'goods', with serial numbers and dates which have to be quoted on your invoices. They look horribly impersonal and commercial but should be filed cheerfully as in fact the best form of acceptance since, if you remember to use the serial number, you will probably get your bills paid more promptly.

Sometimes a letter of acceptance instructs you to go only as far as a first stage, probably that of preliminary designs. When that stage has been passed you should again see that you are properly instructed in writing to go on with the work in accordance with your original quotation letter. Or if relations with your client are good by this time you might judge it sufficient yourself to confirm in writing that you have been instructed to go ahead to the next stage as set out in your original letter to him.

Whatever the circumstances, your letter must now be brought to a graceful conclusion with a request for a written acceptance of it. You will have your own personal turn of phrase which will be better to put in than any stock phrase I could suggest. But since to begin and to end anything written is often a most difficult thing to do suitably, you might round off your letter by saying something like this:

'I hope this letter gives you all the information you need but please let me know if anything is not quite clear. I shall look forward in any case to hearing from you and hope that you will decide to invite me to work with you on this interesting design problem. If you do, may I have your written acceptance of the method of working and the fees which I have set out in this letter'.

With your fee letter in the post, you have probably got to the end of Phase One (b) of the chart on page 15. I say probably because if the response from the recipient queries your fees or makes any changes to the brief, then the negotiations must continue until they are finally satisfactory to both sides and the agreed amendments recorded by you and accepted in writing by the client.

With a satisfactory written acceptance of your fee letter finally received and safely in your files, then you really have got to the end of Phase One (c) of the chart on page 15. In other words you will see if you look back on the chart that you have completed the whole fee contract phase.

Special research, surveys and reports (27)

The sort of research which a designer may be commissioned to undertake *before* he starts designing may be concerned with production methods or materials or with the suitability of a site or premises. The client may want to investigate the possibilities of making an existing product in a quite new material or of using a material which he already produces for making a quite new product. In some cases, such research might be an intrinsic part of your work on preliminary designs and would not, therefore, qualify for a separate fee. In others if the outcome of it might affect the rest of the job, even to the extent of it being abandoned altogether at that stage, it would probably be called a feasibility study and you should quote a separate fee for it thus:

'For investigating various kinds of polystyrene containers with their comparative costs from about half-a-dozen selected suppliers, and submitting six copies of a report to you, with recommendations as to their suitability or otherwise for packaging your products more cheaply than in cartons, my fee would be £xx. This would be your only commitment if, after considering my report, you decided not to proceed with the project'.

Whatever the kind of report you are quoting fees for, always refer, as I have shown above, to the number of copies of it you will provide for your fee. Six would be about average but if you have been able to find out at your briefing how many copies your client might need, you could then adjust your fee accordingly to allow for the production costs. Some clients might need to circulate copies to twenty or thirty people and the situation to avoid is to be asked urgently for a lot more copies after your production process is finished. When you have decided how many copies to include in your Stage One fee, you could refer under 'Special costs chargeable' to extra copies of the report, if required, being chargeable.

Work based on traditional design, particularly for textiles, may involve a great deal of time spent on research. In this case, it would be best to increase your preliminary design fee to allow for this, rather than to charge a separate research fee.

Another kind of research is the survey in depth to which Chapter Fifteen is devoted.

If what your client really wants is market research then it is best to advise him to call in the experts for this. If he is contemplating a new venture is is not sufficient to consult a few wholesalers, retailers and consumers and advise him for or against the project as a result of their reactions. A much wider and more scientifically-conducted survey is essential and there are efficient and reputable market research organizations which do this. Incidentally, they are also interesting and useful organizations for you to be in touch with. Where their services are obviously required, you can do your client and them a good turn by recommending them provided you have satisfied yourself first as to which are the most suitable. The long report with which they will supply him eventually will not only give him a lot of essential information but you also, if the design side of the project goes ahead. If a manufacturer first calls in a market research or business efficiency organization to tell him why his sales are falling, the result may be that he is advised not only to re-design his products and presentation methods but to call in Designer So-and-So to do this. And that might be you, if you and your work were known to the firm making the recommendation.

A survey in respect of interior and exhibition design is generally used in the architectural sense and means a detailed measured survey of a building or site and the preparation of plans and elevations from them, if no such drawings already exist. Such work always carries an extra fee but does not usually entail a report to the client. One other kind of survey might, however. A client may ask his interior designer to inspect several alternative properties and report on them with his recommendations as to the most suitable. This would also be a feasibility study and would also carry an extra preliminary fee or fees if the search is prolonged and you are continually having to inspect and report on different premises. Surveys for exhibition stands are seldom, if ever, needed. The organizer should always provide them. But they could be necessary for stands or pavilions out-of-doors at big agricultural shows and such like, for foundations, levels, drainage and other purposes, where no drawings existed.

Royalties (28)

In the case of anything to be produced in large quantities, you may sometimes negotiate your fees to be paid to you as royalties. These will probably be an agreed percentage of the value of every unit sold, whether the 'unit' be a suite of furniture, a plastic spoon or a length of something.

The fees you would quote for the actual design and development work would be sufficient only to cover your costs and would be considered as an irrevocable advance of the royalties.

Royalties as fees are tricky things to negotiate and it would always be wise to sound your client about them and get his reactions before you leave your briefing meeting. If he is dead against them and says no, you obviously cannot force them on him. In that case it is an either/or situation: 'either you pay me royalties or I do not design for you'. If you are such a famous designer that he is metaphorically kneeling at your feet, then he will probably agree to royalties and negotiations can start. If he seems open-minded or only mildly reluctant it can be explained to him that royalties as design fees imply that you are willing to share with him the risk of success or otherwise of the product when it is on the market. The more royalties he pays you, the more units he is selling and vice versa.

If it is decided that your fee estimates should be based on a royalty arrangement it would be *essential* for such a letter only to outline the suggested terms of such an arrangement which, if acceptable in principle to your client would then have to be incorporated into a proper legal agreement between you, drawn up by your solicitors. The SIAD publishes model royalty agreements for both commissioned and non-commissioned work.

To draft your fee letter, therefore, there should be the appropriate use of Items 1, 2, 3 and 4 of the fee letter structure on page 37. Then Item 5, the fee for preliminary designs as well as the development fees for Items 7 and 8 should be quoted as being sufficient only to cover your costs and considered as an irrevocable advance of royalties. You would then quote the percentage royalty you suggest, based usually on the wholesale price, excluding VAT, of the unit. Then you would probably finish by saying that if your suggested terms seemed acceptable in principle, you would have your solicitor prepare a draft agreement in greater detail and send it to him for his consideration. The next chapter gives you more information about royalties and what further action to take when you have got the negotiations to this point.

Now that you know how to compose fee letters it is obviously necessary to know how to finish them off by putting in the essential ingredients—the fees themselves. When you go into business as a free-lance industrial designer you will be selling your talents, training and experience in the form of the time it takes you to produce a finished piece of work whether that work is a letter-heading or a locomotive and whether your time is spent in thinking, drawing, travelling or research. It is therefore very important for you to know how to assess the value of your time and consequently what you must sell it for in the form of fees.

The secret of all successful fee-estimating is to know the selling cost of an hour of your own time. Now I am assuming that because you are reading this first part of the book, you are still a student. I am not therefore going to take you through the complexities of calculating your hourly rate as it is usually called. This is because you would have to jump ahead into all the financial problems of running your own office, the mysteries of overhead percentages and profit margins, your personal budget and so on. This is all explained in considerable detail in Chapter Fourteen in the second part of this book. Even there you will find that each must work out his own in accordance with the circumstances in which he is working or going to work. One designer's hourly rate may be double or half that of another, depending upon his experience, his financial needs and whether he runs his office in an expensive city centre or a much cheaper country town.

So at this point I am going to assume a *completely fictitious* selling rate of £2 for an hour of your time in order to explain how to use it for calculating fees.

Fee categories
There are five categories of fees for professional design services:
1 Lump-sum or fixed fees
2 Hourly-rate fees
3 Percentage fees
4 Royalties
5 Consultancy and retaining fees
Let us consider first the kinds of design work and design stages to which these five categories are usually applicable.

Lump-sum or fixed fees
When you are briefed to provide quite specific design services it is usual to

quote a lump-sum (which is the same as a fixed) fee. This is because with a clear brief it is up to you to assess how much of your time it will take to fulfil it and what ancillary costs you will incur in order to provide those services by a given date. Therefore the fee for preparing and submitting preliminary design proposals for product, graphic, engineering, furniture, textile and sometimes fashion design is nearly always a lump-sum fee assessed by the designer. This is Stage One in fee letter structures A, B and D(I) in the previous chapter. Occasionally, the lump-sum can be quoted and accepted between fairly narrow brackets (say for instance £200 to £250) if there are any agreed open ends to the brief.

A lump-sum fee would also apply to any special research, surveys or reports which might have to be carried out, submitted and accepted before preliminary designs were to be tackled. See paragraph (27) in the previous Chapter. When, as often happens, your research, surveys, report and recommendations will finish up with your preliminary design proposals, then there should be one lump-sum fee to cover the whole exercise up to the submission of your work at Stage One in fee letter structures A, B and D(1).

The time it will take
As I said above, we are going to assume, solely for the purpose of this part of the book, that the selling value of one hour of your time is £2. But it is only the value of an hour's work. The next thing you must do is to assess as accurately as you can how long it is going to take you to complete the job you are considering. There is, alas, no yard-stick for doing this since there are too many variables—the speed at which you work, the complexity of the job, your success at finding a good solution quickly or only after lengthy experiment and whether you get your best ideas at the drawing board or in the bath. Only you can take all the particular circumstances into account. One thing is certain, however: you will inevitably underestimate the amount of time you think you may need. All designers do to some extent and very much more so when they are inexperienced at this exercise. This can be serious for you financially and you would be wise, therefore, to add at least half as much again to the total time you have assessed for a job, even though you may have thought of and allowed for all conceivable contingencies within that total.

One point may need clarifying at this stage. The time you are going to assess for completing a job, or stage of a job, is not the time you would tell your client you are going to need before you can submit it to him. It is drawing board time, travelling time, time spent on research, letter writing, telephoning, discussions and meetings, all to do with the job but not necessarily consecutive. When you have allowed for all this and added up the hours, they might come to, say, eighty, or about two whole working weeks. But they might have to be spread out over six weeks, sandwiched in here and there with your other work.

Take the case of estimating a Stage One lump-sum fee for designing a letter-heading, a simple typographical one in two colours with one size adaptation and one overlay for a departmental sub-heading. You have worked out that it will probably take you four hours in all on the drawing board to prepare the preliminary designs. Add half as much again to this to bring it to six hours for safety. Then add perhaps another half hour for mounting your designs into a suitable folder and wrapping them up; a further quarter-of-an-hour for such letter-writing or telephoning as you might have to do to get an appointment with your client; a quarter-of-an-hour to get to your client's office, half-an-hour for a meeting with him and a quarter-of-an-hour back again. Total time: seven and three-quarter hours, or say eight for safety. At an hourly rate of £2, this would mean that you would estimate a fee of £32 for the preparation and submission of preliminary designs. You would follow exactly the same procedure in order to estimate what your lump-sum fee would be for Stage Three: finished working drawings, and you would then be ready to drop the two figures into your fee quotation letter, already drafted according to the suggestions given in the previous chapter.

With the selling value of an hour of your time you will soon learn by experience to assess lump-sum fees in the one or more stages required by the job. At first, as I have said, you will greatly underestimate your hours of work on a job. Try to counteract this right from the start by adding 50%, 75% or even 100% more time to your total of hours and keep on doing this until you have enough experience almost to trust your own first judgment. But do not forget that every job has its unknown quantities which may not reveal themselves until you sit down to the drawing board. Therefore a margin of time allowance for the unforeseen will always be a comforting thing to have even when you are at the top of the tree.

In arriving at a lump-sum fee, particularly for a preliminary design, do not forget to allow for any special costs you might have to incur which will not be chargeable. A perspective sketch by a specialist, a model, a bit of specimen typesetting, a specially-taken photograph—any of these you might decide to commission yourself in order to put over your preliminary designs as impressively as possible. Your fees for this stage should be large enough to cover their cost as well as the cost of your time.

But now back to Stage Two in fee letter structures A, B and D(1) in the previous chapter, referred to as 'development work'. Although it can happen that your client will accept your preliminary design proposals just as they are without asking you to change anything but to go straight on to finished working drawings, this desirable state of affairs is rare. What is much more likely to happen is that you will go on to 'develop' your designs, that is to take into account reasonable (and regrettably sometimes unreasonable) criticisms and requests from your client to try it this way and that way until you reach a solution which solves all his problems.

I deliberately jumped over Stage Two in explaining above how to arrive at lump-sum fees for the preliminary designs and finished working drawings for a simple letter heading job. But that did not mean that you could leave this stage out of your fee letter. It merely brings us to the need to explain our second category of fees.

Hourly rate fees
The time to be spent on the development of a design is a completely unknown

quantity. It may never even arise. There is thus no basis on which to quote a fixed fee and this is where hourly rate fees come in. It means that you will only charge your client for the time you spend doing the work he has asked you to do which was not in your original brief. Most clients will reasonably understand this and accept the hourly rate fees, but if they are new to the idea, they may be worried about the unknown amounts they may be letting themselves in for, just as you would be worried at having to quote fixed fees for an unknown amount of work. As suggested in the previous chapter, they can usually be reassured with the explanation that you will render monthly invoices for this development stage of the work, so that they can check at frequent intervals how it is going and call a halt if they feel it is getting too expensive.

In any case, hourly rate fees are becoming so widely accepted that it is a good idea to quote them whenever you can after Stage One in all the fields of design covered by fee letter structures A, B, D(1), D(2) in the previous chapter. This would mean that finished working drawings or finished artwork, the application of a house style or corporate identity programme, adaptions for size, range and colour, the time spent in checking prototypes and samples and in advising on and supervising production could all be quoted for and charged like this, as well as all the items under 'Additional fees' in all the fee letter structures.

If your client still prefers you to quote lump-sum fees for adaptations, these are admittedly easier to compute in time and therefore in lump-sum fees. But in such a case it would be wiser to quote, not an all-in fee for all the adaptations, but a flat rate fee per adaptation, regardless of how many there may be. This fee would be arrived at by estimating your time to carry out an average adaptation and multiplying it by your hourly rate, with all the usual margins for contingencies. When you actually do the adapting work, some may be more, some less, complicated but your average fee should work out satisfactorily on the swings-and-roundabouts principle.

But watch out for this adapting operation. For a big corporate identity programme, when the process of adapting is usually called implementation, the complexity of the work can be far greater when you get down to it than you had bargained for. When you learn from experience to be aware of this possibility it would be safer either to quote hourly rate fees for all the work or to suggest that you would prefer to quote fees for it when you can be given a fairly precise programme of what has to be done.

If therefore you decide to quote hourly rate fees for all stages of a job except the first, your paragraph following your fees for Stage One might read: 'For all subsequent work as outlined at Stages Two and Three above, my fees would be charged at hourly rates based on recorded time. The current rate would be £x an hour'. When you have an assistant and have worked out his hourly rate as well as your own, you would say 'My current rate would be £x an hour and that of my assistant £x'.

When you have a number of assistants, you need usually only quote the lowest and the highest hourly rates.

Since fees at hourly rates are most often quoted and accepted for a programme of long slow development work, this usually means that they may have to stand for two or more years. But what if you have to increase your own 'salary' or that of your assistant, in the meantime? What if your overheads rise, as well they may? (All overheads regrettably do.) You might find yourself working during the second year at an hourly rate which was no longer economic for you. You must therefore always cover this possibility with a special clause in your letters quoting fees at hourly rates. Follow the actual rates with a phrase on these lines:

'These hourly rates would be subject to review at the end of a year's work, to allow for possibly increased costs and overheads'.

Without that clause, your client could quite rightly hold you to the original rates quoted and agreed. When you have an assistant and you know that he will be due for a rise within a few months of starting on an hourly rates job, you will be wise, even with the above clause, to quote a rate for his time high enough to take in his rise in advance. The same would apply to your overhead percentage if you knew it was going up in a month or two—increased rent, rates, taking on a secretary and so on.

Fees at daily rates
In television scenery design, it is usual to agree a daily rate fee and then to estimate and agree the number of working days likely to be involved, according to the type of production. The daily rate fee need present no difficulties since it can be calculated on your hourly rate.

Fees based on a percentage of costs
These are the third category of fees and, like hourly rates, are usually equally simple to quote. They apply to interior design, exhibitions, shops and shop-fitting and so on and are usually on a sliding scale. This means that as production costs increase, the percentage fees come down. If at the time of quoting fees the budget is not settled it is sufficient to give some indication of the scale and leave it at that.

Tight budgets
If often happens that a very low and a very tight budget for an interior or exhibition job means a great deal of extra work for the designer. He will have to spend so much time searching for ways and means to get the best effect on a shoestring, seeking materials that are cheap and yet look good, going hat-in-hand here and there to see what he can beg, borrow or steal to save him a few pounds. It can be stimulating to have to be so economical but it is very extravagant on time. It is therefore some consolation to know that below a certain cost level you can either increase the percentage fee out of the scale altogether or even quote a lump-sum fee or hourly rates. Therefore it would be quite in order to quote a fee of more than 18% for a contract below £2000, basing it not necessarily on a percentage of costs but relating it to the type and

67

amount of work involved, either as a lump-sum or on a time basis.

Furniture from stock
For interior design which is going to involve the selection by you of loose furniture from stock, it would be unreasonable to expect the full percentage fee on its value, since you have not designed it. In this case it is usual to suggest a modest 5% on the total value of such items in the budget.

But even though it can be a very time-consuming activity, it is well worth it. You will be able to seek out just the right kind of furniture to fit in with the areas you will be designing and you will have avoided that almost heart-breaking situation when your client tells you that he has got all the necessary furniture in stock, with usually awful results.

Standard office furniture imposed on your elegant reception area or in your beautiful boardroom can be very hard to bear. It would always be wise to discuss the furniture situation at the beginning of the assignment so that if the worst seemed likely, you might be able to talk your client out of it.

A client's own materials and labour
There is one further point to a watch on an interior job, particularly a large one. The client may decide himself to supply certain materials for the work, either because he makes them himself or has his own sources from which he can get them more cheaply. Or he may decide himself to place certain of the contracts direct for such things as electrical work, plumbing, or ventilation, perhaps through his 'house' architect or a 'house' maintenance builder. In all such cases you are entitled to receive a percentage fee on the value of such materials and services, the full relevant percentage for materials and services which are actually included in your specification, and a lower one, perhaps 5%, for ancillary work not designed or specified by you but which has to be integrated with your work and partly supervised by you. This situation seldom reveals itself at the very beginning of a job but as soon as it does, your entitlement to fees should be clearly stated in writing to your client. When the job is complete you will have to ask him for the value of the orders and contracts placed by him direct, in order to compute your final percentage fee for invoicing.

In the case of exhibitions, a client's own materials are likely to be his exhibits as well and it is therefore a little tricky to suggest that you should receive a fee on their value. Only if they were going to contribute an unduly large part to the production of an exhibit could you reasonably do so. As an alternative, this might be a case where you could more conveniently quote a lump-sum fee for the whole job, and then you could disregard who had supplied what.

You will see in fee letter structure C(1) in the previous chapter, which covers all design work done on percentage fees, that the need to quote a lump-sum fee for Stage One is indicated. This is in order to provide a breaking clause as explained in paragraph (14) in case your client decides not to proceed. It is not a lump-sum fee in the usual meaning of those words but an accepted proportion of your percentage fee—one-fifth. If you have been given a budget you can work out your one-fifth of it on that basis. If you have no budget, you can then only quote it as being one-fifth of whatever estimates of cost you will provide with your preliminary design proposals.

Fees for book illustration
One of the three accepted ways in which fees are negotiated for the illustration of a book will be dealt with further on under Royalties. The other two must be considered separately here as they do not quite fit any previous fee quotation pattern. The most usual way is to quote a lump-sum fee, or flat rate, for an agreed number and size of illustrations, to include full or restricted copyright and for payment on delivery of the drawings. It is usually best to convey only restricted copyright (ie first British reproduction rights) and in this case the designer is entitled to ask for the return of his originals.
The second way occasionally used is what is known as 'flat rate plus refreshers'. This means that when the flat rate or lump-sum fee is being negotiated, a limit of impressions or editions of the book is established. If this is exceeded the illustrator receives one or more 'refreshers' in the form of further fees, which also have to be agreed in advance.
In quoting lump-sum fees for book illustration it is usual to allocate 25% of them to roughs, if these are required to be seen by author and publishers.

Fees for textile design
As we saw in the last chapter free-lance designers in these fields can work in a different way to other designers but having presented their collections, they can then proceed to negotiate fees in the usual way. It is worth remembering that fees for commissioned designs can be considerably higher than for those bought from a collection since your reputation, experience and the importance of the job will have brought the client to you instead of you having to seek him. A fixed fee is usual for preliminary designs with hourly rate fees for development work, putting the design into repeat, additional colourways and so on, also for finished artwork in whatever form that may be required.
It is very important for you as the designer to do all the colourways but some manufacturers still need persuading about this. It is equally important to persuade them to let you see the first strike-offs of colours.
For the purpose of fee estimating, the category of textile design can also include the design of household linens, carpets and rugs, laminates and synthetic fabrics, linoleum and plastic floor coverings as well as wallpaper and wrapping papers. Again fees can be quoted on the basis of a lump-sum fee and hourly rates or lump-sum fees throughout. In this whole category it is also possible to negotiate fees on a royalty basis. More about this further on.
Incidentally, think hard and long before deciding to offer to produce your own textile designs. It is something you have been trained to do and will want to do but it is costly and difficult when you are on your own. A well-known textile designer said to me 'Only very small quantities can be produced in your own studio and printing problems are such that one can spoil whole pieces very easily. To commission printers is costly as print works are becoming more and

more mechanized and demand minimum runs of several hundred metres per colourway. One also needs somewhere to keep stocks and a sales staff of some kind. One does have to have nerves and muscles of steel and real technical knowledge and experience'.

Fees for dress and fashion design
Like textile designers, fashion designers also work differently in several ways. They can be commissioned to produce designs, in which case a fee letter on the usual lines and acceptance of it from the client follows the normal pattern. They can produce a collection of designs on paper and submit them to fashion buyers or wholesalers after which any that are purchased should again be the subject of straightforward fee negotiation by letter. Sometimes however a fashion designer will both design, make-up and cost a sample garment or garments and approach fashion buyers to see if they are interested. If so, then the order to the fashion designer will probably be to supply a given quantity of the garment in each of several sizes, already made up. This situation needs a recosting of the garment in the light of quantities and size range required and confirmation of the firm total cost to the client, with a design fee either separately quoted or spread as a percentage over the total quantity of garments. The latter might be made up in the designer's workroom if it were adequate or the designer himself would contract to have the garments made up to his specification and under his supervision at an out-work factory.

There may well be other ways in which the fashion designer can or will be able to sell his skills both of designing and making. In the present day fashion world almost anything goes and it is therefore difficult to fit him into the patterns of operation we have been considering so far. But, for his own protection and reputation, businesslike he must be in confirming estimates and orders and if he is a member of the SIAD he must of course observe its Codes of Professional Conduct.

Fees according to circulation
The size and whereabouts of circulation can affect fees over quite a wide field of illustration—magazine and newspaper illustration; cartoons and strip cartoons; fashion drawings; technical illustration; greetings cards; drawings for press advertisements and so on. In all cases, the total fee can be quoted either in the usual two-stage way—for roughs and finished artwork or for finished artwork only if the client does not need to see roughs. But where the work is being commissioned by a periodical, the circulation of the magazine or newspaper should be taken into account. The fees should increase by some 50% to 100% according to whether the circulation is local, national or international.

Repetitive work and multiple displays
This might occur in the design of shop fittings, display units and suchlike. The SIAD advises that 'Where extensive works of a simple nature are repeated for the same client and drawings and specifications can be used without revision,

70

irrespective of whether more than one contract is involved, the fees may be reduced on a percentage basis, consistent with the reduction of the work involved.'

You will realize that it might be difficult at the time of writing a fee letter to know whether this situation would arise. It would therefore be advisable to make this concession a tentative one ' . . . should any extensive work of a simple repetitive character arise within this assignment I would propose that my fees for such work be reduced etc. . .'.

The production of multiple displays would produce a fee situation from the start. If you are being commissioned to design, say, a window display unit for an airline, your client's production order will probably be in the hundreds if not thousands. You could quote a lump-sum fee for design, contracting and supervising production, assembly and installation of a first limited batch. But if your fee was to be on a percentage basis, this should first be calculated on the cost of producing a specified number of units and then generally reduced. The extent of such a reduction must depend on the scale of the work.

Fees for contracting
The sort of contracting for a client which interior designers are normally required to do as part of their services is covered by their percentage fees and as the whole operation is a fairly complicated one involving responsibility for large sums of money, it is dealt with separately in the second half of this book in Chapter Sixteen.

But in graphic design, more often than not a client will ask you to look after the production of what you have designed for him and that usually means the contracting too. This should earn extra fees for you because it can take up a lot of your time.

In this case Stage Four under 'Services provided' in fee letter structure D(1) would have to be amended to read somewhat as follows:

'If you would like me to advise you on the most suitable printers (or boxmakers or contractors) to produce the finished work, I would be very happy to do so. I would select and recommend to you not less than three such firms, provide them with detailed specifications, invite competitive tenders and submit these to you. I would then, with your agreement, place the contract on your behalf, and supervise all stages of the work to final proofs, first deliveries and check and certify final accounts'.

If you had quoted hourly rate fees for Stages Two and Three in such a letter it would be equally suitable (and desirable) to do likewise for this version of Stage Four. Otherwise it would have to be a lump-sum fee and a difficult one to compute at that.

Fees for attendance at committees and panels
In the previous chapter Stage One under 'Services provided' included an agreed number of visits to be allowed for in the relevant fee, in letters, A, B and D(1). Visits extra to the agreed number were also dealt with under 'Additional fees.' But it may also have been suggested that you should 'sit in'

regularly at meetings which may have only some slight bearing on the work you are doing and which have not been convened solely to discuss it. Then you could consider charging an extra fee for such attendances. This sometimes happens when a large organization has a design or publicity committee or in the case of trade associations or semi-official bodies. At any of these you might be required to sit for two or three hours in order to spend five minutes expressing an opinion or reporting progress, often an exasperating waste of time and one for which, if it seemed tactful, you could suggest an extra fee:

'Apart from the joint meetings which will be necessary during the course of this work, you have asked me to attend at the regular monthly meetings of your (Design, Publicity, Production Executive, Exhibition) Committee in case matters should arise about which I could usefully express an opinion or be required to report progress. I hope you will consider it reasonable that I should charge an extra fee of £x for each of these attendances'.

I have implied in that paragraph a lump-sum fee as I think the largely unproductive nature of the time spent by you at such meetings would justify a fee rather higher than just your hourly rates. But if you felt diffident about this, hourly rates would do. It would depend very much on the size of the job and the importance of the client. If you were negotiating a retaining or consultancy fee, the above paragraph would not be applicable.

Fees for special research, surveys and reports

If you have been able to establish with your client a fairly precise programme for any of the above important activities then you should be able to calculate how many hours of your time (and of your assistant's if you have one) will be involved and, with very generous margins for over-optimism, unforeseen contingencies and non-chargeable costs, arrive at a lump-sum fee. This is generally preferable from the client's point of view, particularly for surveys which are likely to take several months as the big ones often do.

When a report must be submitted by a fixed date this gives you another way of arriving at a lump-sum fee since there is a limited amount of calendar time in which to earn it. You could calculate that, from starting date to submission date, you would be involved for say three-quarters of your available working hours and your assistant for say half of his. You could then work out the cost of time in days or weeks instead of hours and, again with liberal safety margins, arrive at a lump-sum fee. My experience is that the time spent in research, surveys and reports invariably runs on for longer than had been calculated. That is why I am so insistent about safety margins.

For short quick surveys or where it proves impossible to establish a programme with your client, then hourly rates are the only answer or lump-sum fees within wide brackets.

Measured surveys of premises where no accurately dimensioned drawings exist and the preparation of the new set of dimensioned drawings can take much longer than is usually anticipated. Here again hourly rate fees are the safest to quote. The operation of actually measuring the premises always involves two people, one at each end of the tape and travelling time may also be involved.

Fees as royalties
This fourth category of fees usually only applies when the thing to be designed is likely to be sold to the general public in large quantities—furniture, domestic equipment, textiles, fashion and so on.

The extent to which you are prepared to enter into a fees-as-royalties agreement with a client depends on whether or not you are a bit of a gambler. It *is* a gamble, but not quite so governed by the laws of pure chance as a heads-or-tails situation.

It is obviously worth while going to some trouble to find out all you can about your client's business (if he and it are new to you), about his sales policy, his markets and his advertising and publicity methods, when you are contemplating royalties instead of fees. However excellent and sales-worthy your designs for him may be and however competent his production lines, the finished product is unlikely to sell in sufficient quantities unless his marketing and advertising is expert and adequate. And by 'sufficient quantities' I mean enough at least to bring you in as royalties the amount which you would have earned for the job under the more usual arrangement of fixed fees agreed in advance. If your royalties do not reach such a total, the gamble has not paid off. If they do and even pleasantly exceed it, it may pay you rather handsomely.

Given that you have sized up the situation really carefully, firmly refused to let yourself be dazzled by your client's optimism about the quantities he will sell and still feel that the gamble is worth it, there remains the question of the actual fees and royalties to be negotiated.

The percentage method of computing royalties, based on the manufacturer's selling price excluding purchase tax etc., is the most usual one, but equally you can agree with your client that when he has sold, say, 1,000 articles he will pay you a lump sum of x pounds; when he has sold a further 2,000, he will pay you y pounds, and when he has sold a further 4,000 he will pay you a final z pounds, after which you will require no more, however many he goes on to sell.

There are no hard and fast rules about royalties but a royalty percentage is usually something between 3% and 6%, though for very large sums, a lower figure may be agreed. It is for this reason that it is even more important than usual to see that your agreement sets out clearly all the conditions on both sides and ties up all the loose ends. If your design proves to be a best-seller and the royalties look like mounting up agreeably, a not-too-scrupulous client might look for some loophole in your original exchange of letters to avoid paying you your dues.

You will notice that I referred to your 'agreement' in the previous paragraph and a proper legal agreement is something you must have if you are going to enter into a royalties arrangement with your client. Here are some of the aspects which must be taken into account: How often should the royalties be paid. . . . What about licenses granted by the company. . . . How are you to know how many units they have sold. . . . What if they are very late in paying

you your royalties. . . . What if they stop production or never even start. . . .
Who should own the copyright of your designs . . . and so on.

That is why I suggested in the previous Chapter that your fee letter should
merely broach the subject, so to speak, and, with a favourable reaction, that
you should then instruct your solicitor to get busy on a draft agreement to
cover all the necessary legalities for your client's consideration and eventually
his acceptance.

Consultancy and retaining fees

The fifth category of fees, consultancies and retainers, are unlikely to apply
until you are a fairly well-established designer in private practice with a
growing reputation.

For this reason I am not going into them in any great detail in this part of the
book. You will find more about them and how to calculate them in Chapter
Fourteen. But it may be useful to describe them briefly here.

A consultancy fee is usually negotiated to cover consultancy services only, no
drawing board work. As a design consultant you would be required to advise
on and guide a firm's design policy. If design and drawing board work does
emerge from a consultancy, which it often does, then quite separate fees are
quoted for the actual work, job by job or on an hourly basis throughout. A
consultancy can be for a single programme of work or last for several years.

A retaining fee covers much the same sort of services but is usually on an
annual basis renewable by mutual agreement after one or more years. It often
has an extra and important element: it may 'retain' your exclusive services in a
particular field of design which means that you undertake not to work for any
other client in that particular field. So if you are retained to design
refrigerators, with an 'exclusive services' clause in your fee contract, then you
cannot design them for a competitor until the termination of your retainer
releases you to do so.

'Sprats to catch mackerel'

One of the most difficult decisions for any designer but particularly for you in
the early stages of your practice, is whether to quote an almost nominal fee to
an important new client for a small job in the hope that it will give you a much
sought-after chance to show your talents and so lead to bigger and better
things. It is impossible to advise on this problem since the circumstances vary
so widely whenever it crops up. In your very early days, when you have nothing
to lose and perhaps a really glittering prize to gain, the gamble may very often
be worth it, particularly if it does not mean putting other more lucrative work
aside. However, as your practice grows, it should be less necessary for you to
throw out your sprat. Also, if you are working in a fairly parochial community,
it will get around surprisingly quickly that your fees are low and it will then be
difficult to quote higher and more normal fees to other clients.

There is also Clause 19 of the SIAD Code which might have to be considered in
this situation. It says:

'. . . no member shall knowingly seek to supplant another designer currently
working on a project whether satisfactorily or not'.

Reducing fees

However carefully you assess the enquiries for your services, work out your time and costs and quote what seem to you to be reasonable and adequate fees, there will always be those clients who come back to you protesting that they are too high. If it is a job you really want then you are faced with as difficult a decision as the 'sprat' one above—whether to offer a reduced fee. Again, advice is very difficult to give about this except to say that if you do it too often and by too much, you may tend to get the reputation of always apparently over-quoting in order to reduce your fees if bargained with. You will realize how very undesirable this is for a professional designer and decide that carefully-considered fees should be reduced as seldom as possible and then by very little, just as a token. That may often be sufficient to appease your client's bargaining habits since this situation often arises with manufacturers who are not used to dealing with professional designers. In addition, the Clause referred to above might again apply.

Introductory commissions

These would be of two kinds: a commission offered to you by a contractor, supplier, agent or suchlike in return for the opportunity of working through you for one of your clients; or a commission which you might be expected to pay to a person or business in return for introducing you to a client from whom you eventually received design fees.

Concerning the first kind of commission, the relevant Clause 14 of the SIAD Code says:

'Whilst acting for his client, a member may not divert to his own advantage any discounts, reductions or other financial benefits offered as inducement by contractors, manufacturers or suppliers. Similarly a member must disclose any financial involvement which he may have with contractors or suppliers he may recommend.'

Handling charges and the acceptance of discounts are dealt with in Chapters Seven and Sixteen.

The other kind of commission is a quite legitimate one for a designer to pay (if he is asked to do so) and can usually be agreed on the basis of 10% of fees for the first year. But there is one kind of person with whom no designer should exchange introductory commissions and that is another designer. Clause 20 of the SIAD Code says:

'Neither shall a member charge nor receive a fee, neither make nor receive a gift or other benefit, from a fellow member in recognition of a recommendation to a post or an assignment.'

When you have one or more jobs signed up at last, you then start Phase Two of the chart on page 15 and you will be eager to get down to work on the drawing board. But there are some administrative things which should be done first and a pattern established whereby you can check progress, record time, costs and expenses and generally keep the situation under control. This will prevent panic and confusion setting in later on and is referred to as 'setting up the job' at Two (a) on the chart.

Job numbers

The first thing to consider is a quick and easy way of identifying every job and for this the use of job numbers is much to be recommended. In a notebook you enter consecutive numbers from 1 upwards. (Or you might decide to start at say 51 or 101 to disguise quite pardonably the fact that your practice is in its infancy.) As the jobs come in you write in against the numbers the client's title and two or three words to describe the job. This master list will prevent you allocating by mistake the same number to two different jobs. Your list might read like this at the beginning:

Job No.	1	Smith & Brown Ltd	Stand at Packaging Exhibition
	2	Jones Bros	Letter-heading
	3	Green & Co Ltd	Re-design of cutlery
	4		
	5		
	etc.		

The job number should be used on all correspondence, notes and minutes of meetings, drawings, orders, time sheets, petty cash chits, invoices, statements —in fact on every piece of paper, hand-written or typed, which relates to the job in any way. You will see later on why this is so useful for filing, costing and invoicing.

Progress charts

Next you will need to devise for your pin-up board a large clear progress chart on which to put all the jobs going through your office. It will be a sort of calendar with blank vertical columns for weeks and months across which you can draw in lines with coloured chalk to show what stage a job has reached and stab in coloured pins to show the stages it must reach by certain vital dates. It is usually called a bar chart.

You will find that such a chart is useful to refer to if you are suddenly asked to take on another job which is very urgent. Your chart will show you where there are likely to be troughs of slack time between the peaks of pressure—such as waiting for tenders to come in or waiting for a client to submit your designs to his Board. That is when you might usefully accept a small urgent job which could be started and finished quickly.

Date schedules

As well as a progress chart on which you can compare the progress of all your work together, you will need individual date schedules for those jobs which have an absolute deadline for completion, such as exhibitions, the opening of office or showroom interiors, even for a product or graphic design job which may be geared to the opening of a publicity campaign. These schedules, particularly for exhibitions, will need working out in some detail and if there are dates when you are going to depend on some action by your client to enable you to be on time you should always send him a copy of your schedule. In your covering letter you might refer tactfully to those dates and ask if the time you have allowed for his action and decision is adequate.

The easiest way to work out a date schedule is first to write it down backwards, starting with the completion date. Always do it with a calendar before you so that you will not overlook Sundays and public holidays. Here is a typical date schedule for an exhibition stand. It would serve, with adaptations, for an interior design job.

Opening day: April 28.

Private view and press day: 27 April. (The stand should be ready for photographers.)

Client's exhibits delivered to site for installation: 24 April.

Work begins on site: 17 April. (The organizers usually give this date in the rules and regulations.)

Main contracts and orders placed: 18 March. (This should average four weeks before site work begins but two days have been added to allow for the Easter holiday.)

Client's approval to estimates received: 17 March.

Tenders and estimates submitted to client for his approval: 11 March. (This should allow him a week to get financial approval or perhaps submit the figures to his Board.)

Tenders and estimates received: 10 March. (Always try to allow a day for checking, collating and typing estimates and a covering letter.)

Working drawings and specifications out to tender and for estimating: 23 February. (A minimum of two weeks should be allowed for tendering for a fairly simple job.)

Working drawings ready for printing and specifications for typing: 22 February. (Always allow at least a day for these operations.)

All details of client's exhibits, copy etc. received: 6 February.

Working drawings in hand: 26 January. (This allows just under four weeks but will obviously vary according to the job and your other work.)

Approved preliminary designs submitted to exhibition organizers for approval: 25 January. (This is always required but is usually only a formality unless you have blatantly broken the rules.)

Preliminary designs approved: 24 January. (The client may need at least a week to get departmental, and possibly his Board's, approval.)

Preliminary designs submitted: 19 January. (Try to make this date a Monday so that you have a week-end to finish off if you are rushed.)

Preliminary designs in hand: 29 December. (Allowing for the Christmas holiday.)

All briefing complete: 22 December.

With your schedule worked out to your own and your client's satisfaction, type it the right way round with the dates first, and put it on your pin-up board. The schedule above would certainly need to be sent to your client for his approval since there are three points at which you will have to await his action. If he told you that he was going to be abroad at one of these crucial points, you would have to re-plan your schedule to allow for this.

Some date schedules will be much simpler and briefer, others will need to be even more detailed than the one above but it will serve as a pattern. Without any date schedules at all, unless you are a superman, you will inevitably come to that awful moment when you look at the calendar and realize that you are so far behind that there is no time left in which to catch up. And that can be total disaster.

Time Sheets

We saw in Chapter Four that there might be many occasions when you would negotiate with a client to charge him hourly rate fees. Therefore when a job, or a stage of a job, is finished and can be invoiced you will need to know how many hours you have worked on it and at what cost, certainly to you and possibly to the client.

One way of doing this is to keep time sheets and job sheets. Printed time sheets can be bought from some of the big office system organizations but to start with you could more cheaply get a local typing agency to run you off a hundred or so on a duplicator. They should be for a week at a time so you would get through about fifty in a year. Below is a suggestion for setting them out with some entries to show how they might be used.

In the previous chapter, we used a *fictitious* rate of £2 an hour for time. But that stands for the *selling* price of an hour of time and therefore includes an allowance for running costs (or overheads) and a margin for profit. On time sheets and job sheets, which are part of a simple design office accountancy system, the basic rate which an hour of time *costs* must be used. This is all explained in great detail in Chapter Fourteen and it is not necessary to go into it all here. For the purpose of showing you how time sheets work therefore we will use a basic rate of £1 an hour. Very low by any standards but it is fictitious! Nearly all professional people—architects, accountants, engineers, keep time sheets. Nearly everyone who keeps time sheets finds them an irksome chore

TIME SHEET

Job No.	Job	M	Tu	W	Th	Fr	Total hours	Cost of time
	Name Bill Brown		*Week ending* (date)					*Hourly rate £1*
1	Smith's stand	5	4	1	5	–	15	£15.00
2	Jones' letter-heading	–	2	4	1	1	8	£8.00
3	Green's cutlery	½	2	3	½	7	13	£13.00
Gen.	Filing, correspondence, etc	½	–	–	1	–	1½	£1.50
,,	Enquiry	2	–	–	½	–	2½	£2.50

but essential. Without them you are working in a vacuum. You will never know how long a job has taken or what it has cost you—and it is your time you are selling. They are even more essential if you have agreed to charge fees at hourly rates. They might also be important in the event of a dispute about the time you had taken on a job. They are in fact the necessary first part of a really very simple system of keeping records in a design office, of which the next part is the job sheet.

Job sheets
On every job you will spend time and on most you will also spend actual money—on travelling expenses, prints, reference material, typesettings, photostats, trunk calls, parcel postage and so on. There could be as many as fifty such items of expenditure on quite a small job, many of them amounting to less than a pound each. But they might add up to a total of several pounds and certainly some, if not all, of them would be chargeable to your client extra to your fees. You simply cannot afford to lose that amount of money on any job and there is no need to do so if you can get yourself into the habit of keeping simple job records and remembering always to use your job numbers. There are two ways in which you will spend money on jobs—by direct payment in cash, probably for small amounts, and by cheque to pay bills for larger amounts and for monthly accounts. *Every* time you spend any cash in connection with a job try to enter it with its job number in your pocket diary preferably at the time of spending it but if that is not possible, then at the end of every day. *Every* time you issue a written order for anything connected with a job, either in an order book (see further on about ordering) or in a letter, see that you use the job number. Then at least, all the expenses you incur on a job will be recorded somewhere.
But when the time comes to invoice a client for your work you will find it very tiresome to have to search back for several weeks or even months in your pocket diary, your time sheets, your order book, your cheque stubs, in order to pick out all the items against the single job number you want. And that is where job sheets come in. To start with they could be loose-leaf ruled sheets

with two cash column rulings on the right. You could buy such sheets at any office stationers with a loose-leaf book to keep them in. You would start a new sheet for every new job, put the client's name and the job at the top and the job number good and large in the top right hand corner.

Then on to this sheet you would enter up once a week with unfailing regularity if you can make yourself do it, all the individual items of time and expenditure spread throughout your diary, your time sheets, your order book and so on, under their job numbers. Here is what such a job sheet might look like, with some typical entries:

Client Smith & Brown Ltd		*Job* Stand at Packaging Exhibn		*Job No.* 1
Date	*Record*	*Item*	*Cost of time*	*Expenses*
(date)	Petty cash	Taxi to meeting		£1.50
(w/e date)	Time sheets	Time—15 hours	£15.00	
(date)	Petty cash	Reference books		£2.75
(date)	Order No. 1001	3 dyelines		£0.85
(date)	Estimate	Trunk call to factory		£1.75
(date)	Letter	Jones—for model (Est. £25.00)		£25.00
(w/e date)	Time sheets	Time—8 hours etc.	£8.00	

It is useful to put the dates in particularly for journeys, as you will see when the times comes for invoicing. It is also important to put the order number in (practically all orders books whether specially printed or from stock are numbered serially in duplicate or triplicate) as you will see when we get on to ordering procedure further on. But at the time of entering your order you may not be able to enter the actual amount against it under expenses, only the estimated amount. You must wait for the bill to come in before doing that in case it turns out to be justifiably more, or perhaps less, than the estimate.

You can see how useful this job sheet will be, if you keep it entered up, as a complete record of every job ready with all the necessary dates, facts and figures for your invoicing and remaining afterwards to give you useful data about the time and money you spent on the job.

Order books

There is a golden rule which ought to be engraved in deeply incised letters on every designer's heart and that is—issue a written order or letter for *everything* you need to buy or contract for on a job. And in the majority of cases your orders should be acceptances of written estimates received. Without an estimate or order or both, you are completely at the mercy of your contractor or supplier. If he has done the job on your verbal instructions only, he can charge you what he likes and you have no solid grounds for arguing with him. Moreover your efforts to keep tidy records of a job will get in a terrible tangle.

All you need to start with is a simple order book such as you can buy at any stationers. The leaves are numbered serially in duplicate with carbon paper in between and you tear out and send the top copy, leaving the second one in the book for reference. Always preface the serial number with your job number and write—or rubber stamp—underneath 'Please quote this number on your invoice'. If the order is one accepting a written estimate give the date, reference and amount of the estimate. Don't forget to write your name and address clearly on your order. This may sound ludicrously obvious but it can easily be forgotten if you are in a rush. Then your supplier will be a very ingenious man indeed if he can trace where the order came from.

Job files
When your job has its job number, you need a labelled folder for it for your correspondence filing system. Into this will go all the letters, notes and papers about the job as you deal with and finish with them.
Now your pattern is established—your new job has its job number, new job sheet and job file ready labelled. You have worked out its date schedule and entered the important dates on your progress chart. Your time sheet and order book are near at hand. You are ready to begin work on the drawing-board.

Secrecy
But first a word about secrecy. That may sound a bit cloak-and-dagger but if you are working on the development of a new idea for your client—whether it be a new pack or a new product, he will naturally want to keep it dark until he is absolutely ready to dazzle the world and his competitors with it. So it really is a good idea not to talk about the work you are doing while you are doing it and not to show it to any visitors who might cast inquisitive glances towards your drawing-board. Your casual visitor—a salesman perhaps or even a messenger —might say a casual word in the right ear which could eventually wreck a patent application or ruin a sales campaign.
Clauses 7 and 8 of the SIAD Code refer to this:
'Good professional relations between a designer and his employer or client . . . also depend on the reliance which the employer or client can place on a designer's integrity in all confidential matters relating to his business.' (And further on) '. . . no member or his associates or staff may divulge information confidential to his client or employer without their consent, subject to any requirement under law'. (And as a footnote to this) 'Nor should a member have an interest in any business which might break this principle.'

Identification of drawings
With your preliminary designs nearly ready for submission you must decide how your actual drawings are going to be identified, because on no account should they leave your hands unless they have your name, address and telephone number on them somewhere, with the job number and possibly the date. These can be put, usually on the back, with a stencil which looks pleasantly neat and efficient; on a typed adhesive label, which could come

unstuck; or by means of a specially-made rubber stamp which costs more to start with but is nice and quick to apply. Whichever method you adopt do not forget to use it in the last-minute rush of completion and packing. Your work must be identifiable if it should go astray anywhere, for copyright purposes and to ensure yet again that your name is seen, recognized, remembered, this time in the best place of all—on your own good work.

Submitting preliminary designs

It is worth going to almost any lengths to ensure that you submit your preliminary designs yourself to your client in person. The reasons why you have done this or that need explaining, which could be done by letter, but may also need battling for, which cannot. You may be able to swing a whole meeting round from 'it can't be done' to 'there's something in it' with reasoned arguments and a persuasive tongue. You may be able to stand firm on one important element in your design proposals by conceding reasonable amendments on less important ones. It is a fascinating and stimulating process of give and take which may start with a battle of resistances and end with an enthusiastic collaboration. But if you are not there to speak for your work when your client and his colleagues take their first coldly critical look at it, their initial resistances, if they have any, may set like cement and you may find it very difficult to break them down again later on.

It is sometimes a good idea to show your client informally how your thoughts are working on a preliminary scheme before you finalise it for the more formal submission. The extent to which you do this will depend very much on the kind of job and the personality of your client. But should there have been any small misunderstandings between you during the briefing process they will show up at this point and save time and unnecessary work later on.

A small practical point: when submitting textile designs, either as a collection or commissioned, they are best mounted on very light card or white cartridge paper all of uniform size. The design should be attached by its top edge only and preferably not in a 'window'.

Approval of designs

Now I am afraid you must get back to some letter-writing. With the submission of preliminary designs you have completed Phase Two (a) on the chart on page 15, except for the first invoice and for this see Chapter Eight under 'When to invoice'. You have also completed the first contractual and financial stage of the job and the next stage has probably been agreed. These decisions must be recorded and they could be one of at least seven alternatives:

(a) Your designs have been approved exactly as they stand and you have been instructed to go ahead with finished working drawings.

(b) Your designs have been approved subject to minor agreed amendments and you have been instructed to go ahead with finished working drawings which will incorporate the agreed amendments.

(Both these alternatives would take you straight to Phase Two (c) of the chart on page 15 as no development work would be needed.)

(c) Your designs have been approved in principle but with agreed amendments which your client would like to see as revised preliminary designs.

(d) Your designs have been approved as a basis for interim development work which you have been instructed to proceed with.

(e) Your designs were not approved at all, through no fault of your own, and you have been instructed to start again almost but perhaps not quite from scratch.

(f) Your designs were not approved or the project has been abandoned and you were instructed not to proceed at all.

(g) Your client did not like your designs, felt you had not followed his brief and indicated that he would not pay your fee unless you produced some further designs.

(Both (c) and (d) above would mean the completion of Phase Two (a) on the chart and the beginning of Phase Two (b).)

Alternative (a) needs only a simple straightforward letter recording the approval and the instructions to finish the work. The same applies to alternative (b) except that the agreed amendments should be listed. In the case of alternative (c), if you have quoted lump-sum fees in two stages only—for preliminary designs and for finished working drawings—you may want to suggest a further fee for the revised preliminary designs asked for by your client. It could be a fairly nominal one unless the revisions are going to mean a lot more work for you. Again the revisions should be listed.

If you have quoted your fees in three stages, ie a lump-sum for preliminary designs, fees probably at hourly rates for interim development work and a lump-sum or hourly rates for finished working drawings, there are no complications about alternative (d). You simply confirm the approval and the instructions you have been given to proceed to the next stage. Alternative (e) probably means that the client admits to an inadequate or to a changed brief. In this case you must confirm to him that there will be a further fee for your new preliminary designs and get his agreement to it. This fee could justifiably be as much as the fee you originally quoted. Or it might be a little less, particularly if you feel you can afford to make a gesture in a difficult situation since you may have covered a certain amount of ground the first time and will not need to retrace your steps the second time.

Alternative (f) is a sad situation which can happen to anyone. It certainly calls for a gracefully worded note 'regretting that I was not able to find an acceptable solution to the problem and hoping that there may be further opportunities, etc., etc.' Alternative (g) is the really sticky one, the kind of situation to which I referred in Chapter Three. If you had confirmed your brief in writing before you started work and had then reasonably kept to it, you would have to point this out in writing, at first gently but firmly, later perhaps less gently but more firmly until at last you would have to give a week or two's notice of passing the matter to your solicitors. On these unpleasant occasions this final threat fortunately nearly always produces the required settlement. If it does not then you *must* instruct your solicitor to deal with it for you. If on the other hand you felt that the client had a modicum of right on his side you might then write and admit this to a reasonable extent and try to save the situation by offering to prepare further preliminary designs free or for a nominal fee.

So you see, whichever alternative applies, your letter should record the stage reached and the next stage to be proceeded with. This is important for another reason. In the case of alternatives (a), (b), (d) and (f) you will be able, after a decent interval, to render an invoice for your preliminary fees (see Chapter 8). In the case of (c) and (e) it would be more appropriate to wait till your revised designs have been submitted and approved. In the case of (g) you would certainly submit your invoice if you knew you had a cast-iron case for doing so.

Verbal instructions and decisions

During the course of a job, you may often find yourself taking verbal instructions from your client or someone else in his firm, either by telephone or in an informal meeting. Your first thought should be as to how the instruction or decision will affect your work. Your second thought should be 'will this affect the agreed fees?' Or 'will this cost my client more of his money than he has sanctioned me to spend for him?' 'Or possibly both?' When you have a reasonably definite answer to these questions you should record the instructions in writing and point out clearly that they may, or will, increase the agreed fees and production costs. It is fatally easy to overlook this, particularly in exhibition and interior design and then be faced with horrifyingly expensive extras when the bills come in. These you have to explain away to your client and hope he will pay. He may almost casually have asked for a variation in the work and then say when he sees the bills 'But I had no idea that small addition was going to cost so much. Why didn't you warn me?' It really is your duty to warn him. Equally for your own protection you should record all his verbal instructions to you in case he forgets having given them to you, as well he may over a lengthy job. Then he might repudiate them when he sees them in cold black and white on the bill.

Diary notes

You will find it very useful to get into the habit of writing diary notes of important conversations and meetings where the points discussed do not call for formal confirmation to your client but provide you with useful data about the job which you need to have recorded somewhere—the sort of thing you might literally scribble on an envelope and then lose if you did not get it into some more permanent form. You might also consider using your job sheet as a day-to-day diary of events, as well as for time and cost records. For instance:

(date)   Client rang to ask for six photostats of plan of stand for board meeting.
(date)   Visit to client's factory to inspect three more exhibits for stand.
(date)   Two contractors in to discuss tenders.
(date)   Client rang to ask that office area on stand should be increased.

Such events would be interspersed with the weekly entry from your time sheets of time spent and of costs incurred and orders placed. You would thus build up a complete case history of the job as it progressed.

Development work

If you have negotiated fees at hourly rates for any or all stages of a job which may run on for several months, it is essential to render invoices for these fees to your client at monthly intervals, even if in some cases he has not yet seen the result of your month's work.

This is where all your record-keeping really comes into its own because your monthly invoices must be almost a brief progress report on the work and you would find it very difficult to write them without your time sheets, your job sheets and your diary notes. You will also be charging for the time you spend at meetings. There is more about how to render invoices in Chapter Eight but here is a typical 'formula' for a monthly invoice for a job being charged at hourly rates, to show how it should also be a progress report:

'Fees based on hourly rates as agreed for the completion of drawings for the first prototype; for a meeting on (date) with your Production Manager at the Factory; for making revisions to the drawings as requested and for instructing the prototype maker at a meeting on (date); for work in progress on finished working drawings for transfer of logo-type and for meeting with transfer printer to obtain estimates:

30 hours at £2 an hour—£60.

Submission of finished work

Finished working drawings should of course be clearly identified, as were your preliminary designs and should where necessary be accompanied by separate typed specification notes which your client can hand on straight away to his printer or box-maker or contractor as the case may be. It is a small but useful service which saves him the time of getting your notes extracted and copied if you have put them in a letter which he will want to keep in his files. If you have sent him colour and material references you will need to keep a duplicate set in your work file for checking proofs or prototypes. In the brief letter which will accompany your finished work it is a good idea to reiterate yet again that you will want to see and check proofs, prototype or first run, whichever is applicable. This is a point at which some clients may fail you badly. They are in a hurry to get the job into production, afraid that you may be fussy about production details; and the next thing you get, after a long silence, is a sample of the finished job, a *fait accompli* which may fall lamentably short of the high standards of production you had set. This is a very irritating and oft-recurring situation which may leave the client vaguely dissatisfied with the result and you without that most precious of all designer's assets—a really good example of a finished job in production. So you must nag away as mercilessly as you feel you can about fulfilling your obligations to see the job right through.

Delivering finished work

If the finished job is in the form of finished artwork, try never to send it through the post. With all due deference to the Post Office it may get lost or damaged. If distance makes it essential to send it through the post, expert packing is an obvious necessity and sending it by Recorded Delivery another.

For an oversize package or for a very urgent one, to go some distance, it is a good idea and a fairly safe one to put it by hand on a selected train, having first arranged with your client to have it met at the other end.

Graphic designers, who usually prepare their artwork same-size, will need to know the maximum dimensions and weight of parcels which can be sent by post. It would be a good idea to write out the following and put it on your pin-up board for quick reference when the crisis happens:

Maximum dimensions for parcel post
Length 1·070 metres (3ft 6in) or
2 metres (6ft 7in) length and girth combined.
Maximum weight for parcel post
10 kilos (22 lb).

In most main cities and towns in Great Britain there is a Post Office Messenger Service which is well worth investigating in advance so that you will know what it can do for you when you have an urgent delivery problem. Subject to the availability of staff, the Post Office will provide express conveyance all the way for an article by Post Office Messenger. 'Railex' is another Post Office service whereby a Post Office Messenger will put your postal packet on the first available train. These services will obviously be expensive but if you are a one-man office, their cost should be weighed against the cost of your own time spent more lucratively on the drawing board than a long return journey spent being your own messenger. Your local Head Postmaster could tell you about the service and how it is charged.

Checking proofs and prototypes

Given that you succeed in persuading your client to let you check proofs, prototypes and production runs, do not then let your enthusiasm for perfection so run away with you that you involve your client in extra costs without first getting his approval. If you have genuine criticisms that a production specification is not being adhered to then you must ask and get revisions at no extra cost to your client. But if at that stage you want to make amendments which are outside the specification, you must find out from the contractor what they would cost and ask first for your client's approval of the extra expenditure. In most cases he will probably give it if so asked. But he will not like to find that extra time and money have been spent on a last-minute amendment without any reference to him at all.

When final proofs, prototypes or first production runs have been checked and found satisfactory you will have completed Phase Two (c) of the chart on page 15 except for sending in the last invoice relevant to this phase of the pattern.

Almost any design job needs at least some written notes to accompany preliminary design proposals. If you present these in person, as you always should if possible, you will of course explain verbally why you are proposing what you are proposing.

Design notes
But then it usually happens that your preliminary designs are kept by the client to show to his colleagues, to other departments in the firm and often to his board of directors, with probably an awesome chairman to say the final yea or nay. You may have put forward highly technical reasons for this or that aspect of your proposals and these can get distorted as they are passed on round the firm by word of mouth. So a brief summary in writing could be left with your drawings to state your case for you when you are not there to do it in person. Provide a neat light folder or cover for the top copy and be sure that your full name, address and phone number are included. Use one of the numbering systems from Chapter One for the paper itself and keep it concise and factual, preferably on a single sheet of paper.

A design report
Sometimes you will be commissioned to submit a brief report based on your research, conclusions and written recommendations to support your visual design proposals.
This need not be alarming because it is likely that by the time you are involved in preparing a design report, you will already have mastered the techniques of business letter writing, particularly fee letters and also of structuring and numbering them correctly. The simple design report is really only a longer and more detailed letter but without the dear-sir-yours-truly bits.

First draft of the framework
The secret of writing a design report is to sit down firmly before you start any of the work at all and draft a framework for it. This will help you to get the various parts of it into the proper sequence, help you in planning your programme of work and most important of all, enable you to write the text for each stage as you complete the physical work. This will prevent that awful last-minute panic and pressure if you leave all the writing as well as the designing to the eleventh hour. First jot down the items you are sure about:

Cover
Title page
Brief
Research
Conclusions
Recommendations
That list would provide the basic headings for almost any design report of any length or complexity.

Now write the list again, this time each item at the head of a separate sheet of paper and begin to add to them.

Cover   This is only a reminder that your report should have one and that it could carry either a title plus your name or just a title or just your name, whichever you think most appropriate.

Title Page   Title of the report.

Name, address and phone number of author (you) or authors if you have worked in collaboration with anyone.

Signature/s. It is usual to sign the top copy of a report.

Date

The Brief   This can probably be lifted as it is from your fee letter but could be amplified if appropriate.

Research   If you have not already done so, you will have to start planning your programme under this heading. For instance:

Visits

Materials

Processes

Experimentation

and so on, according to the nature of the job.

Conclusions   This will be your summing up of everything you have previously seen and done, with the conclusions you have come to. This did not seem worth following up, that looked promising, one competitor looked formidable, others did not, the advantages and disadvantages of material or process A against material or process B, and so on. The headings under this section will probably stem from the brief and might be:

Competitors

Existing materials

New materials

Existing processes

New processes

Rationalization of sizes, parts, colours, ranges

Cost element

etc. etc.

Recommendations   These you will have to leave until your designs are beginning to take final shape on paper or in model form. But a check-list of possible subheadings might usefully be put down in advance, say:

Materials
Colour
Dimensions
Range
Cost
etc.

Second draft of the framework
Now let us recap, by putting down the framework so far, leaving out my comments and having a first go at a numbering system:

Cover

Title page

Section A The Brief

Section B Research
1 Visits
  (a) to client's factories
  (b) to other places
2 Materials investigated
  (a) existing
  (b) new
3 Processes investigated
  (a) existing
  (b) new
4 Experimentation in progress
  (a) at home
  (b) overseas
etc. etc.

Section C Conclusions
1 Competitors
  (a) at home
  (b) overseas

Section C *continued*
2 Materials available
  (a) existing
  (b) new
3 Processes suitable
  (a) existing
  (b) new
4 Rationalization
  (a) of colours and sizes
  (b) of colours
  (c) of parts
5 Cost element

Section D Recommendations
1 Materials
2 Colour
3 Dimensions
4 Cost
5 Range
etc. etc.

You really will find that if you draft your report framework somewhat on the above lines, adapting it of course to the special circumstances and before you start the job, you will have almost eliminated the mental anguish of having to write it and probably halved the time it would otherwise take you to do so. This is because everything you have to say, most of it factual, will fall into its already allotted place and in the right sequence.

I have outlined above how to draft the framework of fairly simple reports when the necessity for design or re-design has already been agreed. There are occasions as well when a designer is faced with the responsibility of making a wide study in depth, over a firm's whole design policy or lack of it. The technique of drafting and writing the resultant report is exactly the same but the process is rather more elaborate. Chapter Fifteen deals with this.

Contracting for a client means either advising him how to spend his money on the production of something you have designed for him or actually spending it for him yourself, with his agreement of course or within an agreed budget. In those fields of design where your client may not have the facilities for producing what you design for him—print, displays, exhibitions, interiors, the chances are that he will ask you to look after the contracting and production for him. Although this means a good deal of extra work for you it is much to be desired since you will probably be able so to control the production of your design as to ensure the high standard it will undoubtedly merit. Otherwise your client may be the kind of man who 'always goes to a little jobbing printer' or who has 'a good handyman who fits up interiors in his spare time' with the usually lamentable results.

It also means that you take on considerable extra responsibility to three people:

(a) to your client since he will probably accept your recommendation as to the most suitable contractor and it is then your professional responsibility to see that he gets the best possible value for the money he will be spending on your advice;

(b) to the selected contractor to see that he also gets a fair deal (particularly if your client is difficult and unreasonable) and to see that the contractor's bills are paid as promptly as possible. In the event of any dispute you would have to arbitrate unless it were serious enough to go to law in which case you would be an important witness;

(c) to yourself—yes, to yourself. Unless you are aware of and follow meticulously the legal rules about acting as your client's 'agent' or as the 'principal' at the moment of placing an order or contract you may in the event of a major difficulty or dispute unwittingly find yourself under a legal obligation to pay the bill with little hope of recovering any of it from anyone. If the bill were a big one that might mean bankruptcy for you.

Contracting procedure

This goes through a quite specific drill:

(a) completion of working drawings or artwork

(b) writing the specification

(c) selecting contractors

(d) informally inviting the selected contractors to tender

(e) writing a formal letter to the selected contractors inviting them to tender, with a full set of working drawings or artwork, the specification and the date by which tenders must be submitted

(f) if asked for by any of the contractors, having a meeting with them to explain any points of detail in the drawings or specification and agreeing or not with any suggestions they might usefully make to amend a method or material which might ease work and cut costs

(g) if any such amendments are agreed between you and one contractor, notifying immediately the other contractors before they tender, to give them the opportunity to make and price the same amendments

(h) receiving the tenders on the agreed date and making a comparative summary of the prices and of each contractor's special clauses added to the specification

(i) comparing the summary with the agreed budget, if any

(j) if the lowest tender is seriously above the budget asking the two lowest tenderers (if there is not much between their prices) to discuss with you how drastic cuts might have to be made, less expensive materials used and asking them to re-estimate for such items by an agreed date

(k) receiving the revised figures, collating the now lowest tender into a budget summary with any other single estimates for ancilliary items which you have been getting, adding your agreed fees and submitting to your client, pointing out where savings could be made

(l) receiving your client's *written* acceptance

(m) agreeing with him whether he or you will pay the bills (DANGER POINT, see below)

(n) placing the contracts *in writing* with copies to your client, telling the contractor at the same time to whom his bills should be made out and to whom they should be sent (DANGER POINT, see below)

(o) writing to the other contractors to tell them with polite regret that they have not won the tender

(p) supervising the work at all stages wherever it is being done until it is completed to your satisfaction and delivered or handed over

(q) during the course of the work, confirming *in writing* to the contractors, with copies to your client, any agreed variations to the original specification *as they occur* and which will involve your client in extra costs

(r) agreeing any reasonable requests for interim payments by the contractors and certifying the invoices

(s) checking the contractors' final accounts, meeting them to discuss any items which are not clear or which seem unreasonable, finally certifying and passing them for payment

(t) defects liability period—this usually only applies to interior and permanent exhibition design and is therefore dealt with in detail in Chapter Sixteen in the second part of this book.

That all looks pretty formidable and it *is* pretty formidable and it needs to be. Nowhere is a designer's professionalism and administrative efficiency more necessary than when he is contracting for a client. If he makes serious mistakes a lot of money and several reputations may be at stake—his client's, his own and that of the contractors and suppliers. It can even be that a designer in addition to having to pay out of his own pocket for his mistakes may also be threatened with litigation by his client who may have lost valuable time or customers.

Some categories of designers may never get involved in contracting for a client. This is obvious where the design work is for something which the client produces himself—furniture, products, dress, etc. The most which might happen would be the need for a special prototype for which the firm had no production facilities, or a specially-designed component. In both cases or in any other similar ones the appropriate parts of the contracting procedure which I have outlined above should be meticulously followed.

Another category where contracting for a client need not arise is all aspects of graphics. But if a designer offers voluntarily to get his work produced this will probably be accepted gladly by say an engineering or furniture manufacturer who may have no adequate department to cope with the mysteries of paper and print, ink and foils, box-making, illuminated signs and suchlike.

In this case the designer's responsibilities are precisely as I have set them out above except that he may, quite correctly, advise his clients that competitive tendering might not be appropriate where the production process he is advising is only available from one specialist firm.

The design categories where the contracting procedure can seldom if ever be avoided are those of interior and exhibition design and it is in these categories where the largest sums of money are likely to be involved. The rare exceptions might be if you were designing special interiors for say a building contractor who would probably want to do the work in his own workshops. Or a design for a small exhibit at an overseas trade exhibition where the firm's local agent might have to get it built and installed locally to avoid heavy travel expenses for the designer. But when a client commissions a designer for an interior or an exhibition, a shop or a showroom, he needs and expects to get, not only the creativity of the designer but also his expertise in getting the job built and installed. It is just the same as the collaboration between client and architect and the interior designer is trained to, and must accept, the same sort of responsibilities.

Although the contracting procedures I have set out above are the same for all fields of design, they need more amplification for interior and exhibition designers than for others. I am therefore dealing with them separately in Chapter Sixteen in the second part of this book but I hope that interested students will take in both chapters while they are still studying.

Here I am only going to enlarge on some of the items in the contracting procedure as they apply to less complicated and less expensive productions.

The specification

Before you can ask contractors to tender for a job (to tender really means to estimate but in this context it usually means to estimate in competition with others), you have got to write a specification. This is a very detailed description of the whole piece of work, specifying precisely what you want done, the materials and processes to be used, all to be read in conjunction with the working drawings or artwork you will have prepared. It will form the basis of the contract which will eventually be placed with one of the contractors.

It is no concern of this book to deal with that part of a specification which describes your design and the way it is to be produced. Your training will have taught you how to do that. Here we have to consider the general clauses and the administrative instructions, which are almost as important but some of which may get overlooked. A typical example would be a print specification.

A print specification

The design part of a print specification will detail the dimensions, the number of pages in addition to the cover pages (if it is a book or brochure), the method of printing, the number of colours, the paper and so on. The more general points would be in connection with:

Quantity It may be that your client is not certain at the time of inviting tenders how many copies he needs or can afford. You therefore specify a price for a basic quantity with the additional price per extra multiples of hundreds or thousands.

Run-on prices If the print job has been designed for immediate short-term use (a special leaflet, say, for an exhibition stand or an exhibition catalogue) where it is difficult to estimate 'consumption', it is useful to ask for a run-on price per multiples of hundreds or thousands. This means that if the printer were given an order for further copies while he was still finishing the original order he would run it straight on, on his machines, at rather less expense.

Delivery date If an actual date cannot be specified the printer can be asked to give one calculated from the date when he receives the firm order and the art work.

Delivery address The question of deliveries is often overlooked when writing a print specification. Then it is disconcerting to be faced with an extra charge for this, which may run into several pounds on a bulky print order placed with a country printer for town delivery. If your client cannot give you a specific delivery address you can put 'delivery to city centre address' in your specification which is sufficient for the printer to price the cost of transport. If you are not able to do this then you must ask for a price 'ex works' and point out to your client that delivery charges may be extra.

If your client is going to want his print job packed into several parcels and despatched or delivered to several different addresses (agents or branch offices perhaps or even overseas) this too should be specified since it will certainly involve extra labour, packing and transport charges.

Blocks If the job involves the use of blocks the specification should state clearly whether the printer should allow for getting these made himself or whether they will be supplied.

Colour proofs For a job of elaborate colour-printing and particularly if time is short, some printers charge extra if a full set of colour proofs is required. This requirement should be stated in order that the printers can allow for their charges, if any.

A display unit specification

Some of the points under the print specification above would also apply in the case of display units, window or counter displays or any similar three-dimensional device designed for production in quantity. But packing would be a more important item and you would need to specify whether the units were to be just wrapped, provided with light protective packing or elaborately packed, boxed and even crated. If they are for export, this must be mentioned since packing then becomes a major issue. You might even decide to have the packing estimated for by a separate firm, experts in the designing and making of export crates. If your display unit contains items which your general contractor will mount or fix but not produce himself—photoprints for instance or models or captions—this should be clearly stated in your specification . . . 'to be supplied by another contractor' is the usual phrase.

Display units often travel unassembled and are then put together by the recipient on the site. Your specifications should therefore usually allow for the printing and inclusion of assembly instructions and diagrams. You and your client will almost certainly want to see a prototype of a display unit. The contractor should be warned of this in the specification and asked to quote a separate price, if any, for it. Usually a single prototype is more expensive than the cost of one unit in a bulk order.

Inviting tenders

Whenever there is time you should always invite not less than three contractors to tender for a job which you are handling for your client, whether it be print, displays, exhibitions or interiors. It is his money which you are going to spend for him and it is up to you to get the best price for the work. 'Best' does not always mean 'lowest'. It means the most reasonable price from the most suitable contractor who is likely to produce the most satisfactory results in the time available.

To ensure that you get three really competitive prices, you should pick three firms whose size, facilities and reputation are roughly comparable. Then you will be pretty safe in recommending to your client that he should accept the lowest tender. But if you invite tenders from, say, two top-class firms and one small back garden firm which is eager to show you how good it is, the chances are it will put in a rock-bottom price a long way below the other two. This may be merely because its overheads are very low or because it wants to win the contract at any price or because it is not very good or experienced at estimating.

Whatever the reason (and you are not likely to know it at the time of receiving the tenders) it puts you in a dilemma. If you say to your client 'Here are three tenders, from A for £1,000, from B for £1,800, from C for £1,900. I recommend that B's tender is accepted because I think that A would be too small and inexperienced to handle the job' your client is going to wonder why on earth in that case you invited A to tender, and may suspect your judgment. Equally he may be attracted by the low price and insist that A gets the job. Then you may really be in trouble unless A miraculously turns out to be all that he claimed. It is unfortunately more likely that he will not have sufficient experience to do the job properly and finish it on time; not enough reserve capacity to deal with the unforeseen crisis and that his bill at the end will be heavily loaded with extras.

But of course there are a number of small contractors in any field who do excellent and conscientious work and who have the advantage of giving close personal service. If you hear of one, preferably by personal recommendation from a fellow-designer who has used the firm, go and see them on their own ground and judge for yourself their capacity and workmanship. Try them out on a small simple job or two until you are satisfied that they could handle larger ones. Then you could more confidently invite them to tender in competition with larger firms, particularly for jobs with shoe-string budgets. To find and get used to working with a good small firm in this way can eventually be a great asset to you. It is worth taking considerable time and trouble with a promising one, so that they get to know the way you like things done and take a pride in doing it for you.

But before we go on, bear in mind Clause 14 of the SIAD Code of Professional Conduct, already referred to on page 75:

'While acting for his client, a member may not divert to his own advantage any discounts, reductions or other financial benefits offered as inducement by contractors, manufacturers or suppliers. Similarly a member must disclose any financial involvement which he may have with contractors or suppliers he may recommend.' And Clause 15:

'On the other hand, if a member is also a manufacturer, retailer or agent in his own right, he may accept those financial terms which are normally honourably offered within the trade, provided they accrue to his company or his organization and not to himself privately.'

As time is nearly always running short when you get to the tendering stage on a job, it is a good idea to ring up your three or more selected contractors a few days before your drawings and specifications are ready and ask them if they are interested and able to tender. This will avoid that maddening situation whereby you get one or more of your three firms returning the drawings during the tendering period with regrets that their programme is too full. You will have lost a valuable week or so and have to start all over again.

If the design part of your specification is impeccable and your selected contractors know your work, it may be that they will need no further briefing from you before they put in their tenders. Otherwise you will always find it useful to go over everything with them, either severally or together, so that they are quite clear about all the details of the work for which they are tendering.

How long to give your contractors to prepare their tenders depends on the size of the job. A week would probably be a minimum for any job; ten days to two weeks for an exhibition stand of average complexity; three to four weeks for a large and complicated one, six to twelve or more weeks for an interior design job, depending on its size. Don't forget that in the case of print you will probably have only one original. Each of your printers' representatives will want to take this away to show his estimating department unless you are able to provide photo copies, though these are no use in the case of a complex colour job. In fixing your tendering date you must therefore allow time for this.

Single tenders

There will be occasions when you will agree with your client that a job should not go out to competitive tender. This may be due to lack of time, to the client's wish to give the job to his pet contractor or to mutual acknowledgment of the fact that the selected contractor has advantages for doing the job which outweigh any financial considerations. There may be other reasons but these are the most likely ones. Each needs a closer look since there are obvious dangers in single tenders. If the contractor knows that he has no competitors there will be nothing to curb his pricing of the work except his integrity and his desire to retain your goodwill.

Collating tenders and estimates

As soon as possible after you have got together your competitive tenders, original or revised as might have been necessary and any single estimates which you have had to get as well, collate them into a single document with as much detail as seems necessary to explain and justify the cost of each item, put them into a neat slim folder and send them to your client with a covering letter. This is how collated estimates for a print job might be set out for your clients, say Robinson Limited:

ROBINSON LIMITED   *(Your job reference no.)*
Estimated cost of design and production of booklet '(title)'

1 *Paper and printing*
Cost of printing photolitho 5000 copies of 16-page booklet and cover on paper and card as specimens enclosed, with six drawings and four photographs, the inside pages black and white, the cover in two colours, trimmed size xx mm by xx mm, wire-stitched and delivered to city centre address. Tender (number and date) from (printers' name) attached £...

2 *Photography*
Cost of special photography as agreed, including photographer's travel expenses to site and supplying two prints of selected shots; also copyright fees for use of two photoprints from (name) Photo Library, including retouching £...

3 *Illustrations*
Artist's fees for six drawings from references supplied £ ....
4 *Production and miscellaneous costs*
Typesetting for cover and titles, copy negatives, photostats travel
and delivery expenses, etc. say   £ ....
                                                                                            ─────────
                                                                                            £ ....

5 *Fees*
As agreed for the preparation of preliminary dummy for booklet,
and for finished artwork for the cover and 16 type-estimated page
layouts for the printer, research for photographs, supervision of
artist's and photographer's work on illustrations, obtaining tenders
and estimates from printers, submitting to you; and supervising
production, proofing, completion and deliveries   £ ....
                                                                                            ─────────
                                                                                            £ ....

6 *Notes*
(a) Other tenders received for Item 1 were
     Printer's name   £ ....
     Printer's name   £ ....
(b) The run-on price for Item 1 if required would be £ .... per X00 copies
(c) The above costs do (or do not as the case may be) include VAT
(d) Delivery is promised for x weeks after the contract is placed.
(date)   (Your name, address
                                                                            and phone number)

Just a few points about the items in that document. If the prices on the right
come to pounds and some pence always round off each total upwards to the
nearest pound so that 747.59 would become £748. Nobody, least of all a busy
client, wants to be bothered with anything but round figures in these sort of
estimates.
Item 1 would have been the subject of competitive tender and you would send
with your collated budget the original or a copy of the tender you were
recommending for acceptance. Items 2 and 3 would have been single estimates
and Item 4 would be your own estimates of costs which you had already
incurred and might continue to incur. The useful word 'say' indicates that the
total is not a firm one. An alternative is to start the item by saying 'Allow
for . . .' The travel and delivery expenses referred to there would of course be
those of your own office, as the printer's price at Item 1 includes delivery of the
finished job.
The great thing to remember about preparing collated production budgets is to
put in everything—all those things for which you have been able to get firm
tenders and estimates and an allowance for those items for which you have not
(but there should not be too many of these particularly if your only excuse is

lack of your time). The main thing the client will want to know is what the *total* job is going to cost him and whether he is going to get it on time. He will be justifiably irritated if you keep coming up with prices for items which you had forgotten and even more so if these only come to light when the final bills come in. This does not of course refer to extras or amendments which he had asked for during the course of production.

The covering letter
Now for the covering letter, which should contain the following information/ explanations/requests for decisions etc. in that order and suitably worded:

1 Here is the production budget for . . .
2 It is based on the lowest tenders received . . .
   (If it is not, explain why you are recommending the next lowest)
3 Point out that it is within the agreed budget of £ . . .
   or
4 As it exceeds the budget by £ . . . savings could be made by cutting this . . . or amending that . . .
5 Ask for instructions to proceed . . . by not later than (date)
6 Ask if the client will be placing the contracts direct or would he prefer you to do this on his behalf
   or
7 Would he prefer you to place the contracts and orders in your own name, pay all the final accounts and re-charge them to him in a single invoice?
8 In the event of the Item 7 above, you would be entitled to quote a handling charge for this service of something between 2½% and 10% on all costs (more about this below).

But before you write such a covering letter, I must digress now in order to explain the DANGER POINT to which I have been so ominously referring and also to explain about handling charges.

Financial DANGER POINTS
If you have received tenders and estimates from a contractor or supplier and if you write to them on your own letter-heading and say in effect 'I accept your estimate for £ . . . dated . . . Please go ahead etc. . . . .' you have established to the contractor and his accounts department that you are acting as what is known legally as the 'principal'. In other words the contractual arrangement is between you and the contractor direct and he will make out his bills in your name, send them to you and you will be financially responsible for paying them.

If on the other hand you say in your letter, in effect: 'I accept your estimate for £ . . . dated . . . *on behalf of my clients Robinson Ltd.* Please go ahead etc. Your account should be rendered as followed:

                    Robinsons Limited
                    (full address)

but sent to me first for checking and certifying after which I will pass it to my clients for payment to you direct . . .' then you have correctly indicated that you are acting as what is known legally as the 'agent' (ie on behalf of your client), that the contract is between the printer and your client direct and that it is the latter's responsibility to pay the bills. If you had written the first kind of letter without thinking but had really meant the second situation to apply, there would still be time to remedy it if the final bill came to you in your name. You would send it smartly back to the contractor's accounts department with an apology for not having instructed them properly in the first place and ask them to re-render it with the correct name and address on it.

Then you would send it on to your client for payment direct and apart from this irritating bit of extra work for all concerned, all would be well *provided the job had gone through smoothly from start to finish and the client was entirely satisfied*. But if the client found the job unsatisfactory or delivered too late to be of any use and refused to pay all or part of the bill and the contractor stubbornly said it wasn't his fault, then—oh dear, you are in great trouble if you had written the first kind of letter by mistake. Because if your client refuses to pay then the contractor will hold you responsible for paying him, whether the amount be £5, £50 or £5000. The same situation could apply even if the job had been entirely satisfactory but the client had suddenly died, gone bankrupt, been taken over or fled the country to avoid paying his debts.

Unfortunately, and this is the biggest danger point of all, it happens all too often that nothing about a contract gets recorded in writing at all. For reasons of lateness all round (not necessarily your own) and the pressure of delivery promises which must be kept, you get a verbal estimate from your contractor, you get a verbal OK to it from your client, you give the contractor a telephoned instruction to go ahead and to hurry, hurry. You confirm nothing in writing to anybody and then if anything goes wrong, you are even deeper in the mire, particularly if the contractor's bill has a lot of unexpected overtime added to it when it flutters inexorably through your letter box.

Now let us see how to circumvent this danger point.

Your client's acceptance
When you have sent in your collated estimates the chances are that your client will telephone you to discuss them and eventually to say go ahead. Then you must be certain of getting his instructions to you recorded in writing. Just as the contractors are not legally empowered to proceed with the work until they have your (or the client's) written instructions, so you too are not legally empowered to issue those instructions without your client's written approval. If he gives you in the first place a verbal OK to go ahead, he should be asked at that time for confirmation in writing and he (or his secretary) must be persistently asked for it if days go by without any sign of life from him. If you continue to be unlucky and you suspect that because he seems inefficient, over-worked or a doubtful customer anyway, you may never get the required letter from him, then you can do one of two things. Write and tell him firmly but politely that all work is suspended pending his written instructions or write

yourself to confirm his verbal instructions, referring to your telephone conversation, its date, your estimates, their date and their total. Such a letter could finish by saying 'unless I hear from you to the contrary I shall assume that you agree the content of this letter.'

The first alternative should be used if you have good reasons for suspecting your client's integrity. The second might be sufficient to cover you if later your client refused to pay up. Either is only a last resort. Much better and safer is to get it in writing from him.

If your client decides in answer to the sixth paragraph in the outline covering letter above that he will place all contracts himself, there is no problem or danger point. This is often done by large firms who have purchasing departments. If your client asks you to place the contracts on his behalf (ie as his agent), ask him to return the originals of any tenders and estimates you may have sent him, write the second kind of letter I have indicated above and *be sure* to send him a copy of it and all other such orders or order letters. He is eventually going to have to pay the bills and he *must* be kept informed of how you are dealing with every stage of the contracting procedure.

I am going to repeat here in more detail the contractually important part of this all-important letter:

ABC Printers Ltd
(address)   (date)
Dear Sirs
Booklet (title) for Robinsons Limited

My clients Robinsons Limited have instructed me to place with you on their behalf the contract for the production of the above booklet in accordance with your tender dated . . . reference number . . . for the sum of £ . . . and to ask you to proceed at once with the work. Your accounts should be made out to

Robinsons Limited

(full address)

but sent to me for checking and certification after which they will be forwarded to my clients for payment to you direct.

In the first paragraph of that letter, the total amount of the tender has been referred to as 'the sum of £x' on the assumption that it was being accepted in its entirety. If however you were omitting certain items, separately priced, or if you had made cuts which had necessitated part of the tender being repriced and re-submitted, you would have to refer to such omissions or any further documents received from the contractor (their dates, reference numbers and amounts) at the same time and in the same letter. And again I repeat, you would send to your clients a copy of all such letters placing contracts and orders.

When the selected tender has been accepted and the relevant contractor informed, it is normal, and courteous, practice to write to all the other contractors who tendered and tell them, with suitable regrets that their tender was not accepted.

With that letter and the copy of it on the way to contractor and client you will have successfully passed the danger point on the second alternative. But now you will be surprised to find that I am going to tell you what happens when you deliberately accept the third alternative, that of being the principal in contractual arrangements, paying the bills for your client and re-charging him. Why accept the danger point you will say? Well the risks are there but there are advantages as well.

Paying bills for your client

This situation is obviously not one to be entered into lightly and *never* when really large sums of money are involved. But it will probably arise to a limited extent in connection with almost any job where a number of small disbursements have to be made, small items bought for cash and a succession of small orders placed, possibly with firms with whom you have monthly credit accounts for such things as typesettings, photographic work and so on. These might be the sort of things covered at Item 4 in the example of collated estimates above. Most clients would probably agree that it would make for mutual convenience, ease and speed of working if you were the principal for such orders and purchases.

They may equally ask you for their own convenience to finance the whole job so that their own possibly over-worked and under-staffed accounts department is not called upon to deal with a multitude of copy orders, invoices and payments but one final collated invoice from you when the work is complete. Providing, as has already been stressed above, this does not involve you in substantial amounts of money and provided also that you are assured of your client's financial stability and integrity, you may decide to accept the position of principal and to place all contracts and orders in your own name. But in addition you must be reasonably certain that your bank balance could stand the strain if you had to pay the contractors and suppliers before you get repaid by your client. Finally you can and should agree a handling charge with your client before you go into action.

Handling charges

If your client has asked you to be responsible for paying bills for him, you are tacitly accepting a certain degree of financial risk and you will also be involved in extra accountancy overheads: entering invoices, receiving and checking statements, issuing cheques in payment, entering receipts for cash purchases and so on. In mitigation of all this, you can agree with your client that you should add what is usually called a handling charge to the amounts you are paying for him. This will be shown separately on your final collated invoice to him and would normally be 2½% to 5%. In special circumstances and again by agreement, it might be higher but *never* higher than 10%. This percentage has, of course, nothing to do with a percentage *fee* and is quite separate from it.

Final accounts from contractors and suppliers

The checking of final accounts from contractors and suppliers must be done with patience and great attention to detail. This is the final moment of spending the client's money for him and you must ensure that he is charged accurately and fairly for what he has had. Equally if he has asked for extra work you must ensure that the contractor gets a fair payment for it. In the event of any argument from either side you must be the arbitrator unless or until the argument becomes serious enough for it to go to court. With a reasonable client and a responsible contractor this should very seldom happen if the rules for placing orders and sanctioning extras have been kept. Then it only remains to check each item in the light of the materials and workmanship provided, decide whether both were up to the required standard and query any which were not. For some extras agreed at the last moment in the frenzy of completion, the contractor may not have had time to submit prices and you will see these for the first time on his final account. They need looking at with a particularly critical eye and discussing with the contractor if they seem to you unduly high. He must give you a satisfactory explanation of their apparent costliness before you can pass them on to your client with equal conviction.

The process of to-ing and fro-ing to get a complex contractor's account agreed can sometimes take weeks or even months but the issues must be faced and the battle must be fought to a conclusion which satisfies the three parties concerned—your client, your contractor and yourself. When this happy stage is reached and the client is going to pay the bills, you should type or write on each 'Certified correct for payment' with the date and your signature beneath. You should always send them with a covering note to your client, listing the three essential details of each invoice: number, date and total amount. Send a copy of your letter to the relevant contractors so that they will know that their invoices have been cleared by you and sent on. Then if the client is a slow payer, they will worry him and not you.

If you are paying all the bills you will probably have recorded them on your job sheets or job records, as was suggested in Chapter Five. Here again, you have to wait till the very last one is in and checked before you can render the final collated account for the whole job. It is a good idea to try and set out this final account to match up as far as possible to the form of the collated estimates since this makes for easy comparison and checking by your client. The summarized items in the estimates would however have to be broken down into greater detail on the invoice. Extras go best at the end divided according to whether the exigencies of the job required them or whether they were requested by your client.

If you are an interior or exhibition designer, turn now to Chapter Sixteen where you will find more information about contracting especially applicable to these fields of design.

When you have tied up the agreement on fees for a job and established your method of recording the time you will spend and the expenses you will incur on it, it remains for you to do the job itself, until such time as you have completed the first stage of it in accordance with your fee letter.

Then comes the great moment when you render your account or invoice which is another way of saying send in your bill.

When to invoice

How soon to render an invoice after you have completed the first stage of a job needs some consideration. You could, if you needed to badly enough, submit your preliminary designs to a client on Monday and render your invoice to him on Tuesday. But it would be à pity and create a bad impression. I would say that as a general rule preliminary designs submitted and approved within the first three weeks of a calendar month could reasonably be invoiced on the last day of that month. But preliminary work submitted during the last week of a calendar month might more decently wait until the end of the following month. That is, if you can afford to wait.

If preliminary designs are submitted and approved in principle but have to be held for the final endorsement of, say, a board meeting, you should wait to receive this final clearance before sending in your invoice, unless it is unreasonably delayed. In fact, it is always worth trying to find out if your client is reasonably satisfied with what you have given him so far, before invoicing for it.

If your fee arrangements are for development work to be charged hourly rates, we have already seen in previous chapters that you render your invoices every month regardless of the stage you have reached. The interval between submitting finished working drawings and rendering your invoices for them should be on the same basis as for preliminary designs but with one difference. Your invoice in this case may be the absolute end of the job and of your collaboration with your client, at any rate for some time. It is necessary therefore to make quite sure that your invoice includes, as well as your final fees, all remaining costs and expenses to be charged in addition—drawing office prints, models, special artwork, long distance calls and so on. Your order books and job sheets should show you whether you have yourself received all such relevant costs for recharging and only when you are certain that this is so should you set about drafting your final invoice. Much better to hold over your own invoicing for a further month while you wait for some dilatory supplier's account than to risk forgetting it altogether and then receive it a month after you have rendered your final invoice to your client. Legally he must still pay you, even up to seven years, but he and his accounts department will be very irritated at small items continuing to come in, in dribs and drabs, after they had thought that their account with you was closed for a particular job. You also may feel diffident about charging such items and may decide instead to pay them yourself. This is something you can ill afford to do and the necessity for which should never have arisen. Such items overlooked and consequently not charged to clients could add up to a sizeable annual sum even though individually they do not amount to more than a few pounds.

When you have rendered your final invoice (professional people always 'render' their invoices) you will have completed Phase Three (b) of the chart on page 15. What you do about Phase Three (a) is dealt with in the next chapter.

Setting out an invoice

Now for the invoices themselves. You will use your ordinary letter-heading and *always* take at least one carbon copy for your accountant. Sometimes when you receive a formal order for a job it will ask for your invoices in duplicate. The firm in question will have its own good reasons for this request and it should be respected. The end-of-the-month date will go at the top of your invoice and the firm's full name and address. Never address your invoices to an individual in a firm, always impersonally to the firm itself.

Centred below the date and address should go the word 'invoice' in capital letters. This is to differentiate it from its follow-up 'statement' and later, if you have been unlucky or inaccurate, 'credit note'.

If you have ever had to write to or ring up one of your own suppliers to query an invoice you have probably found a serial number on the printed invoice form to use as an easy reference. For the same reason you should use a reference number on your own invoices and this should be your job number, as you will need this for your own records as well.

So your 'reference' number should come next and be followed by a brief general heading descriptive of the job. This will be very useful later on for everybody's quick reference and particularly when you are carrying out several different kinds of work for one client. It is a kind of chapter heading and might read 'Packaging for Bigga Biscuits', or 'Stand at Food Fair'; or 'Sign for Manchester Factory'; or 'Treatment of Van Sides'; all of which might be jobs for the same biscuit manufacturers. Your heading would tell the accounts clerk at a glance from which department the order for your work had come.

Invoicing lump-sum fees

Now we come to the actual wording of the invoice itself and let us assume that this is to be a simple straightforward charge for preliminary designs with an additional fee for amendments. It might read thus:

(1) Fees as agreed (Mr J. R. Jones' letter of (date), for the preparation and submission of two alternative preliminary designs in the form of coloured dummies for a new pack for your Bigga Biscuits, excluding copyright in the designs—   £xx

(2) Fees as agreed (my letter to Mr J. R. Jones of (date) for amendments to one of the above coloured dummies to show enlarged logotype, as requested—   £xx
                                                                                   ———
                                                                                   £xx

(3) Costs incurred as follows:
   (a) travel and subsistence expenses in connection with visit to your Glasgow Factory on (date)   £xx
   (b) long distance call   £ x   £xx
                                                                                   ———
                                                                                   £xxx
                                                                                   ———

There are several useful things to notice about that comparatively simple invoice. First, each item or sub-item which is going to end in a sum of money is numbered or lettered for ease of reference and general tidiness. Second, a precise reference is made to letters of agreement about fees with names and dates. If instead of a letter you had received an order you would refer to its serial number and date. This will speed up checking in your client's accounts department. Third, you have summarized the job in a few words by referring to the quantity of designs, the form in which they were submitted, what they were for, the copyright position, and the agreed fee. Fourth, the costs you are charging are itemized separately and the date of your journey is given. It is always worthwhile being very precise and factual about these sort of costs. A few pounds-worth of them are more likely to be subject to suspicious scrutiny by a conscientious accounts clerk than several hundred pounds-worth of fees. The same pattern of wording and layout as given above for an invoice for preliminary design fees would serve with the appropriate amendments when you come to invoice your fees for completing the job.

Invoicing hourly rates
When fees are to be charged on the basis of hours worked the formula needs to be more explicit, almost like a brief progress report. For instance:
Fees based on hourly rates for making amendments as requested to the selected preliminary design; discussing this with you and receiving your approval; visiting Manchester on (date) to meet your Production Manager to discuss the making of a first prototype; preparing the necessary working drawings and specification for this purpose; further meeting in Manchester on (date) with your Production Manager to discuss working drawings and

subsequently making further modifications to prototype drawings, before passing them over for prototype production—55 hours at £2—£110 If, instead of that sort of wording, you had merely said on your invoice that you had 'prepared prototype drawings, 55 hours, etc.' your client might well have thought that you had taken an unreasonably long time over a fairly simple set of drawings and might have protested at what he was getting charged. But when he sees that your 55 hours have included preliminary amendments, a meeting with him, two day-long visits to his factory out of town and modifications to the final drawings, he will realize that the total hours and fees are quite reasonable.

Your next invoice following the one above would pick up from where it left off, again as a sort of progress report and would probably refer to 'meeting at your factory on (date) with you and your Production Manager to inspect first prototype; preparation of further working drawings incorporating agreed modifications and passing these to your Production Manager for second prototype, etc., etc.'

Each of these invoices should have as a second item all your chargeable expenses up to the date of each invoice for such things as travelling and subsistence expenses, drawing office prints, long distance calls and so on. Just as it is bad psychology to invoice all your hourly rate fees in one grand and terrifying total when the job is complete, so also is it a mistake to do likewise with your expenses. 'Little and often' not only lets your client down gently but, equally important, it keeps your own revenue flowing in regularly. It is much, much better to have to wait only one month to receive £100 in fees than to leave it for six months in order to receive £600. You may have gone bankrupt in the meantime for want of ready cash.

Invoicing percentage fees
As we have seen in Chapter Four, your fees for interior and exhibition design will almost certainly be based on a percentage of total production costs. Therefore you cannot compute your final total fee until the job is finished, all the accounts received and agreed between you, the various contractors and suppliers and your client. But this does not mean that you will have to wait for several months or even, in the case of a big interior design job, a year or more, before you get any fees at all. It is quite in order to invoice in stages which are related to the stages of your work. In fact these stage payments should already have been included in your fee letter under 'fee instalments'.

If you will turn back to fee letter structure C on page 41 you will see what these stages are under 'services provided' so I am not going to repeat them here. But because the invoicing of the stages of percentage fees is rather complicated, I will show it in stages applied to an imaginary job without, to start with, any of the usual invoicing phraseology or lay-out, just the sequence.

Let us assume a job where the costs were estimated at £6000 and the percentage fee therefore 15%. This would give a total estimated fee of £900 and this is all you can work on to start with. Let us also assume that the actual final costs worked out at £6150. The sequence of invoicing will then be like this:

Stage One Fee
One-fifth of 15% of *estimated* costs
of £6000, ie, one-fifth of £900   £180

Stage Two Fee
One-third of 15% of *estimated* costs
of £6000, ie, one-third of £900   £300

Stage Three Fee
One-third of 15% of *estimated* costs
of £6000, ie, one-third of £900   £300   £780

Stage Four Fee
Total final fee of 15% of *actual*
costs of £6150   £923   (in round figures)
less amounts previously invoiced   £780

Final balance of fees due   £143

That example is based on the first alternative of 'positioning' Stages Two and
Three referred to on page 41, whereby the adjustment of fees based on actual
instead of estimated costs comes at the end of Stage Four. If you chose the
second alternative, the example above would vary like this:

Stage One Fee
One-fifth of 15% of *estimated* costs
of £6000, ie, one-fifth of £900   £180

Stage Two Fee
One-third of 15% of *estimated* costs
of £6000, ie, one-third of £900   £300   £480

Stage Three Fee
One-third of 15% of *contract* costs
of £6150, ie, one-third of £923   £308

                                       £788

Breaking the sequence for a moment, let us assume that the absolutely final
costs of the job, based on all final accounts, is higher than the contract cost, as
happens more often than not. Then there would have to be a further
adjustment at Stage Four, like this:

Stage Four Fee
Total final fee of 15% of all final
costs of £6300   £954
less amounts previously invoiced   £788
                                            _____

Final balance of fees due   £157
                                            _____

There would be one further variation to the Stage Four fee only and that would be if you had agreed a retention (by your client) of 5% or 10% of your final fees until the end of the defects liability period, when you had seen that the contractor had done all the remedial work he had to do under his contract. In this case that final item under Stage Four would be

Final balance of fees   £157
Less 5% retention until the
end of the defects liability period   £8   (in round figures)
                                            _____
                                            £149   ,,   ,,   ,,
                                            _____

When the contractor had finally finished to your satisfaction, you would then invoice that final £8 of your fees.

Other invoicing and payment problems
I have given you above the three basic ways of invoicing fees—lump-sum, hourly rates and percentages. There are however other invoicing and payment problems to know about but as they are more applicable to free-lance practice and are therefore rather more complex, I have put them in the second part of this book in Chapter Seventeen. If you have time as a student to read them and better still really to study them, you will be all the more prepared to cope with the problems when they begin to happen to you in real life, even if your first job is a salaried one.

Throughout your whole career as a free-lance designer from the bottom of the ladder to the top, the importance to you of specimens and records of your finished jobs will never diminish. You can tell possible clients with modesty but conviction that you are a good and experienced designer but they will probably remain unconvinced, unless they already know you well, until they can see for themselves what you have done. One specimen or photograph of a completely finished job is worth dozens of lunches and weeks of public relations work, provided you make good use of it. And this is where you have to become your own publicity manager. There is no mystique about this. A few basic rules, meticulous attention to detail and a bit of common sense will bring you almost as much useful publicity as would the money you could ill-afford in the early days to pay someone to do it for you. The first rule is that you must be prepared to give the time to it and at the appropriate moment. It is no good sending out expensive photographs of an exhibition stand to a weekly magazine a month after the exhibition has closed. You might as well put them in your wastepaper basket.

For some kinds of work it is necessary to start making plans for publicizing it right from the start. In some cases, as you can see in Chapter Twelve under 'Publicizing your appointments', even before you begin, by announcing a new appointment.

For a completed job, we are now going to deal with Phase Three (a) of the chart on page 15.

'Before and after' stories

Editors of technical publications find a visually well-documented 'before and after' design story almost irresistible. It must be because everybody responds to the romance of a Cinderella situation, which this is. That which was out-of-date, shabby, unimpressive has, under the designer's magic wand, been given a new look, attractive, contemporary, colourful. And it is not only for editorial publicity that you will find 'before and after' stories so useful but also as case histories for your records, your photofiles and, in the form of 35 mm colour slides, for illustrated lectures and teaching jobs.

So whenever you are going to re-design something it is well worth going to some trouble and even a little expense to make sure that you retain for your own subsequent use one good clean specimen of the job 'before' or (and this is where the modest expenditure might come in) photographs of it, if it is an interior, shop-front, sign or anything which will have to be demolished altogether to make way for the new. Such preliminary photography is sometimes necessary, as a complement to a survey, for doing the job itself. As such it could justifiably be charged to your client. Or he may be able to produce existing photographs from his archives. But do make sure that you get these records somehow even if you have to pay for them. It is a point so very often over-looked and then, when it is too late, comes the irritating realization of a good opportunity missed.

In the case of printed material, it is not enough to assume that the 'before' specimens which you will have in any case as references from which to start re-designing, will eventually do for publicity purposes. By the time they have knocked around your studio for months and become dirty and dog-eared they will be fit only for the wastepaper basket. Get two sets if you can, wrap one up in tissue paper and put it safely away. If you can only get one set, have it photographed right away before you begin to make use of it. If your one and only set is flat printed material, slip it into a flat Cellophane bag so that you can see it for reference without too much handling. It is, incidentally, a good idea to lay in a stock of these bags. They are made in several sizes, and are very useful indeed, not only for 'before' and 'after' specimens of your work but for photographs and even small pieces of finished artwork—anything which must be kept as unfingered as possible and yet be visible on both sides.

Specimens of work in production
In the case of print and product design, where for some regrettable but unavoidable reason you are not going to be concerned with supervising production, you may find it difficult to get specimens of the finished jobs for your records. We have already seen under Free Specimens in Chapter Three, how you may decide to stake your claim to certain free specimens at the time of quoting fees. Otherwise, when you send in your finished working drawings, put it *in writing* to your client that you would like to receive copies or sets or lengths or whatever seems appropriate as to quanitity in the case of product design.

Your client will then have your letter as a reminder. You will have your carbon copy of it to prod you into ringing him up or writing again if the specimens have not arrived after a reasonable interval. This is really worth doing. Once an old job is off your drawing-board and you are absorbed in all the problems of a new one it is surprisingly easy to realize, months later, that you have never done anything about getting those all-important specimens of it. By which time it may be difficult, if not impossible. Neither should you feel that any job is too insignificant to bother about in this connection. You may have designed the programme for a local concert. A small job, elegantly done but not a world-shaker. Years later a design or musical magazine may approach you for specimens of suitable work to illustrate a special feature on 'Concert programmes past and present'. Your contribution, suitably credited to you might bring you some useful publicity.

There will be many other such occasions as your reputation grows when you will be asked for specimens of your work. Apart from such special magazine features as I have indicated above there is a steady output of illustrated books and annuals about all aspects of design all over the world. It would be a great pity ever to have to refuse an invitation to contribute to such publications because you had not got specimens or photographs of what would be exactly right to send them.

There will be design exhibitions, too, to which it will be exciting and flattering to be asked to contribute your work for display. And immensely useful to you.

I hope I have sufficiently convinced you of the importance of keeping your 'museum' of work a living, growing, usable one. A further point—however many specimens, photographs or colour slides of each job you succeed in getting, put aside in a separate drawer, box or file an absolutely sacrosanct master set of each one, *which never leaves your office*. This is a good resolution which is easy to make and fatally easy to break. Once your last specimen, photo-print or slide has gone out on loan to someone who promises faithfully to return it, the chances are that you will never see it again.

Record photography

For interior design, exhibitions, stands and displays and many product and engineering jobs, you will obviously have to rely on photographs and colour slides for your records. This can be an expensive operation for you if you have to bear the full cost of it, but it is one which must be faced and not in any cheese-paring frame of mind. You will be proud of your work and you will want the best possible photographs of it for your own all-important publicity purposes, quite apart from your client's.

It is a good idea in the early days to try to find a photographer whose work seems really promising and who has still a small enough one-man type of business to be able to give time and close personal attention to your particular demands. You must be infinitely fussy about your photography and, if necessary, persuade and train your photographer to be so as well. If you have chosen him with judgment both your reputations will benefit from the collaboration.

As to the cost of it, there will be a number of occasions when your client will pay all or a share of the photographic bills. You will have to judge each case on its merits. Obviously a large organization with a big advertising and publicity department is not likely to want to pay anything toward the costs you will incur in getting your own special kind of record photographs of, say, a range of packs you have designed for them. After all, they have the packs and will get all the publicity they want from advertising their contents. But an exhibition stand, a display unit, an interior is another matter. Here a sensible client will probably agree that the finished job should be properly photographed and may be quite willing to pay for this, particularly if you undertake to lay on your own special photographer, supervise the job and send out the prints for publicity purposes afterwards. This might not apply to colour slide shots which would be largely for your own use.

Whoever is paying, it is wise to keep a rein on your enthusiasm when ordering shots and prints. It is so easy to get carried away on the site and tell your photographer to shoot now this detail, now that. When the bills come in for all these shots at several pounds each the total can be alarming. You will know your photographer's charges and you will probably know, too, how much you or your client will want to spend on photography. Work it out so that when you go to the site you can say firmly 'not more than four shots' and select them within that limit. But don't be cheese-paring on the colour slide shots: one for your master index, a duplicate for loan purposes and if you can afford it, one to send to the Design Council Slide Library is money well spent.

Your photographer will bless you if you get into the habit of giving him a bulk order for prints on each new job instead of ringing him every day or so to order a few more as you think of new uses for them. He may also give you a small discount for printing in quantity instead of in ones and twos.

Your client's permission

It is essential first to ask your client's permission to send out photographs to the press. Otherwise you might unwittingly anticipate or overlap his own wider publicity campaign or he might have good reasons for wanting to hold back all publicity about his new product for the time being. In the case of new shops, showrooms, offices, there may be plans for a press preview and an accompanying publicity campaign.

You may well know all about such plans in advance and already have made your own to fit in with them. But if not, here is how to set about the whole important operation.

The most efficient way to ask for your client's approval of what you propose to do is to draft the captions and credits to go with each photograph and any additional editorial notes you are going to provide; to make a list of all the publications to which you are proposing to send the photographs and then to send the whole lot to your client—photographs, captions, notes (if any) and press list. The chances then are that he will be impressed with your thoroughness, appreciative of the publicity you will be getting for his firm as well as for your work and will give you his enthusiastic permission to go ahead. Incidentally you might always suggest that he keeps for his own reference the set of captioned photographs and notes which you have sent him. This way you can be sure that he has at least one good set of photographs of the work you have done for him.

Your press list

It is unlikely that any national daily or weekly newspaper or consumer magazine would publish photographs of your work unless it were something of national importance, such as a new coin, or of intrinsic news value, such as a chair without any legs. In such cases the publicity would probably be handled by experts anyway. So you can really leave out of your press list all such publications and concentrate on the technical press. Consult the current issue of the Advertiser's Annual (listed in the Bibliography.) You will find in the section called 'Trade and Technical Publications' a truly fabulous list of weekly, monthly and quarterly magazines concerned with every profession, trade and industry you ever heard of and a great many you have never heard of. The section is usefully classified, the address of each magazine is given and the whole thing as it stands can be, in fact, your own press list from which to select. But you must try to get to know the magazines in some of the classifications you are most likely to use frequently. It would be very expensive and wasteful to send your photographs to all of them, since many are small, fairly localized and may not even use illustrations. There are usually not more than two or three leading magazines for any profession, trade or industry and sometimes only one. These are the important ones for you.

In selecting your list for a particular job try to think of all the separate 'ingredients' of that job which might be interesting in a particular field. Here is a brief description of a hypothetical job with, in brackets, any profession, trade or industry whose leading magazines might be interested to publish photographs of their particular aspect of it:

You have designed a new showroom (architecture, design, possibly building) for a glass manufacturer (glass, pottery), who is a big national advertiser (advertising, publicity). It contains wall units which show the glass in quite a new way (display, shopfitting) with specially designed light fittings (electricity). The decorative panels by a well-known artist (commercial art) have been reproduced in plastic (plastics). The rather unusual information desks were specially designed and made (furniture, cabinet making) but the chairs were a well-known standard make (contract furnishing). The carpet and curtains are nylon (textiles, carpets, man-made fibres) and the photo-mural of glass blowing is one of the longest ever mounted (photography).

That is perhaps a rather exaggerated example but it will serve to show how widely you may be able to spread your photographs of a single job and how important it is to remember this when choosing your shots and writing your captions. These are the sort of magazines in which it is really useful to get published. Many readers of them—manufacturers, industrialists, business and advertising men, are potential clients. Your glass showroom may catch the eye of a rival glass manufacturer when he is browsing through his weekly trade journal and put useful ideas into his head about his own shabby premises.

Writing captions

The kind of caption to put on the back of a photograph to send to an editor is not necessarily what he will eventually print. He will want all the facts as briefly as possible from which to distil his own much briefer caption.

The essential ingredients of a caption should be the title, so to speak, of the job, with the full name of the client firm and the name of the product if it is different; a brief description of the job factual and uneulogistic and the credits. Here is a simple example:

NEW 'PAROTEX' CONTAINER

A new metal container for 'Parotex' cleaning fluid manufactured by Jones and Co Ltd. The design is printed on the container in brown, red and blue with a simplified version of the original symbol in the centre of the lid.

Designer—John Brown

Tin printer—Robinson and Smith Ltd

Sufficient copies of this would be typed on flimsy paper and lightly attached to the back of each print so as not to obscure the negative number and your rubber-stamped copyright instructions referred to a little further on.

If you are going to send several different photographs of the same job, as would be the case with interiors or exhibitions, it is a good idea to devise a short general description of the job and use it as a first paragraph for every caption. The second paragraph should then be specific to each photograph. For instance:

NEW SHOWROOMS FOR SMITHS LIMITED

New showrooms which have been opened at 10 Main Street for Smiths Ltd., glass manufacturers, cover an area of some 8,000 square feet on the ground floor. They are intended for wholesale buyers only and have been designed in dark rich colours to display the glass to best advantage. This photo shows the decorative plastic panels on 'the wall at one end of the showroom. The pattern is carried out entirely in black and white on grey.

Designer—John Jones

Artist for panels—Mary Maggs

General contractor—Green Brothers Ltd

When final captions are being typed it is a good idea to take as many extra copies as possible. These can go in your photo file with your master print and spare prints and are then ready if you need them suddenly after a lapse of time. There is another thing which should go on the back of every photograph you send out, provided you have paid for the photography yourself (*see* Chapter Nineteen, under 'The Copyright of Photographs'). That is a rubber-stamped statement which says 'No reproduction fee provided this photograph is credited to (your name)'. This will reassure the editor who is wary about having to pay reproduction or copyright fees on photographs and will help to prevent your photograph being used by the thoughtless or unscrupulous without any reference to you or your work. It is a good idea also to add your address and telephone number to the rubber stamp so that the print can always be identified with its owner.

Writing editorial notes

If a job is large enough to need editorial notes as well as captions, these should likewise be factual and brief, in fact merely an amplification of the captions. They are usual for larger interiors, shops and showrooms, permanent exhibitions and perhaps to go with a series of photographs illustrating a house style. They should give all the technical details of materials and processes used, touch on problems of layout and circulation, if any, and describe any special decorative treatments, colour schemes and so on. They should be followed by all the credits in full, and finish with a paragraph 'For further information apply to . . .' with your own or your client's address, whichever is appropriate. Such notes could give the editor of a technical journal sufficient material for a short illustrated article. You would, of course, get your client's agreement to the notes in draft before sending them out.

Sending material to the press

So with your captioned photographs and notes ready to go, all you need is a brief covering letter, addressed always to the editor:

'Dear Sir

I enclose a photograph (or photographs) and some notes of the new showrooms which I have recently designed for my clients Smiths Limited and hope you may find these of interest for editorial use. I shall be grateful to have the photographs returned when you have finished with them.'

The material should go in a well-stiffened envelope to make sure that the prints do not get damaged in the post.

When you get to this point you will have completed Phase Three (a) of the chart on page 15. The reason why it appears there before sending the final invoice is in case your client has agreed to pay some or all of the photographic costs.

Press cuttings

You are probably appalled by now at the amount of work involved in publicising your own jobs. But if you do not do it, nobody else will until you can afford to pay someone to do it for you. And it is *absolutely vital* to the growth of your practice to tell the world in every possible way what you have done. Jobs beget jobs but only if enough people know what jobs you have done. The design world is a highly competitive one and is constantly being replenished with the up-and-coming products of the art schools and colleges. If you fail to do everything you can to keep your name in your public's mind it will sink all too soon into obscurity beneath the rising tide of new ones.

One of your minor and more immediate rewards for all this hard work will be when your first batch of press-cuttings arrives on your desk. It is advisable to subscribe to a press-cutting agency otherwise you will never know who has published your material. Find a reputable long-established agency which gives a really good coverage of the world's press. You will be charged a small sum for every cutting they send you but they will require you to pay them in advance for, say, a hundred cuttings, or any other total you like to agree. There is a list of such agencies in the *Writers and Artists Year Book* (see *Bibliography*).

Do not be discouraged if the cuttings are slow to come in at first or if you send out photographs to twenty magazines and only get one cutting as a result. It is a slow process but it will grow steadily as your practice grows. If you keep to a very high standard of photography, with good clear captions and notes and everything always sent out promptly while it is still news, editors will begin to appreciate your material and use it more frequently. And do not forget that even one published photograph out of twenty issued is wonderful free publicity for you, seen by hundreds or thousands of readers any one of whom might become a client as a result. If the cost of sending out a batch of photographs were, say, £5 and half a day's work, as a result of which one got published; if that one published photograph brought you a job with a £500 fee, the outlay would have been minute in relation to the return. And it can happen that way.

Try to find the time, or persuade someone else to find the time, to keep your press-cuttings pasted into a large guard-book as they come in instead of letting them accumulate in a dusty unorganized heap. Then you will be able to look through them occasionally, not only for the pride and pleasure they will give you as they increase, but also because you will begin to assess which publications tend to publish which kind of material you send them and trim your distribution accordingly.

Your slide and photo files

I have already referred several times to colour slides. In this context I am only concerned with colour shots of completed work, which are a *must* for every designer. They are the only way nowadays to show your work to a would-be client provided of course that you have even minimal facilities for projection at your office (projector, screen, sufficient length of throw and black-out blinds) and that your office is presentable and reasonably accessible. If none of this applies, it is worth asking your enquirer if he can provide the black-out facilities in his offices so that you can take along your projector and portable screen.

But you will need photo albums or folders as well when a slide showing proves impossible at either end. To begin with, two might be sufficient. One would be large and impressive into which you would mount special enlargements of your most impressive jobs. Where you have actual samples in colour of flat print jobs—labels, leaflets, letter-headings—they also could be mounted in. This album would stay always in your office, ready to show to visitors. It should be on the loose-leaf principle so that you can add new and better photographs and eliminate some of the ones which may begin to look less important by contrast. The second album, also loose-leaf, would be almost a duplicate of the first but smaller and portable so that you could put it into your brief case to take to someone who has asked to see your work.

If you are going after an enquiry for, say, your packaging design services, you will probably make up your portable album or your slide show to contain mostly examples of packs you have designed. But if you practise in a fairly wide field, do put in some quite different kinds of work as well. Your enquirer for packs might be very interested to find that he could ask you later to design his exhibition stands, his showroom, his van sides. I have known of cases where a designer had worked for years in a narrow specialized field for particular clients, who were then surprised and delighted to find, on looking through his photographs by chance, that their designer could do other kinds of work for them with equal success. It is when such a client gets into the desirable habit of turning to you for help with *all* his design problems that retainers start getting talked about and vistas loom up of long years of the best and most rewarding kind of collaboration.

Work finished

The Phase before the last on the chart on page 15 is to send in your final invoice and this is dealt with in Chapter Eight. Now we come to the very last one,

Phase Three (c) 'Filing essential records'.

By the time you get to this point you are probably well away on the next job but it really is a good idea to tidy up the previous job rather carefully, not only because of the past or the present but for the future as well. The essential records would be in five categories: correspondence, drawings, job sheets, record photographs and slides and probably a miscellaneous collection of samples, discarded prototypes, proofs, components, tatty models and so on. You will already have provided suitable filing for all of these except possibly the miscellaneous collection and that can really be a problem, growing gradually into a dusty heap of junk unless you take it firmly in hand and quickly. If you have even the most embryo library then any samples or components, *provided you label them* could be useful again and should be suitably filed in boxes. Whether or not you keep proofs of typesetting would depend on the job. For an exhibition, probably no. For a range of stationery, packs or labels or for a house style, probably yes because your client might well come back later for more adaptations or applications of the basic typography. Unless you could provide a separate filing system for this material, it could go in the portfolio or drawer of your plan chest with the original drawings for the job.

Tatty models? Unless they are worth spending time and money on to refurbish them my advice is throw them firmly away. They are formidable space-occupiers and dust-collectors and it is sheer sentimentality to hang on to them. But if to throw away your first model (which you probably made yourself with loving care working into the small hours to get it finished) gives you a pang of regret, you need not suffer this the next time. While a model, either made by you or someone else, is new and in mint condition, take photographs and colour slides of it and then it is recorded for all time. Such record photographs could be very useful to show a prospective client with your other work, if the job in question did not go through to completion.

Job histories

There is one further file you must make in this tidying-up phase and that is some sort of job history. This would be a gathering together from all the material referred to above of essential facts about the job, such as:

(a) a financial summary to show its profitability or otherwise

(b) the amount of time spent on the job from start to finish, but broken down into the relevant stages

(c) total production costs if relevant and particularly for interior design, shops, exhibitions, etc., related to areas so that you can calculate square-metre costs (See Chapter Eighteen 'Estimating production costs' for more advice about this).

(d) comments on the excellence or otherwise of the contractors, suppliers, specialists you used on the job.

(e) any particular technical difficulties which arose in respect of methods or materials and which proved soluble or insoluble.

That list is just a guide. You will certainly be able to add to it, particularly while it is still all fresh in your memory. It will probably all go on a single typed sheet and then into a folder marked 'job histories' which always stays near at hand in your desk drawer. Two or three years later when a similar job comes up you might find it extremely valuable to be able to refer to such an *aide memoire* for quoting fees, estimating time programmes and production costs and to remind yourself of snags to be avoided if possible.

This is the way in which true professionalism builds up and your increasing expertise (which is another word for know-how) enhances your reputation.

Part Two

Introduction

Designers who set up in free-lance practice are immediately 'in business' to a much greater extent than most other professional people. They have to deal directly with business men, who are seldom likely to be sentimental about creative work. The design services they buy have eventually to sell and sell well. The relationship between designer and client is therefore a strictly business one. The designer's codes of professional conduct are the foundation on which this relationship is built and they protect both sides of it. But the rest of the structure depends to a great extent on the designer: not only on his talent but on the degree of efficiency with which he runs his office. His absorbing years of training and his first staff jobs do not always prepare him adequately for this situation.

The absolute genius may get by. There are never enough of him to go round, and there will always be a few long-suffering wealthy clients to put up with his probably muddled and unbusinesslike eccentricities for the sake of the work which he finally produces. Most business men however, anxious to buy design services, would probably define their ideal designer as one who produces the very best work of which he is capable within the given circumstances, delivers it on time and keeps within the agreed production budget. All the training and experience which the designer has had will enable him to fulfil the first of these requirements. It is hoped that what follows in the second part of this book may help him to fulfil the other two.

It is meant for designers who are new to free-lance professional practice and design office management. It assumes, as I think text books should, that the reader will know little or nothing of the subject. Therefore little or nothing is taken for granted. This inevitably means a lot of detail but good organization is built up on attention to detail.

If the activities which it suggests seem at first sight bewilderingly elaborate, it should be remembered that few designers would need to adopt all of them and no designer would need to adopt those applicable to his practice all at once. Moreover those which he did adopt would very soon, I hope, be adapted to his own way of working.

The main thing is that there should be a plan and that the plan should gradually become a habit. Then, even though the free-lance has to be his own telephonist, secretary, filing clerk, book-keeper, messenger, press officer and public relations expert, he will still have time to clear his mind of detail and be a designer as well.

There are three things which you, the trained designer, should have in order to start your free-lance career. The first is at least one client who has given you a definite and fairly large commission. The second is some money in the bank with which to finance yourself until your client pays you. The third is somewhere to work. If the money in the bank is enough to give you a safe margin you may decide to set up your office first and then find your client. If there is no money in the bank but the first client has been signed up the solution is to work at home. This is of course the way in which many free-lance designers begin but the advantages of having no initial capital outlay, very few overheads and probably someone always around to answer the telephone are often soon outweighed by the distractions of domesticity-while-you-work and a possibly remote address.

Let us assume that there is enough money in the bank (the next chapter will advise you about that) to allow you to give time and thought to the setting up of your first design office, however modest and with or without benefit of client. If you have or can get a steady part-time teaching job, that will provide very useful revenue during the first years of your free-lance career. Some of the suggestions which follow may seem very obvious to practical people but I do not apologize for them. They are meant to be helpful to those who may find it easy to design but not so easy to organize.

Position

You are unlikely to be able to afford the rent of a city centre address and this matters very little at first. Until you are better known a good address in the snobbish sense is not important. Neither is it likely at first that your clients will often come to you. But because you will have to go frequently to them, try to find somewhere near to convenient transport to the centre to save time and fares.

Requirements

The first absolute requirement is good natural daylight in which to work. This will not only save your eyes but your electricity bills. Another very important thing to look for in choosing an office is that it should offer some facilities for taking telephone messages for you when you are out, that is if you are going to start quite on your own. Many a rising young designer has lost many a useful commission when some harassed client has said in his desperation 'Ring up young so-and-so and ask him to come and see me right away' only to be told that there is no answer to the telephone call.

So until you can afford a secretary or an assistant try to arrange for your telephone to be an extension through someone else's switchboard, or install what British Telecom calls a Plan 107: two instruments connected to one line or extension. A switch on the main instrument will transfer all incoming calls to the second instrument which you might persuade a friendly co-tenant in an adjacent room to house, in order to take messages for you. The modicum you would pay for these services, plus the slight extra telephone rental, would be very well worth it. Telephone answering services are increasingly available in cities now. They are expensive but the ideal solution for the one-man office.

Another thing to look for in choosing an office is storage space. Not only will you want to keep your drawing materials clean and tidy but as your practice builds up you will accumulate sketches, artwork, proofs, dummy packs, bottles, prototypes, samples, magazines. These will submerge you like a rising tide unless you start with a strong-minded plan to cope with them.

A suitable office with cupboard space already fitted with shelves would be a very lucky find. An unfitted cupboard would be next best as you could probably make and fix cheap shelving into it yourself. If no cupboards offer themselves then a corner or recess in your office will have to be used and this means rather more outlay.

If you are taking a short lease with high hopes of moving to larger and better premises at the end of it, it would be worth considering the advantages of buying some of the excellent standard industrial or library shelving which is free-standing. Then when you move you can take it with you. The cost of fitted shelves and cupboards always seems unduly high for what one gets while the price, if any, at which one is able to re-sell it to an incoming tenant is usually much less than its original cost.

Room heating should also be thought about if you are in a position to choose between several different offices. Whatever form it takes, it will be quite a big item in your annual budget. Central heating, provided it is adequate and efficient, is much the best and if available would probably be included in the rent. An open fire or some form of slow-burning closed stove is the cheapest kind of room heating but you have with it all the complications of fuel storage, fire-lighting and ash removal. A gas fire or gas convector heater is next cheapest and much cleaner. An electric heater is cleanest of all but the most expensive form of space heating. If it is to be a gas or electric fire it is important to see that it is big enough to heat the room adequately. Your speed of work in cold weather will be seriously slowed down if your room is not comfortably warm, never less than 36°C. (65°F.) The local gas or electricity people will advise you about this if you give them the cubic dimensions of the room and also, most important, of the windows. Something like 20% of your room heat is lost through glass windows or skylights in cold weather.

Finally you must make sure that the rent includes the use of an adequate lavatory and wash basin and facilities for that indispensable twice-daily comfort—the morning cup of coffee, the afternoon cup of tea. You should also

124

find out whether the landlord will let you have access to your office out of normal office hours by giving you a key to the main front door as well as to your own. This is important because at the beginning of your free-lance career you will have to, and want to, work hard and long, late into the evenings and sometimes over a week-end. On such occasions it will be very irritating to have to take home all your work and materials if your office premises close promptly at 5 pm. on Mondays to Fridays and stay firmly closed on Saturdays and Sundays.

To sum up and if the district in which you are searching for an office gives you sufficient choice, here are the requirements to keep in mind for economy and efficiency before you make a decision:

(a) Good daylight; (b) telephone message-taking facilities; (c) storage space; (d) cleanest and cheapest possible room-heating; (e) lavatory and wash-basin amenities; (f) facilities for making tea or coffee; (g) access out of office hours.

The lease

Your first design office is probably a big venture for you and therefore a short lease, perhaps not more than three years, is a good idea. If the venture is unsuccessful you will not be too committed. If it is you will certainly want to move on to something larger and nearer the centre. If by a lucky chance you do happen to find a small place at a bargain rent which is already sufficiently central, a short lease is still a good idea for the first reason. But it might be negotiated to carry an option to renew, particularly if the premises seem likely to give you room for expansion.

There are three ways of approaching the actual legalities of the lease. If you know your landlord well enough, both personally and as a business man, to trust him to be fair then you *could* dispense with the law and merely exchange formal letters confirming the terms of your tenancy. This would only cost you the postage stamps on the envelopes. I would regard this as undesirable even if the would-be landlord were a member of your own family. You might prove to be as unsatisfactory a tenant as he to be an unsatisfactory landlord. If a dispute then arises it is likely to be far more acrimonious and difficult to settle if the tenancy agreement between you has been only loosely defined. Even members of the same family have been known to take each other to court.

The second approach is, by mutual consent, to leave it to the law to draw up a tenancy agreement by exchanging suitable formal letters of contract. These define precisely the terms of the tenancy and what the landlord and tenant covenant (which merely means promise) to do for each other. This is a much better method and quite adequate for a short-term small-rent tenancy if both sides agree to it. Moreover it will only cost you fairly modest fees to your solicitor.

The third method may be forced on you by circumstances. If there is an existing lease for the premises you want to rent, the landlord's solicitors and yours have to get together to make the legal arrangements for assigning the lease to you and for exchanging the necessary letters or documents of agreement whereby you take over the lease for the agreed terms and covenants. This involves you not only in solicitors' fees but certain stamp duties as well. If your budget for initial expenditure in setting yourself up is a very tight one, these kind of legal fees can be a nasty shock when the bills come in unless you have discovered about them and allowed for them in advance. Most of them relative to leases and tenancy agreements are on a standard scale and your solicitor can easily tell you what they will be in relation to the proposed rent.

Your professional advisers
I have already mentioned several times 'your' solicitor and I shall frequently mention further on 'your' accountant, 'your' bank manager, 'your' patent agent, 'your' insurance broker. These may sound rather awe-inspiring people for a free-lance designer to have at his beck and call but they are indispensable and must be budgeted for. You will not be able to do without their expert professional services at certain stages of your career any more than you can do without a doctor when you are ill.

Moreover you will find, if you have been wise in your choice, that they will be interested in the progress of your practice and very useful advisers to turn to if ever you are faced with a problem which cannot be solved on the drawing board.

But do not rush at the first solicitor or accountant whose brass plates you see. Make a few enquiries, collect a few recommendations, try to meet them if at all possible. Then make your choice. If you choose well you may have started what will prove to be life-long associations of the greatest value to you in many ways.

Getting a telephone installed
If the room you are taking has no telephone your most urgent job will be to make an application for one at the earliest possible moment. There may be a waiting list in your district and nothing is so frustrating as having to operate without a telephone for several weeks. Until your own telephone number is allocated to you, you will also be prevented from getting your letter-heading printed.

So get an application form from the local Telephone Manager's Office (you will find the address in the Telephone Directory) and send it in as soon as you have chosen your premises and are reasonably likely to complete the negotiations for them. A small scale plan of the room marked with your suggested position for the telephone junction box should go with it and if you want your instrument on an extra long cord you should apply for this at the same time. You can have 5 metres free. Above that a small charge is made.

You will be entitled to one free entry in the Telephone Directory and this a 'trade' entry, ie John Brown, Designer, instead of just John Brown. This is because you will be paying a business instead of private rental. But if you are going to call your practice by an abstract title such as Design Services or Studio Ten, it might be advisable to have a second entry under your own name since this is the one you will be known by best until your abstract title gets established. This extra entry will only cost a small extra amount a year.

Registering a name

The law requires you, if you are going to work on your own or in partnership, to register the name of your business if it is not the 'true surname' of the proprietor of that business. Design Services or Studio Ten would have to be registered. 'George Jones' or 'G. Jones' or 'Jones and Robinson' would not. To register a business name is quite simple. You write to the Registrar of Companies & Limited Partnerships (Board of Trade), Companies House, 55 City Road, London EC1. Telephone 01-253-9393, and ask him to send you a form on which you provide the details of your business, the names of its proprietors and the title under which you wish to register it. This will cost you about a £ in Stamp Duty. It could cost you a fine of £5 a day if you omit to do it within fourteen days of formally opening your office.

The Registrar will file your application and 'he shall send by post or deliver a certificate of the registration thereof to the firm or person registering and the certificate or a certified copy thereof shall be kept exhibited in a conspicuous position at the principal place of business of the firm or individual. . . .' (Registration of Business Names Act, 1916.) So you will need to frame it and hang it up where it can be seen by allcomers to your office. In addition, and this is important, your letter-heading and any other printed matter you send out about yourself *must* show the 'true names' of you and any partner you may have, as well as the title, Design Services or Studio Ten.

Nameplate and letter-heading

There is no need to tell you, as a trained designer, anything about how to design and produce your first nameplate and letter-heading. But you must be warned not to have printed anything with an address and telephone number on it until your solicitor tells you it is absolutely safe to do so. Any tenancy negotiation can fall through right up to the moment of final signatures even though a deposit may have been paid. As for the nameplate, there may be reasons, applying either to the building or the district, why an outside nameplate is not permissible and it is important to find out about this from your landlord. Wherever it is finally fixed, choose a material for your nameplate that does not need daily polishing unless you can be sure of a very efficient daily cleaner. If the main nameplate is outside you will need your name repeated on your own door and probably also one or two directional signs on staircases or landings.

Decorations

If you take on a decorating lease you will start at no extra cost with clean redecorated rooms for which, if your landlord is cooperative, you may even be able to specify the colours and finishes. But this also means that you will have to pay for redecoration when you move out at the end of your lease.

If you have to take the rooms unredecorated, it is immeasurably worthwhile to try to get something done to them (or do it yourself) before you move in. Once

127

you are settled and well away you may never again be able to find sufficient time to give much attention to your surroundings. This is likely to be detrimental to your practice and reputation. So many offices, shops and studios are so lamentably dreary and unkempt that a clean and tidy suite of rooms with good colours and finishes, cared-for plants and well-planned lighting will always make its mark, be remembered and talked about by many who visit you. It is one of your best selling points.

And here it may be worth putting in a point about prospective clients which can easily be overlooked. *Everybody* you may meet, who runs his own business or practice or who is in a senior position in somebody else's, is a potential client. The contractor who fixes your shelves may one day want you to design a fitting for him. The printer who prints your letter-heading may one day want some typographical advice about his own or a customer's. A removal firm might want its van-sides re-designed. Your landlord might admire your own well-designed nameplate and decide to have his own improved.

There is more about finding clients in Chapter Twelve but right from the start the firms and individuals who may be helping you to instal yourself in your first design office can be interested in what you are setting out to do, will respect your insistence on high standards of work and may be encountering for the first time a real live designer and finding him a sensible likeable chap. They may remember that, if ever the time comes when they need a designer themselves or are asked to recommend one. It is surprising how often the largest jobs can be traced back to the smallest beginnings.

Light fittings

You will probably need as a minimum for each room, one ceiling fitting for general light, a desk lamp and a lamp for each drawing board. A fairly average fluorescent ceiling fitting may cost about twice as much as a fairly ordinary flush or pendant fitting for tungsten lighting. The tube will cost about four times as much to renew as a 100-watt tungsten bulb. On the other hand, the fluorescent tube will last about six times longer than a tungsten bulb and give about two-and-a-half times as much light. These are only very approximate comparisons since there is such a variety of types and price of fittings of both kinds. They should be sufficient to show that the running cost of fluorescent lighting is the more economical of the two.

It is an equation to be worked out in relation to how much natural light you have in your room and whether you can more easily afford a little more at the capital outlay stage or on the subsequent running cost stage. Your local electricity showrooms will tell you the current local cost of a unit of electricity and how many units an hour each size of tube or bulb will use.

If it is to be a fluorescent fitting, what is known as a 'warm white' tube will be best for general lighting particularly for colour matching. In a small room the over-bright light from even the smallest fluorescent tube can be toned down with a louvre fitting or diffuser which clips on quite easily to the trough carrying the tube.

Desk and drawing board lamps should ideally be of the spring-loaded or counter-weighted extension-arm type either with a table or clamp-on base or for wall fixing. The clamp-on kind can be used on a desk, table or drawing board and easily removed from them. The table base kind only sits well and safely on a flat surface and is no good on the slope of a drawing board. The type fixed to a wall is all very well in its first position but a necessary re-arrangement of furniture or a move to new premises may mean that it can no longer be suitably placed.

If the initial budget will run to it, it is a good idea to lay in a small stock of the kind of bulbs you use. If a bulb goes when you are working late to finish a rush job, it could be infuriating not to have a replacement and to know that the shops were shut.

Some designers also find it useful to have some blue daylight bulbs in the store cupboard as these are useful for colour matching.

Good lighting, daylight or artificial, is definitely something on which you should not economize. Better at the start to do without a floor-covering or an elegant chair for your guests and have instead good, strong efficient light just where you need it and no makeshifts.

Furniture and fittings

The basic pieces of furniture you will need for your first office are a drawing table or trestle with an adjustable stool; another table or work top of some sort on which to lay out large drawings; a plan chest or deep shelves for filing drawings; other storage in the form of a cupboard or shelves for files, stationery, drawing materials and a spare chair for your visitors. If the budget will stretch beyond these essentials, a small pedestal desk will be useful for letter-writing and telephoning, with a comfortable desk chair. A filing cabinet is an expensive item but would be invaluable not only for correspondence files but for photographs, reference materials, catalogues and even small drawings and proofs of typesettings.

A pin-up board on the wall is an essential item. Strawboard painted white and screwed to the wall is inexpensive and quite effective. If you can give it a simple frame it will look even better.

You will need at least one deep drawer or small cupboard which you can lock as you may need to keep in it a cash box, stamps, private papers and even a bottle of something hospitable in case your most important client decides to call. It would be nice, too, to have a small cupboard for the tea things instead of letting them stand around in a dismal clutter.

Office and studio equipment

Then there is the typewriter problem and the use of it. Letters must be written and some of them at any rate must be typed: those of which it is essential that you keep a copy.

You may be able to type or you may decide to teach yourself. It is surprising how much can be done with the two-finger technique. You may be lucky enough to have a girl-friend, a sister or a wife who is a trained typist and who would type your letters for you for spare-time pocket-money. Failing any of these expedients you will have to pay for part-time secretarial help. Many ex-secretaries who have married like to keep their hands in at shorthand and typing by doing a few hours regular work every week provided a long journey is not involved.

But from whatever source you get your secretarial help, a typewriter you will certainly need sooner or later so it ought to be allowed for quite early in your budgeting. A portable machine will be the least expensive and the most practical to start with as you may often need to take it home for evening or week-end work.

The extent to which you budget for photographic and projection equipment will depend on the fields of design in which you practise and what you can afford. For the graphic designer, photography is so essential a tool of his trade that it is difficult to see how he could do without a camera, dark room facilities and equipment.

Photography, except for initial record purposes, is not so necessary for other designers but a slide projector and screen for showing examples of your work and presenting your preliminary design proposals is almost a must for every designer.

The cost of buying any or all of this sort of equipment is pretty formidable, particularly for a first-year budget. Fortunately all of it can be hired as required and this is a good solution for the freelance beginner (provided he remembers to insure it while it is in his care).

A very useful but again very expensive item of office equipment is a photo-copier. The range of types and prices is very wide but even if you could manage the simplest and cheapest you would find it invaluable, particularly if secretarial services were a problem. But again there are other solutions for the very tight budget. Coin-in-the-slot document copiers are all over the place and this could be a stand-in solution until you could afford your own.

Floor-covering and curtains
Floor-covering may depend on the type and condition of the floor of your room and of course on what you can afford. If you have an evenly boarded floor compare the cost of having it sanded and polished with the cost of buying and laying linoleum or carpeting. It would look pleasant and professional and is easy to keep clean. If the floor cannot be sanded and polished, good linoleum is a much better buy than cheap carpet, particularly if you can run to an underlay as well. A rug under your desk or work-table would look pleasant and keep the winter draughts from your feet.

Curtains would, on most windows, be something of a luxury, would keep the cold out in winter but would very soon look squalid unless they were regularly laundered or cleaned. On some windows they might be a necessity. Bright sunlight is a rare and delicious treat but not when it falls dazzlingly across your drawing board. Venetian or linen blinds are the answer to this problem, but if they cannot be afforded, the alternative would be curtains made of fine white cotton lawn or nylon to draw close across the glass. If they are fine enough they will keep out the sun but not too much of the light. Again they will need very regular laundering to prevent them looking dingy with city soot but if you have two sets made at the beginning you will always have one to wash and one to wear.

As for the smaller items of equipment, you will need a really large wastepaper basket or two, almost what the manufacturers call a bin. Buy them in metal if you can afford it, they will last years longer than wire mesh or basket. You will need ash-trays (*not* old tin lids), hooks and a hanger or two for coats and hats, a few filing trays to keep your papers tidy, a calendar and perhaps a blotter. Unless your office is very near to a chemist's shop, a small first-aid box will be useful for dealing with cuts, burns and headaches.

There is no need to tell you of the drawing equipment and materials you will need. This is so much a matter of personal preference and the kind of work you do and you will have discovered your preferences during your training.

Filing

If you decided that you can afford to start with a three- or four-drawer filing cabinet this will serve nearly all your needs for a year or two while your practice builds up.

Instead of a filing cabinet, large strong cardboard boxes into which foolscap files will fit upright as if they were in a filing drawer will make a good substitute, particularly with the strong alphabetical divider cards which you can buy at most stationers.

Large drawings, prints, perspective sketches, tracings—all must be kept flat and clean. A plan chest is the perfect solution but an expensive one. Instead you may have to make do with large portfolios on deep slatted shelves, fitted into a recess and covered with a curtain.

For addresses a small card index box to stand on your desk; for telephone numbers you most often use, a flat alphabetical index to hang on the wall close to your telephone.

All these are easy, inexpensive and probably very obvious ways of dealing with the filing problem. But alas, there is no suggestion I can make for easily keeping it tidy and always up-to-date other than the irksome discipline of frequently and regularly 'doing the filing'. Otherwise it will swamp you rather than serve you, until you can afford someone to do it for you.

Cleaning

The simplest way to find an office cleaner is to fix up with one who already works in your building—either as a caretaker, or 'freelance' or who is employed by an office cleaning firm. You will pay her so much an hour and as she normally cleans early in the morning or late at night you will have to provide her with a set of keys. If she works on her own you will also have to provide her with her cleaning materials and equipment—brushes, dusters, polish, etc. If you place a contract with a cleaning firm the price will include all materials and if your regular cleaner is ill or on holiday, they have to provide a substitute. It is well worth the slightly higher cost. Usually the same firm can also supply you with window-cleaning services.

Amenities for your staff

There is an Act called the Offices Shops and Railway Premises Act 1963 which lays down certain minimum working conditions for the places in which employed people work. If you should take on an assistant or secretary, the most important of its provisions are that you must provide your staff with a minimum space of forty square feet (3.72 sq. metres) per person in which to work or where the ceiling is lower than 10 feet (3.048 metres) there must be 400 cubic feet (11.32 cubic metres) per person. You would be well advised to get a copy of the Act from the nearest branch of Her Majesty's Stationery Office for a very modest sum since there are other requirements in it regarding light, heat and sanitary facilities which are also obligatory.

The requirements are minimal enough to sound obvious, with or without the Act. But there are, even to-day, rooms in old buildings which might be offered at temptingly low rents just because of their lack of such amenities. It is a temptation to be avoided at all costs.

A sole trader

You will have realized that throughout this chapter I have assumed that you are going to set up on your own. This means that you will be what the law calls a 'sole trader'. The advantages are obvious. You have only yourself to think about and cope with and you can do what you like with your business.

One of the disadvantages is equally obvious—you carry the whole financial responsibility yourself but there is another not-so-well-known disadvantage to take into account. If you get into serious financial difficulties, can't pay your bills and have to go officially bankrupt, then the law can take from you all your belongings, business *and* personal in order to sell them to produce money to pay off your debts. You may therefore decide that to set up as a sole trader is more suitable for people whose work does not require the purchase of a lot of stock and equipment.

A partnership

When you come to budgeting for your capital outlay on setting up your office and for your first year's revenue and expenditure, which is what the next chapter is about, you may find that there is not going to be enough money in the bank to pay for everything even if you cut out all the frills and set up with only the bare essentials.

There is only one possible solution, short of raising some more capital, and that is to set up with another designer who wants to do likewise and is in the same dilemma, take a partner in fact.

The advantages are considerable. Most of your heaviest initial costs and running expenses will be halved. You can arrange not to be away from the office together so that there is always someone to answer the telephone and receive visitors and you may together be able to take on jobs which individually you could not tackle.

Nearly all the disadvantages might stem from personal relationships and if they go wrong, they may wreck the arrangement almost over-night. To try to prevent this happening it would be wise to choose as your partner someone you have known long enough to be sure that you like each other; someone whose work you respect and particularly who works in a design field different to your own but perhaps complementary to it. This will avoid rivalry and enable to you work together on jobs which call for different design experience. A book called *Group practice in design* by Michael Middleton makes interesting reading in this context. (See *Bibliography*.)

In spite of your care in making a choice of partner and even after some months or even years of sharing offices and jobs, the clash of temperaments may come and you may decide to part. The only crumb of comfort in this dismal situation will then be that you were both wise enough at the very beginning to put the sharing arrangement on a proper partnership basis. Your solicitors will help you to write contract letters to define how you will share the costs, the work, the income; how much notice you must give each other if either of you wants to end the arrangement; how in that case you would divide the assets—the furniture and equipment, the balance in the bank and such clients as still remained on your books.

With such a written agreement between you from the start, you can put it away and forget it and work together to build up a joint practice, knowing that if the worst happens and a split must come, you have both agreed to a pattern of action which will be fair and reasonable under the circumstances and enable you to part company with a minimum of argument, acrimony and unpleasantness.

I cannot stress too strongly how important this is since I know how often it is overlooked or dismissed as unnecessary because 'it couldn't happen to us'.

It does happen and without that agreement between you, the closing down process can be devastating in every way and usually to one side more than the other.

A word of warning: a partnership rates in law in the same category as a sole trader if it gets into financial difficulties. Moreover a single partner can be held responsible for the liabilities of all the others if things go financially wrong for any of them individually.

A limited company

In law a limited company is like a completely separate person. What the owners of the company do is really what the company does, not what they do separately as people. If you are going to form a company you decide beforehand how much money you are going to put into it. Then if you get into financial difficulties and the company fails and has to 'go into liquidation' your liability is limited to that amount of money. This has the advantage that your own personal finances and possessions are not involved at all. If your company had to be wound up your creditors would share only what was available in your business—furniture, equipment, stock, etc.

There are few disadvantages in setting up your business as a limited company but it must be done properly and legally with the help of a solicitor who will tell you what it will cost. It must be a quite separate legal entity with its own bank account, letter-head, invoices and a registered office. It must also have not less than two directors. It must also have its accounts audited annually, produce an annual balance sheet and send in annual returns to the authorities. There are distinct tax advantages and as a company grows and establishes itself, it can be that it more easily earns the respect and co-operation of other firms with which it needs to do business rather more than would a sole trader or a small partnership.

It is well worth discussing all this with your solicitor before you decide which of these three alternatives to choose.

Chapter Eleven   A budget for the first year

At the beginning of the previous chapter we saw that one of the essential things which you must have before setting up your own office as a free-lance designer is some money in the bank with which to finance yourself until your clients start paying you.

How much do you need? Taking time and trouble to find the right answer to that question may make all the difference between success and failure a year hence; between being able to hang on for a few extra months if clients and fees are known to be just round the corner or having to close up because there is no reserve cash left in the bank.

You will need money for three things. Firstly, and obviously, for your own personal needs: bed and board, clothes, daily journeys and leisure—in fact the things you would spend a salary on if an employer were going to pay you one. Secondly you will need money for capital outlay which means the expenses which you must incur to start you going but many of which will not recur: legal expenses in connection with your lease, buying furniture, insallation of the telephone, initial decorations, a nameplate, light fittings, a typewriter. Admittedly some of these will want renewing, but not for some years.

The third thing you need money for is those office running expenses which recur weekly, monthly, quarterly or yearly. These are such things as rent, rates, light, heat, cleaning, telephone, drawing materials, stationery. For budget purposes running expenses divide into two: those which are already fixed in advance, such as rent, rates, gas and electricity standing charges, telephone rental, cleaning; and those which you will have to guess-estimate because they all depend on usage—electric current or gas consumed, phone calls, drawing materials, stamps, stationery, travel to visit your clients and suppliers.

Now I am going to suggest how you should work out your three budgets and then show you how enormously useful it will be to have done so, not only to enable you to decide whether you can afford to set up on your own but also as a fundamental basis for later knowing how to do that trickiest of all designer's jobs—estimate your fees.

But first I would like to sound a loud warning note. To show you how to make use of your three budgets it will be much clearer and easier to use a few fictitious figures. *But they are fictitious figures*, not in any way related to the cost of anything anywhere at any given time or to any specific kind of designer or the personal budget or office set-up he might need. These will vary according to person, place, time and many other things. In order to avoid the slightest chance of misunderstanding I am even going to assume a fictitious designer, John Brown, when I have to refer to figures. My figures and 'John Brown', I repeat, are fictitious. If you applied them to your own circumstances you might be wildly and disastrously wide of the mark. You *must* work out your own.

Your personal budget

The first thing to tackle is your own personal budget which is not easy if, like so many of us, you have never kept personal accounts. But it must be done since, to you, it is much the most important part of your finances. What you have to arrive at is a minimum but safe sum of money which will enable you, and your family if you have one to support, to live for at least a year.

When John Brown has done this, and his total is, say, £1420, he should add 10% to it, that is £140, for those wreckers of budgets and businesses — 'unforeseen contingencies'. They may never arise. Then he will be £140 to the good at the end of the year. But if they do—car needing a major repair, an illness needing a holiday to convalesce, new clothes for a very special occasion—he will have reserved for them in advance for this first all-important year and they will not unduly rock the boat.

Your capital outlay

Next comes the capital outlay budget—your starting-up expenses. It is easier to help with suggestions here since most of them have been touched on in the previous chapter. Here is a list; it may not all apply, but from it you could extract your own according to your needs. In the reading room of the nearest public library you could consult the technical magazines for the names of suppliers of special equipment—office furniture, light fittings, etc. and then write to them for catalogues and price lists.

Travel expenses in finding your offices, visiting your solicitors, landlord, etc. These should be quite easy to guess-estimate.

Legal expenses in connection with the tenancy agreement or lease and fees for the registration of an 'abstract' name, for a partnership agreement or for 'floating' a limited company. Your solicitor can estimate these for you to within a pound or two. He may also know the current name registration fee.

Installation costs for the telephone. Your nearest Telephone Manager's Office will give you these.

Decorations, pin-up board, coat hooks. A local builder will give you an estimate. If you are going to do it yourself then you need only assess the cost of brushes, paint, wallpaper, strawboard, hooks, etc.

Nameplate and any inside directional signs. A signmaker will give you an estimate for making and fixing, from your own designs.

Heating appliances and the cost of fixing them. Your gas or electricity showrooms will give you these or your local builder if you decide to install a solid fuel stove.

Floor covering and the cost of laying it and possibly a rug. A local furniture store will work out how much you would need and the costs. Your builder would estimate for sanding the floors.

Curtains and the cost of making and hanging them. Again a local furniture or draper's shop could work this out for you.

Light fittings and the cost of fixing them and possibly installing socket outlets. The appropriate catalogues will give you the cost of these and if fixing, other than just plugging in, is needed, your electricity showroom will tell you the cost.

Furniture: drawing table or trestle, drawing stool, long table or work top, plan chest, storage cupboard, visitor's chair, desk, desk chair, filing cabinet. The cost of all these can be found in the catalogues of firms specializing in drawing office furniture and equipment and ordinary office furniture, that is if they have no showrooms in your town. If you can put up with slightly battered and possibly out-of-date-looking furniture, try a second-hand office furniture showroom.

Shelving for general storage and instead of a plan chest. Your builder will estimate for you or you must work out the cost of materials if you are going to make them yourself.

Typewriter and carrying case, metal wastepaper bins, strong cardboard boxes for filing, divider cards, manilla folders, portfolios for storing drawings, card index, telephone index, blotter, filing trays, cash box, scissors, rubber stamp pad. A good office stationer will give you all these prices.

First-aid box   Nearly all chemists sell these.

Cleaning equipment if your cleaner needs it (dusters, brooms, mop, bucket, lavatory brush) and a special duster and small soft brush for your own use; roller towels, tea-towels; tea-making equipment, kettle, tea-pot, coffee pot, crockery, cutlery, storage jars, tray and ash-trays. All these can be found and priced in good general stores, hardware shops, china shops and drapers.

Initial printed stationery costs   Typesetting, block or die for letterheading, visiting card, compliments slip, etc. A printer will estimate for these separately. The cost of paper and printing is a running cost, as it recurs.

Drawing equipment   This will depend on what you may already have acquired; what you need for your own particular work; and what you like to use. Catalogues and price lists from suppliers of drawing office equipment will give you all the costs.

Sending out 'new address' notices   When you move and if you decide to do this the notices could take the form of a specially printed card or be overprinted on your new letter-heading. A printer would estimate for either method.

Sundry oddments such as electric light plugs, picture wire, flex, nails, tools and so on and any transport or delivery costs for the things you buy or move. All such things necessary to almost any move may seem trivial as to cost but the small amounts each that they cost can add up to a surprising number of pounds so it is wise to budget a lump sum for them.

Special equipment such as photographic and projection. These could only be included if the budget could stretch that far.

It may look a pretty formidable job to price everything on that list. But maybe you already have some of the things on it; some you may not need. I have tried to include everything that anybody might need to start up a small office from scratch.

When you have made from it your own, possibly shorter, list, a day going round the shops and suppliers and an evening writing for catalogues ought to be sufficient time spent on bringing you in all the prices you need. And how else are you going to arrive at that important second budget figure—your capital outlay or starting-up expenses?

Let us assume that John Brown has made and priced his list and that it totals £500. If he has done a really thorough job of estimating, he would not need to add any contingency sum to that. But if he has done a bit of guessing here and there then it would be wise to add 10% for contingencies, making £550 in all. Whatever your own total, it will probably seem a rather frightening one but do not forget that most of what it buys—furniture, fixtures and fittings, furnishing and equipment—should last you for many years and will have *some* resale value if you ever have to sell up. Also most of it will go as assets on your balance sheet and an annual allowance for this depreciation will help you with your Income Tax.

Your overheads

Running expenses or overheads as they are more usually called, are all the recurring and expendable items and while a few of them may be known and fixed, others will need a good deal of guess-estimating based on all the facts you can gather. I am afraid that another list and some more price research is essential but obviously this can be done at the same time as your capital outlay list. All the figures should be annual totals but each one may have to be paid in either weekly, monthly, quarterly or annual instalments.

Rent If you have already found your office premises you will know the rent. If not, ask at one or two estate agents in your chosen locality for average costs per square foot for single offices or small suites of rooms. These are fairly constant and can be taken as a reliable guide.

Rates Again, if you have already found your office premises and assuming that they are not newly built with you as the first occupier, the rates will be known and fixed. Your landlord may know what they are, otherwise the Rating Office at the Town Hall will tell you. If your office is in a brand new building it will be difficult to find out what the rates are to be until you have moved in and the rateable value has been assessed. Equally it is difficult to know how to budget for rates before you have even found suitable premises. As they are likely to be a heavy item in your overheads however, it is very important to try and reach a safe estimate for them. You might ask one or two friends with offices of about the kind you are looking for what rates they pay.

Estate agents could also guide you on this point.

Insurances If you are working alone, the only compulsory insurance is National Insurance which is referred to later on in this chapter. But it would be foolish to grudge the premium on an all-in office policy which is somewhat on the same lines as a all-in householder's policy. At this stage you will have to find the first of the professional advisers to which I referred in Chapter Ten—your insurance broker. He will make no charge for advising you about the kind of insurance you should have and will estimate for your budget what the premiums would be.

Lighting Assuming that your office has reasonably good natural daylight and that you are going to work an average 8-hour day for a 5-day week, you should only need to use artificial light for six months of the year, from October to March. During that time you will probably have your lights on for a total of about 500 hours. Your electricity showrooms will tell you how many units an hour different-sized tungsten bulbs and fluorescent tubes use and also the cost of a unit of electricity. The rest is simple arithmetic, plus an allowance for standing charges which are usually worked out on a square foot basis. If your offices are dark and you are going to work longer hours, you will need to step up the total cost considerably.

Heating Allowing for the English climate to do its worst, you will probably need room heating from about the end of September to mid-May, 30 weeks in all. An 8-hour day—5 day-week would thus give you 1200 hours of room heating. If it is to be by electricity, you can estimate the cost of this as for lighting, at your electricity showrooms. If by gas, the gas showrooms will help but the estimate is more uncertain since gas heating is more flexible than electricity. If by solid fuel, the estimate will depend on the type of grate or stove and the fuel you use for it. A good coal merchant might help, otherwise write to the Coal Utilization Council (address in the London Telephone Directory). They will advise you free.

Telephone The installation charge will not recur and has therefore gone into your capital outlay list. The charges for rental, calls and any extras are what you must budget for on this overheads list. Rental is fixed and the local Telephone Manager's Office will tell you the cost. You will find that a business or professional subscriber pays rather more rental than a private subscriber. 'Extras' might be additional rent for, say, a Plan 107 instrument and anything you might have to pay an office neighbour for taking your calls on it; also for an extra directory entry. The cost of calls is quite an unknown quantity but somehow must be allowed for. If you are starting your design practice on your own from scratch, an *average* of ten local calls a day for the first year might be about right. To this you ought to add an allowance for long distance calls.

Cleaning and cleaning materials If you are going to make your own arrangements direct with a cleaner, you will probably pay her the rate per hour which is current locally for charladies. An hour a day should be ample for her to clean one or two rooms. To the cost of this you will have to allow for buying her expendable cleaning materials. If you are going to use an office cleaning firm, they will give you an all-in estimate.

Postage   This must allow for parcels as well as letters and there may be quite a lot of the former, as you will have no messenger to deliver finished artwork for you. Moreover, all such parcels should be sent Recorded Delivery unless you risk the loss of time and fees if a precious bit of artwork goes astray. Allowing for normal correspondence, orders, invoices, and paying bills, say, twenty letters a week as an average, and an allowance for packets and parcels. An average of two a week ought to be safe for the first year. In Chapter Five there are suggestions for making use of the Post Office Messenger Service, where this is available.

Typing   If your outward 'post' is going to average twenty a week, someone is going to have to type the letters, invoices, envelopes and labels. So this is where you must budget for the services of a shorthand typist, either hired by the hour from a nearby secretarial bureau (who would give you their charges) or paid for as pocket money to a willing friend or relative. Unless you are going to start by doing it all yourself.

Office stationery and materials   The basic essentials will include typewriter ribbons, eraser, carbons, flimsy copying paper, staples, paper clips, pins, ink, pencils, biros, blotting paper, note pads, adhesive labels, tie-on labels, strong brown paper, corrugated and tissue paper for wrapping, sheets of thick cardboard for stiffening flat parcels and packets, string, sticky tape, order books, scissors, adhesive, etc.

Printed stationery   You will probably start with just a specially printed letterheading, visiting card and possibly a compliments slip, so all you need budget for is your printer's estimate for paper and printing a year's supply.

Drawing materials   This will be a very difficult item to budget for and only your own experience in art school or a staff job will guide you. It is worth knowing that if you can afford to buy in bulk rather than ones and twos, most standard drawing office materials show a useful reduction for quantity.

Domestic items   These would include electric light bulbs and fluorescent tubes, soap, toilet paper, the laundering of your hand-towels, tea-towels and dusters; and your groceries for tea-making. A housewife friend could best advise as to possible consumption and costs.

Subscriptions   These would be for technical magazines, professional societies, any directory entries other than the Telephone Directory; any clubs or societies to which it might be essential for you to belong. You will probably know already most of the costs involved and any others are easily collected by letter or telephone.

Accountancy   This covers the whole important business of keeping your books (and buying the necessary ledgers and cash books), producing regular balance sheets and dealing with your Income Tax. Chapter Thirteen will tell you more about this but you must budget for someone to help you with it all—another of your professional advisers, your accountant. He should be able to give you a fairly safe estimate of his fees and expenses for your first year and they are likely to be quite modest. No audit fee will be involved unless you have formed yourself into a limited company.

Bank charges   Most banks no longer make charges for the day-to-day handling of your account with them, provided it does not fall below a specified amount. But you should allow for having to pay bank interest at the current rate on any overdraft you might have.

Travel   Visits to your clients, contacts, suppliers and contractors, following up enquiries, in fact all journeys except the daily one between home and office must be allowed for in the budget, as a total of fares or car mileage. This will have to be a very hit-and-miss guess-estimate but can be quite a large item. In Chapter Three I explained how quite a lot of such travelling expenses should be charged to jobs as extras to fees.

Entertainment   This will probably be your biggest 'public relations' expenditure and a very important one while you are building up your practice. (See Chapter Twelve.) It would be wise to budget for one lunch or dinner a week to someone useful and one or two rounds of drinks a week.

Advertising   The SIAD Code of Professional Conduct now permits its members to advertise their services so you should make some allowance, possibly a quite modest one, for this activity in your first-year budget. Read the more detailed information on page 162 on what to do about advertising and how to find out what it costs. You should then be able to budget for what you decide is appropriate.

Record photography   Good photographs of finished work are absolutely vital. (See Chapter Nine.) Sometimes a client will pay for the taking and you will only have to pay for the prints for your files. But quite often you will have to pay for it all. Budget for, say, two dozen shots during the first year and several dozen prints for record and publicity purposes.

Reserve for redecoration, replacements and additions   This is always an essential item in an overheads budget but need only be a modest one particularly for a first year in a newly-decorated newly-furnished office. But a modest sum should be put aside each year so that the money accumulates and is there when refurbishing does become necessary or if an expensive addition suddenly becomes essential.

National Insurance   This is compulsory whether you are employee, employer or self-employed. The rates change regularly (usually upwards) so it would be essential for you to check them currently at your nearest Social Security Office or any Post Office. The rates are different for men, women and self-employed people and will cost you a considerable sum of money so this is a very important item to budget for. The increases are usually widely advertised well in advance and should also be budgeted for within the year on which you are working.

Staff   If you are going to start up rather grandly with an assistant, obviously the salary you will pay should be added to your running costs budget, to start with at any rate; also the contributions which you must make towards his or her National Insurance.

Income Tax   You are very unlikely to have to pay any Income Tax for your first year. The fund in your bank with which you are going to start your practice and pay yourself a 'salary' has either been saved by you, in which case it has already been taxed, or is a loan or guaranteed overdraft, neither of which is taxable. It is your profits which will be taxed. Nevertheless you will have to make an Income Tax return, profit or no profit, each year and practically all the overhead expenses listed above will qualify for tax relief, provided you have kept a proper record of them and receipts wherever possible.

VAT This is the Value Added Tax which you must add on a percentage basis to your fees when you invoice them but showing it as a separate item. But it does not come into operation until your gross earnings have reached a statutory annual level. At the time of writing (mid-1983), this level is £17,000 and the relevant percentage is 15%. Your accountant will explain all the mysteries and do it all for you, when your earnings look like approaching the current minimum level.

When this third list of estimates is complete you will be able to arrive at your third budget total. It is even more important for this one than for either of the other two that you should add a substantial percentage for unforeseen contingencies, however accurate you may feel your estimating to have been— at least 5% and preferably 10%, if it can be managed. Assuming that John Brown's estimates total £910 his final total, allowing 10% for contingencies, would be £1000.

Expenditure

Now at last the results of these irksome labours can be put to good use. First they are the ingredients of a simple addition sum (but as previously mentioned, the figures are completely fictitious. Inflation would probably have doubled and trebled them by now):

John Brown's capital outlay budget, say	£550
John Brown's personal expenses budget, say	£1560
John Brown's overheads budget, say	£1000
	————
	£3110
	————

John Brown now knows that to set up and run for a year his own design office, he will need £3110 from *somewhere*. The first item for capital outlay he must have already in the bank, either as his own money, as a loan or as a guaranteed overdraft. Without it he cannot start. But having got it, spent it and opened his office, he then needs £2560 to run it and to live for a year. He will not need it all at once but at weekly, monthly, quarterly or yearly intervals. It should be quite easy to go back through all your own detailed estimates and split the amounts up under these four 'time' headings, when the bills are likely to come in. Do not forget that some things, like rent for instance, have to be paid in advance for a **week**, month, or quarter according to your tenancy agreement. Do not forget, also, that if your initial fund in the bank is a loan or an overdraft, you must allow for the regular repayment of it with interest. John Brown's figures assume that the fund has been saved by him.

If John Brown is starting up with no clients at all then he would be wise to ensure that he has in the bank all the money he needs for a year, £3110, since he could be unlucky enough to take that time to find clients and start earning fees.

But if he has already got—as is much more likely—one or two definite clients and jobs lined up and fees for them confirmed in writing, then the simple addition sum could be recast to include a little subtraction as well and would take on a slightly rosier aspect.

Expenditure and Revenue
Let us assume that John Brown knows for certain that he is going to earn fees totalling £500 during his first year of operation; then

Capital outlay budget, say		£550
Personal expenses budget, say	£1560	
Overheads budget, say	1000	
	———	
		2560
		———
		3110
less definite fees to be earned		500
		———
Net total required for the first year		2610
		———

Since it is undoubtedly true that jobs beget jobs, the sum above could be recast again to allow a small element of optimism to creep in. This, however, will be pure gambling and the extent to which John Brown brings it in will be entirely according to his nature, his estimate of his own abilities and his considered judgment of his future chances. Still, every new venture must be a bit of a gamble so here is the third sum which recognizes this fact:

Capital outlay budget, say		£550
Personal expenses budget, say	£1560	
Overheads budget, say	1000	
	———	
	£2560	
less definite fees to be earned	500	
	———	
	£2060	
less estimated further fees to be earned, say	500	
	———	
		1560
		———
Net total needed for the first year		2110
		———

It is the figure which John Brown puts against that second 'less' above which is the gamble.

By the time you have read as far as this you are probably dismayed at the idea of so much research, budgeting and figuring. But please do not let yourself be discouraged. The process is a simple and straightforward one if you work your way through it step by step, using the 'John Brown's pattern *but your own figures*.

The results are very important indeed. First they enable you to know, not just to guess at, how much money you need for the first year. On that knowledge you will presumably take the basic decisions: 'Can I afford it or can't I?' 'Is it entirely a gamble or a reasonable certainty?'. Secondly you will see how, in Chapter Fourteen, two of your budget totals will give you the fundamental information on which to assess your fees—the cost and 'selling price' of your time.

This will be the main battle of your whole free-lance career: not only to find clients to start you going but constantly to be finding clients to keep you going. It is a battle which has to be waged more or less ceaselessly until you retire and one which will never allow you to rest on your laurels. With a growing reputation and work coming in, you may be able to see ahead to several months of exciting creative jobs and think that your client-finding activities can be safely relaxed for some time. But at the end of your long spell of concentrated work those clients who were queueing up for your services will have gone elsewhere because they could not wait. You and your reputation will have tended to get out of circulation because you have not been seen around for some months and you may find yourself with some nice fat cheques for the work you have completed but with also an empty order book and possibly one or more idle assistants. Their salaries, with all your other overheads, will eat into those nice fat cheques in no time while you spend weeks or months looking for new clients again.

What you have to find by experience and firmly maintain is a proper balance between the time you can afford to give to the work you have got and the time you must afford to give to your constant client-finding activities. The incidence of the latter should not be less than weekly but the proportion of it will naturally be very much higher at the beginning of your career. It may be as much as one-third or one-half of your first working year.

Action

There are three main courses of action open to you. The first is to get yourself on to the SIAD's Designers' Register as soon as you have been accepted as a member; and on to the Design Council's Designer Selection Service. The second is to 'promote' in every way which is now permitted by the SIAD Code of Professional Conduct, yourself and the work you have done. The third is to make and keep yourself as a personality as widely known as possible, professionally and socially.

Now let us take each of these in order and see what can be done about them.

The SIAD (Society of Industrial Artists and Designers)

Even if you are not already a member, you will probably know about this important body, which was the first society of industrial designers in the world and was incorporated by Royal Charter in 1976. You can read all about it in the Appendix (page 233) and you should apply for membership as soon as you think you are eligible. A letter to the Membership Secretary will bring you all the information about how to apply. The standards are high but don't let that deter you.

The proud day when you can add for the first time the letters MSIAD after your name will not only establish your own professional status but will involve you in the stimulating obligations of maintaining and improving the status of the whole design profession, alongside the several thousand fellow-designers who are already members of it. In addition, you will receive your free copy of the Society's monthly publication *Designer* which is an excellent 24-page printed and illustrated magazine with all the news and pictures about members, their work, correspondence (often heated!), useful articles on technical processes, forthcoming events and so on. You can take out a paid subscription even if you are not a member and it would be well worth it.

The Society also publishes a regular flow of small pamphlets for its members, each dealing with some specific aspect of design practice (see Bibliography page 229).

On becoming a member, you can also apply to be registered in the Society's Designers' Register which aims to 'match skill and experience to meet the needs' of potential clients. The Register contains a biographical sheet for every registered member and would contain your relevant professional details: training, qualifications, length of time in practice, size of practice, particular experience, awards and so on, with of course your address. Linked with the Register is the 'Visible Record of Designers Work' and again, potential clients looking for just the right designer to meet their particular needs can inspect, at the SIAD's Headquarters in London, your photoprints, slides, proofs, specimens, sample swatches, descriptive brochures and so on, and then make up their minds. And don't, *oh don't*, forget how very important it would be for you to keep your file in the Visible Record right up-to-date with the newest material representing your most recently completed jobs.

Another useful service provided by the SIAD to its members is its Staff Vacancy Register. If you decided, after completing your training, to spend a year or so as a salaried staff designer (and how *very* wise that would be in nearly all cases) your name and professional details would be on the Register to be matched against vacancies notified to the Society. And that might bring you face to face with a potential employer and finally a job.

The Design Council

Most readers of this book will already know how much the Council has done and continues to do to improve the standards of design in Great Britain and how vitally important it is to professional designers in every field. You will find full information about it in the Appendix (page 242) but there is far more to do than just read about it. Visit the Design Centres in London or Glasgow (there is also a small exhibition in Cardiff), however far away you may live. You will find its permanent but changing exhibitions of well-designed consumer goods endlessly interesting and stimulating whatever your own field of practice. A subscription to its monthly magazine *Design* is a must and can be ordered from your newsagent or from the Council's London address. Most important of all, aim to get your name on to the Council's Designer Selection Service.

As soon as you feel that you are sufficiently qualified and experienced apply for an interview to the Council in London. When you are granted this interview, take your elegantly-presented specimens of work with you. If your work and experience are considered to be up to the Council's high standards, your name will go on the Record and hundreds of industrialists from all over the country apply to the Council every year for the names of suitable designers to help them with their design problems. Once on the Record, your name has a fair chance of being one of these important and useful recommendations. All this will cost you nothing except your fare to the Design Centre in London. Even if you live at John o'Groats do not begrudge the time and money to make this journey.

For those practising as product designers and/or engineering design, read the paragraph under The Design Council on page 243 and decide whether, under the sub-heading 'Design Advisory Service', you can offer engineering expertise as a result of your training and experience; and hope that this will eventually result in your name being put forward as a Design Advisory Officer.

Other organizations concerned with design

As well as the all-important SIAD and Design Council, there is information in the Appendix about other societies and bodies concerned in one way or another with design. As soon as your budget can manage it, membership of some of them at any rate will help to widen your knowledge of the national and international design world and its activities and keep you in touch with what other designers are doing. Even if you are geographically remote from their centres of activity their literature and publications will be useful and interesting to receive.

That more or less completes your first course of action for finding clients. It should have got you right into the heart of the design world, national and international but for that reason, the very breadth of coverage it offers and consequently the competition you will be up against, may make it slow-moving in producing clients for you, short of a minor miracle.

Nevertheless, to quote a splendidly mixed metaphor I was once privileged to hear 'You must just cast your bread upon the waters and hope that it will eventually come home to roost!'

But the second course of action can be carried out nearer home and may therefore produce quicker results. This is the active promotion of your design services by you.

Promoting your services

'Promote' in this context means 'to publicize and sell' in all appropriate and permitted ways and includes advertising, editorial publicity, writing direct to potential clients, appearing in public and on the air, and eventually paying experts to do all this for you. But before I go any further, may I suggest that you turn to page 233 in the Appendix and read Clause 9 of the SIAD Code of

Professional Conduct, and the relevant Notes. This is the Clause, hotly debated in the drafting and still held by some to be very controversial, which has largely untied the hands of the designer seeking clients. Until it was finally accepted and the whole of the rest of the Code revised around it, a designer who was a member of the SIAD was forbidden, along with the members of many other professional organizations, from paying to advertise his services, from writing direct to potential clients to offer his services, from producing printed matter, displays, etc. about his work and from paying an advertising or public relations expert to blow his trumpet for him.

Contrary to what the gloomsters predicted when Clause 9 became an accepted Code, the design profession has had the good sense not to rush jubilantly into the media, with full-page advertisements in *The Times* and the colour supplements and slots on commercial television. Apart from the fact that they probably couldn't afford it, established designers have realized that to be discreet in their approaches is far more professional than to be blatant and far more helpful to those young fellow designers who are only just beginning to climb the ladder.

Which is where we came in because this chapter is still concerned with how you can set about finding clients during your first difficult year or so in private practice. But before we go into more detail about all these new-found activities, I must sound a warning note.

It will be *no good at all* spending precious time and money to promote your services if you have not already got a fairly impressive visual record of completed work to show, when the promotion produces a positive reaction. Work which didn't go through to completion, projects carried out while you were still in training, big jobs in which you played only a small part as a salaried designer—none of these are likely to impress the hard-headed industrialist. He will be just as much concerned to see proof that you have been able to handle some 'live' jobs efficiently, with an eye to the time-table and the budget, as he will be with the excellence of your design abilities and a thin collection of specimens will be sadly unconvincing.

But let us hopefully assume that, since you are about to set up in private practice, you are doing so on the basis of sufficient good free-lance work and work you may have handled entirely on your own as a salaried designer, all carried through by you from start to finish and in production. So what is your best way to start your promotion campaign? I would choose the 'direct approach' since this is the easiest and least expensive.

The direct approach

If you are setting up your office in the city, town or area in which you also live, which seems likely, you will start with the advantage of knowing something of who's who and what's what around you—the businesses, industries and professions, the big shops, services and so on. And if you are hoping to make the direct approach to as many of them as possible, which means a personal letter to the managing director or the head of a department, it would be worth doing quite a bit of 'sleuthing around' in order to finish up with an accurate list (on a card index) of names and addresses (and by names I mean if possible the personal names of the men to write to), their phone numbers, a note of their activities and a comment on whether their premises, their 'images', their products, services, look as if they might ever, or never, have used the services of a professional designer.

At this point also, you must refer to Clauses 17 and 19 of the SIAD Code (see page 240) to make as sure as you can that in writing any of your direct approach letters, you would not be likely to supplant a fellow designer if you were offered any work.

Now the letter itself. (See page 16 for advice about writing business letters.) It should be short and to the point and might be somewhat on the following lines, but with your own personal touch to it:

> I have recently set up my own design office at the above address and I am writing to ask if I may have an appointment to show you some of my work, in case you might have need of professional design services in the future.
> I specialize in the fields of (insert whatever is appropriate) and have carried out design commissions for (names of two or three clients) amongst others.
> I look forward to hearing from you.

Make sure that the letter is laid out and typed beautifully on your elegant new letter-heading, make a note of its date on the appropriate index card and post it, and all the others, hopefully. For important future reference, record the gist of any replies you get on your index card (not interested, already have a designer, will get in touch later, etc.), follow up those in the latter category in a few weeks (see below under Following up) and put those who have offered you an appointment joyfully into your diary, after sending a brief note thanking for the appointment and confirming that you will be there.

After you have worked your way through your initial list, add to it from time to time as you come across new and potentially useful names. And you will find it very useful to keep that card index right up-to-date, with comments, dates, replies, appointments, etc. for future reference.

Introductions

During your initial 'sleuthing' operations, you may be lucky enough to come across someone you know reasonably well who knows personally someone whose name you have already got, or would like to have, on your list. Ask right away if the friend or acquaintance you have encountered would give you an introduction and you will probably get it.

The best and tidiest way to be given an introduction is to be given a copy of a letter which your contact has written giving your name to the recipient and asking him to see you when you get in touch with him. You then know exactly who he is and where he is, and he has also seen your name in print and connected it with that of the friend or colleague who has recommended you. He is therefore under a fairly strong obligation to see you. Even so, *never* follow this up with a telephone call. You might catch him at an awkward or irritating moment. Write a brief note instead, a day or two after your contact's letter, saying perhaps:

Dear Mr C

Mr A has suggested in his letter to you of (date), of which he has sent me a copy, that you might spare the time to see me in case the kind of work I do might be of interest to you.

I wonder, therefore, if your secretary would ring me to suggest a date and time convenient to you?

Yours sincerely, etc.

If nothing comes of this after about a week *then* you might follow it up with a telephone call to him or preferably to his secretary.

Another way of getting an introduction is for Mr A's letter to Mr C to be given to you, usually in an unsealed envelope, to deliver yourself to Mr C—a sort of passport into his territory. *Never* deliver it by hand and wait outside like a travelling salesman expecting to be interviewed there and then. Send it with a covering note of your own, on the lines, and for the same reasons, as I have suggested above.

A less satisfactory form of introduction is when your contact says 'ring up so-and-so, mention my name and ask him if he will see you.' However you must be thankful for small mercies but again, never ring up. A note mentioning your contact's name and asking for an appointment is more likely to get you one.

Perhaps the least satisfactory promise of help is if your contact merely says he will mention your name to so-and-so, unless he remembers not only to do it but to let you know that he has done it so that you can follow it up. If you hear nothing for two or three weeks you might then try a polite note to him:

Dear Mr A

I wonder if you have had time yet to mention my name to Mr So-and-so as you kindly promised to do? If so, I will get in touch with him direct to see when he could give me an appointment.

Forgive me for troubling you about this as I know how busy you must be.

With kind regards, etc.

If nothing comes of that, there is little else you can do. Mr A will have proved a broken reed.

Following up

I have already suggested, under 'The direct approach' that you should make a card index of the potential clients to whom you have written direct. As and when you get any introductions, the card index should also be used to record the necessary data about the firms, with also a note of the contact who introduced you and any other useful information, such as the function or status in the organization concerned of the individual member of it who interviewed you—managing director, art director, advertising manager, works manager.

150

When you get as far as an actual interview with someone to whom you have written direct or to whom you have had an introduction, several things may result from it. The best would be a definite request for your services in which case Chapters Three and Four advise how you should act on this. Or there might be a promise, apparently firm or vague, to get in touch with you in the near future about some possible design job. In this case, another brief note from you, expressing thanks for the interview and looking forward in due course to hearing more about the possible assignment, would round the matter off for the time being. But after a month or two, or whatever lapse of time seemed appropriate in the light of the interview a gentle reminder note could be sent if you had heard nothing in the meantime. 'Since meeting you on (date) I wonder if you have had time to consider whether I could be of use to you in connection with the design of your . . . etc.'

The worst, but not necessarily a hopeless, outcome of your interview would be that depressing phrase 'We'll file your name and reference.' People *do* file names for reference if their offices are efficently run and they *do* refer to them, particularly when an emergency arises. So don't despair but equally don't expect anything to result from such an interview. Also it would probably be a waste of time to send a follow-up note.

Finally, whatever the outcome of your interview, if it was the result of an introduction, write and tell your introducer that you have had it, thank him for the introduction and refer briefly to the possibility or otherwise of a job emerging from it. You may by now be appalled at the amount of letter-writing which I am suggesting you should do, particularly if you have no secretary. But I am quite unrepentant about this. The Note Courteous will always be appreciated by even the biggest businessman, in whose mind may build up a useful mental image of your name, your work and your good manners. And, to be less hard-headed for a moment, a genuine expression of gratitude for help given is surely always worth doing for its own sake. The Note Confirmatory is equally important since it is a small revelation of organizing ability, a characteristic which most businessmen think that most designers lack. The Note Following-up is a useful reminder of your existence which may genuinely have been overlooked in the meantime.

In any case your whole campaign for finding clients, particularly at the beginning of your career, is based on being seen, read, heard and consequently talked about so writing letters on every possible occasion is obviously essential.

Artists' agents

If you are a graphic designer or an illustrator there is another way of finding clients—or rather of having them found for you—which you ought to consider: that is to put yourself in the hands of a really good artists' agent. But for this service, of course, you pay a price, usually not less than 20% of the fees which the agent negotiates for you. You would find the names of some such agents in *The Writers and Artists* Year Book and also in *The Advertisers' Annual* (see page 229). It is a wise precaution to choose one of the better-known agencies and to know exactly what their terms are before entrusting them with your work.

Textile design

This is a field of design where the clients you will be seeking—textile manufacturers—have traditions of buying design which differ from others. They prefer to be offered 'collections' of designs instead of commissioning them, although this too is sometimes done, in the more normal way of other trades. If you are a textile designer you will therefore have to compile lists of manufacturers likely to be interested in your particular branch of textile design and make the first approach to them at regular intervals, asking for an appointment (this is essential) to show your collection. The buying time can be almost any time of the year but your assault on Manchester, the heart of the British textile industry, would best be made after the summer holiday since many factories close completely for staff holidays in August. *Never* leave your designs with prospective clients unless a sale has been definitely arranged. This also means that textile designs should always be presented in person, never through the post. Another tip: don't show to or discuss with would-be buyers, designs you have already sold to actual purchasers. It is a very competitive world.

Working 'on spec'

The SIAD, with two exceptions, does not permit its members to work 'on spec'—that is submitting preliminary designs for which you will get no fee if they are rejected.

The first exception is in the case of textile design (see above) and the second is explained in a footnote to the SIAD Code Clause 10: 'In certain circumstances a member may make no charge to a charitable or non-profit-making organization, provided that by doing so he gains no advantage over a fellow member.'

Even if you are not a member of the SIAD I should like to be able to say that working on spec is something you should never do. But to a beginner searching for work there could be circumstances which offered irresistible temptations. If the client offering the temptation were as honest as he should be he would not do it because he is blatantly taking advantage of your inexperience, lack of reputation and need for work. All that I can suggest therefore is that you try to avoid it at all costs; that you only do it if the need is very great and the (possible) rewards very dazzling and that, in any event, you see that the transaction is firmly tied up business-wise and in writing before you start work.

Advertising

Before you set about deciding if and where you are going to start advertising your services and how much you are going to spend I recommend you to do three things. First, if you hope to be or are already a member of the SIAD, read carefully through the Code Clause 9, all about promotion, on page 239. Second, get hold of a current copy of the Design Council's *Design* Magazine and study the way in which other designers are doing it under the Heading 'Directory of Designers' Services' in a special section at the back of the magazine. And three, buy (even if it seems expensive) a copy of the *Advertisers' Annual*. It will be money well spent as you will also need to consult a copy when you send photographs of your work to the technical press (see page 113). And although it is an annual (sometimes also called the Advertising Blue Book) it will, for your purposes, last you for several years.

The first action needs no amplification here. The Code provides the guidelines within which you will want to work. The second is an excellent example of how professional designers are exercising restraint in their newfound freedom to advertise—brief, factual and no loud trumpet blowing, as befits a professional. The heading of the Directory invites you to write for details and advertising rates and I would advise you to do this right away.

The third action brings you nearer home. Wherever you live, there is bound to be a local weekly paper and, if you live in or near a big town or city there will probably be a daily or evening paper covering your area. This is where the Advertisers' Annual comes in because it lists all of them everywhere. Now you can make a modest list: *Design* Magazine at the top, your local papers to follow and finally you must consider the technical magazines, all of which are listed in their hundreds under subject headings. If you have had experience during your training or in any subsequent jobs of some rather special aspect of design, say plastics technology, book typography, shop fittings, ship interiors or what have you, look for the relevant technical publications and add them to your list.

Now you must write to the advertising manager of each publication you have listed and ask for a current rate card, which will tell you how much different sizes of space will cost you, what 'series discount' you would get, if any, by booking several insertions at a time and what the press day is for copy.

And then it is a question of adding it all up to see what you might like to do and then, more soberly, what you think you can afford. Tentatively, I would suggest that you ought to try and afford regular, though not necessarily consecutive, insertions in *Design*, in your local daily paper and in any appropriate technical magazine. And it is worth knowing that you will, generally speaking, make more impact by buying small spaces regularly than larger ones infrequently or once only.

The third course of action
Having made your plans for promotion of your services, you now have to look at the third course of action, which is really to promote yourself, by making and keeping yourself as a personality as widely known as possible. This takes some doing and also some courage if you happen to be a shy retiring character. But it must be done and you will probably find that the shyness soon wears off when you meet and mingle with more and more people.

Local activities
The myth of the typical designer dies hard in this country. 'One of those

unpractical undependable artist chaps—long-haired, unshaven, corduroy-trousered, sandal-shod, generally unkempt, probably amoral, thinks he knows everything.' Many businessmen, industrialists, manufacturers, who have never met a designer in the flesh, might still think in those sort of terms. But if they find that the competent, presentable young man or woman with whom they play tennis or golf at the local club, or who sits across the table of some committee concerned with local activities, is in fact a designer, the myth begins to disperse, interest may be aroused and when their need for design services arises they may, putting it at its lowest, prefer the devil they know to the devil they don't. You have to be a bit hard-headed about your social life, at any rate until you have completed enough jobs for them to begin to speak for themselves. Until then, no party invitation, however uninteresting, should be refused. No opportunity should be lost for going to local functions and taking an active part in them. Pick a good 'local' and drop in regularly for a drink. Join your local amenity, art, music, dramatic society. If you are politically minded you may already belong to your local party organization. At its meetings and social functions you will come in contact with people with whom there is a ready-made basis of mutual interest in one respect at any rate. If you work in or near a big town or city, there will be a number of useful clubs, societies and organizations which you might join. Subscriptions to these will already have been allowed for in your overheads budget.

Other designers and architects

It would be very useful to try and make contact with any other designers and architects practising near you. If you could get them listed, a suitable 'direct approach' letter might be written to each, suggesting that you would like an opportunity to show them your work in case an opportunity for some sort of collaboration ever arose. The established free-lance designer who is getting more work than he can handle himself is often reluctant to turn any of it down and prefers to farm it out to a fellow designer whose work he knows and respects. Or he may get a big job which includes some field of design in which he does not specialize and in which you do. Best of all, he may like to render a client the service of recommending you direct for a very specialized job which he could not tackle at all.

The same applies to architects. Often they seek the collaboration of a specialized designer for interior design, for lettering and numbering for public buildings; for custom-designed carpets, textiles, furniture, light fittings for showroom and office interiors; for permanent exhibitions, displays, murals, charts, pictorial diagrams for entrance halls, boardrooms and the like.

Competitions

There is, also, a perfectly reasonable and legitimate 'on spec' activity for which you should always be on the look-out and that is to enter for design competitions. These may be organized by businesses, manufacturers, associations, advertising agencies, even Government Departments and charities, for the design of a poster, symbol or trademark, a manufactured product, a textile, carpet or wallpaper, a medal, coin or stamp and so on.

Such properly organized affairs, with published rules and regulations, may take the form of an open competition which means that you only get your 'fees' paid, so to speak, if you win a prize. With a prize, of course, also goes a good measure of very useful publicity. Even without a prize, your work will have been seen and noted by a panel of high-level judges, may be on view somewhere and may even get published as a runner-up.

The limited competition is the other kind and this is unlikely to come your way until your reputation is very well-established because it means that the organizers *invite* a limited number of named designers—perhaps not more than three or four—to submit designs in competition with each other for a fixed fee, payable whether they win or not. Government Departments often use this method. Big businesses sometimes do if they are perplexed about the right approach to their particular design problem. They are prepared to pay rather more in preliminary fees to buy a wide variety of creative ideas to help them to make up their minds.

The SIAD advises that 'the prizes, together with any professional fees for design development, should be substantially higher than the fee which would normally be paid for the same design project if it were undertaken as a direct professional commission.'

The open competition will usually be announced in the appropriate technical magazines. Given that you need work, contacts and publicity and can spare the time, competitions are usually well worth considering if you think you have at least an even chance of winning. But check up first to see if your competition is being properly conducted. Most of them are but there are occasional back-sliders. The SIAD's Clause 21 of the Code states: 'Members should assure themselves that competitions they may be invited to assess or may wish to enter are in accordance with the Society's regulations for the holding of design competitions.' Their leaflet 'Design Competition Regulations' is useful reading for both promotors and designers.

Publicizing your appointments

As soon as you have half-a-dozen or so finished jobs to your credit, enormously valuable reinforcements are added to your client-finding campaign. There may even be certain jobs which you can legitimately publicize before you have started them.

If you were lucky enough to land a job as a specialized design consultant to a firm on a retaining fee; or to be selected to design an important interior or exhibition stand, or even to be appointed as a part-time lecturer at an art school, you could, with your client's written permission, send the information about your appointment as a brief item of news to your local papers, to the relevant technical press and to the *Designer* (if you were an SIAD member) and to *Design* Magazine. I would stress: *with your client's written permission*, since his firm may wish to keep its proposed design developments as secret as possible for competitive reasons. This almost invariably applies to the design or re-design of product, pack or presentation material and it would be wasting your time and not very tactful to ask for permission to publicize your appointment to design it.

But with your client's consent you might draft a brief news item on the following lines:

John Brown (letters after name) has been appointed by Robinson & Company Limited to design the interior of their new showroom in White Street, Newchester. John Brown was responsible for the interior design of John Jones' showroom in Black Street and is a part-time lecturer in interior design at the Newchester Polytechnic.

This tells the press about a definite appointment and a definite job completed —just the bare facts in the best professional manner. When you have the brief paragraph drafted to your liking, send it with a covering note to your client asking if he would have any objection to your sending it to a selected list of periodicals and send him your proposed list as well (again from the *Advertisers' Annual*). The chances are that he will not object. He may even be rather pleased at the idea of a little free publicity for his firm's name.

When you have his permission you will find in Chapter Nine, all the 'drill' for issuing editorial material to the press. But don't be disappointed if only one out of twenty periodicals publishes your news item. Even that one is well worth the trouble and money which the operation has cost you. It is your name in print again and out of the thousands who read it disinterestedly, one reader might file it at the back of his mind 'for future reference' when *he* wants something similar designed.

Finished jobs

But it is your finished jobs—the facts and figures about them, their case histories, the illustrations, photographs and actual specimens of them which are your most vital assets and which will bring you more clients than anything else, if you are meticulous to collect and record the material about them and make good use of it. Again, Chapter Nine gives all the details about how this should be done. It might be a good idea to look back at this stage and skim through it before going on to the next chapter. There are certain basic things to remember to do at all stages of a job, some of them even before you begin, in order to build up not only your eventual publicity story about it but very useful records and reference material for later use on similar jobs as well.

Publicity literature

This is another activity which the SIAD allows its members under the new Code—printed literature, probably in brochure or folder form, containing illustrations and descriptions of completed jobs. Such a brochure, if well designed and produced, can be very impressive but it is a very expensive exercise and can also be a very frustrating one as well since such brochures so very quickly go out-of-date. When the urgent need to send one to a potentially important new client arises and you realize that all the jobs illustrated in it are at least a year old, you will feel that your expensive stock of brochures is not much use to you.

One way out of this difficulty, until you can afford to be extravagant and reprint every six months or so, is to devise and have printed an elegant little folder with just your name, address and phone number on it and with two open pockets inside into which you can slip suitably captioned photographs of your most recent jobs. To keep a stock of photoprints in your files, ready-captioned and the folders which will not date, will be much less expensive and wasteful, even if not quite as impressive as a fully-printed brochure.

Entertaining

Now the bugbear of entertaining has to be faced and it is a must for every professional man who wants to build up his practice. The little rituals of ordering drinks, choosing a meal, initial small talk and offering cigarettes all help to provide a relaxed friendly setting in which it is very much easier for two people who are virtually strangers to find out what interests they have in common and whether they can, and want to, be of use to each other.

Having said which, I realize only too well how difficult it still may be for a young designer, possibly shy and inexperienced at any kind of entertaining to face the ordeal of being the host at a business lunch or dinner for the first few times. However like all unknown and dreaded things, it is never as bad as you imagine and soon gets progressively easier as the rituals and formalities become habit. There is one way too of hastening this process. If you can find and try out a small intimate type of restaurant where the food is good and perhaps a little unusual and the service excellent, use it as often as you can. You will find that your inhibitions about playing host will quickly disappear when the menu and wine list become familiar and you can recommend your guest to try this or that and when the waiters get to know you as a good regular customer. *Always* book a table in advance and always insist that you get one, perhaps the same one, in a good position. Your guest may then be impressed with your good judgment and may find it a pleasant change not to be taken to the usual hotel dining-room, vast and impersonal, which is the conventional place for business lunches.

The woman designer has one problem facing her as a hostess which over-rides all others. No male guest is going to like it if she pays the bill or is even going to let her. She will then be very embarrassed if she fixes up a purely business lunch or dinner and finds at the end of if that her guest insists on paying the bill for both of them. The way out of this dilemma is to join one of the ubiquitous credit card organizations for a few pounds annually and pick the kind of small restaurant suggested above where your particular credit card will be accepted. Then your bill for a meal only needs your signature on it and will later be charged directly to your office on a monthly account.

Entertaining in your office should only be embarked upon if it is either very central and fairly presentable or very presentable indeed if rather remote. Moreover, in either event there should also be an impressive array of finished work in evidence. Planned entertaining in your office is therefore best left for a year or so. The overheads budget in Chapter Eleven has allowed for *ad hoc* entertaining so that if an important visitor calls on you, you can be ready to offer a good cup of tea or coffee or a drink.

Wherever you plan to entertain the chances are that it will be arranged verbally, probably on the telephone. In that case I would suggest that you *always* confirm the appointment in writing. A busy man may jot down your name and the appointment while he is talking to you on the phone and then mislay it. A brief note from you will not only be a pleasant courtesy but may show him for the first time your well-designed letter-heading and your name in print. It helps to establish you and your set up much more firmly in his mind and he can pass your note to his secretary for her to remind him of the appointment and record your name and address for future reference. Such a note need only say something like this:

Dear Mr A

I am so glad you are free to have lunch with me on (date) and I shall look forward to seeing you at (time) at the 'Bon Appetit' Restaurant, which as you may know is on the corner of White and Green Street.

Yours, etc.

At no stage in your career will you lose anything by sparing the time to be meticulously courteous about 'thank you' notes when *you* have been a guest.

To a rather illustrious host you might say:

Dear Mr B

Thank you for a very pleasant lunch yesterday and for sparing me so much of your time. I am also most grateful for the (advice, information, introductions) which you gave me, which I know I shall find very useful.

Yours, etc.

A less formal note but on the same lines will always be a pleasant courtesy to someone of more equal status, even with someone with whom you may be on Christian name terms, if he has stood you a meal and helped you with a problem.

Summary

To sum up, try to look on your client-finding activities as an essential part of your work. For instance, make yourself do at least one thing in this direction every week. Decide on Monday what it shall be, fit it into your programme for the week and on Friday evening check up with yourself that you have actually done it. Too many small design offices fold up too soon because the principals seldom looked further ahead than the absorbing jobs on hand.

While you are busy and absorbed in finding clients and working for them, there is another activity which must not be neglected and that is running your office. Otherwise the whole machine will slow down and your other activities will suffer severely in consequence. A smooth-running well-ordered office organization, however small, however simple, is the often unseen but always fundamental basis of every successful professional, commercial and industrial undertaking.

There is no mystery about it. No particularly expert knowledge is needed. It consists almost entirely of getting into the habit of doing the things that require to be done regularly and often. Otherwise you will constantly be exasperated and delayed because there are no stamps and the Post Office is shut; no petty cash and the Bank is closed; a supplier returns an order because you have forgotten to pay his last three bills; a magazine does not turn up because you forgot to renew the subscription; the telephone is cut off because you overlooked the Final Warning; worst of all perhaps, an important letter cannot be found in a hurry because the filing has not been done for weeks.

It sounds like an exaggerated tale of woe but there are many small offices which muddle along in such a context, with frenzy and frustration as their middle names. It is hard to believe that they can for very long continue to produce creative work—or any work for that matter—of any great merit, or grow and expand as most undertakings will want to do.

Assuming that for the first year you cannot afford a secretary (and I shall come back to this desirable solution further on in this chapter) the golden rule is to give small amounts of time frequently to your office chores, rather than to let things pile up until you have to break off doing other important work for a long spell in order to clear the accumulation.

Try to be very strong-minded therefore and set aside, say, an hour a day to write your letters and make your telephone calls, enter up your expenses and your time sheet, pay in cheques received, do the filing (all kinds) and tidy up generally. On one day in the week, extend your hour to two, in order to replenish your stamps, cash a cheque for the week's petty cash, check bills that have come in against orders, enter up your job sheets, bring your progress schedules up-to-date, pay any weekly bills (your milkman, laundry, cleaner?). Once a month set aside a half-day for paying all monthly accounts, sending out your own invoices and statements and having a session with your accountant. There is more about him further on, but first let us go back over some of these activities and see what is involved.

Bank accounts

You will already have a personal bank account and presumably therefore a bank manager who knows something about you. As we saw in Chapter Ten, a friendly bank manager can be a most helpful adviser to you on money matters. If therefore you had thought of opening a separate bank account for the finances of your practice, why not do this at your own bank, but make it a 'No. 2 account'? This means that your bank will keep your No. 1 and No. 2 accounts quite separate as if for two different people. You would merely put the number of the account on your paying-in slips and you would have two separate cheque books, each prestamped with the account number. You can, of course, transfer funds from one account to the other when you want to.

If the branch of the bank where you are known is near to your home but remote from your office, your bank manager can quite easily arrange for you to pay in and draw out (usually up to a limited amount on any one day) at whichever branch is most convenient for you, while still keeping your account at the original branch. This is well worth considering because it is very time-wasting to have to make quite a journey every time you want to pay in or cash an office cheque in a hurry.

Petty cash

You will see later on how important it is to keep a record of what you spend in connection with the office. This is easy enough when you pay for things by cheque because the 'cheque drawn' slip is there to remind you to fill it in. But it is much harder to remember when it comes to petty cash expenses. These are all the smallish items for which you would probably pay in cash—travelling expenses, stamps, parcels, entertainment, tips, oddments for the stationery cupboard and so on. If you get into the habit of paying out for these from the personal cash in your pocket you may find it hard to remember to pay yourself back and harder still to remember what you have spent it on.

It is a good idea, therefore, to get yourself a small cash box (provided you have somewhere to keep it locked away) and in it a little pad of blank petty cash chits which you can buy at any office stationers. Then draw a regular weekly cheque to keep the cash box in funds and enter up something on a chit, as a reminder, when you take cash from it. The date, the amount and, say, 'For journey to Manchester' or 'Lunch John Brown' will be sufficient help in jogging your memory when you have to make up your expenses. Some of them—travelling expenses, for instance, may be chargeable to a client and therefore not to be overlooked on any account.

Postages

For a one-man-office it would not be necessary to keep a post book—that is, a book in which is entered every day the names on the letters and the amount of stamps put on them. As soon as you have a secretary she should do this for you, however, and at the end of each week the value of the stamps used should (but all too seldom does) add up to the value of the stamps bought.

'Stamps £1' would be a sufficient sort of entry on one of your petty cash chits when you buy stamps, but parcel postage and particularly Recorded Delivery parcels should be entered as separate items with a clue as to their destination because they may later on be chargeable to a client.

Filing

Filing anything anywhere is probably one of the world's most boring chores. In an office it is unfortunately one of the most essential and particularly in a design office where, to the ordinary correspondence filing, will be added the filing of drawings, artwork, proofs of typesettings, copy negatives, photo-prints, slides, catalogues, samples and all kinds of reference material. There is no royal road to it, it just must be done regularly and frequently, like the washing-up in a kitchen. When you have a secretary she will do it for you. While you are on your own, every moment of your time will be doubly precious and to have to waste any of it searching wildly for something which ought to be immediately to hand in its appointed file will be exasperating and expensive.

Elaborate filing 'systems' as provided by office equipment manufacturers are not necessary for a small design office. They *may* come later but are usually more applicable to large commercial or industrial undertakings. As we saw in Chapter Ten, all you would need to start with would be a three- or four-drawer steel filing cabinet, if you could afford it or large strong cardboard boxes if you could not.

One drawer, or box, could be used for correspondence, filed alphabetically, Letters from John Smith should be filed under S, not J. Perversely, letters from Johnson Smith & Co. would be filed under J, not S. A second drawer could be for trade catalogues and flat reference material—very useful and vital stuff this which, if properly filed and kept reasonably up-to-date, may save you hours of research when you are on a rush job. This filing should also be done alphabetically but under subject matter. You may not know or remember the names of the firms sending you their catalogues, but you will want to be able to turn up quickly all the information you have on, say, 'End papers,' 'Floor coverings', 'Lettering', 'Sign-makers' and so on.

A third drawer or box could be for small pieces of artwork, typesetting proofs, photoprints, etc. filed alphabetically under clients' names. If you have a fourth drawer use it, or yet another box, for flat specimens of finished jobs and record photographs. If your practice is a varied one, these might be filed under kinds of work—'Booklets', 'Stationery', 'Window displays', 'Exhibitions', 'Wall-papers'. When you begin to collect three-dimensional specimens of finished jobs these present more of a storage problem. First they must be kept exquisitely clean. Tissue paper, cellophane and polythene bags are all cheap and there should be a very generous store of them maintained in your stationery cupboard. Then if you are going to put away in boxes or cupboards your precious specimens of packs, bottles, jars, products, they should be protectively wrapped and if necessary labelled. When you can afford it, design a long shallow hanging cupboard with sliding glass doors for your room. In this dust-proof setting at eye-level you can then arrange your three-dimensional specimens to make an impressive display for visitors.

Your samples will be filed in boxes of different sizes and shapes, one each for, say, pattern pieces of materials, wallpapers, carpeting, plastics, cut-out letters, board, tiles, coloured card, papers, timbers. But there is one thing to know about keeping and filing samples. Unless they retain their manufacturers' labels on them they are virtually useless, an anonymous jumble, useful only occasionally for colour reference but otherwise taking up valuable space.

Large drawings go best into a plan chest but if you are making do with the large portfolios on slatted shelves suggested in Chapter Ten identify the contents of each portfolio on a tie-on (*not* stick-on) label. This will then hang down in front of the shelf and can be read easily.

Retention of letters and drawings

No office, however vast, can find room to keep all its filed material for ever. And fortunately it is not required to do so. Correspondence should legally be kept for seven years but a lot of it need not be kept for anything like as long as that. With limited filing space in a small office you will find it essential to have a half-yearly 'spring clean' of all your files. Correspondence files for jobs which are still current or which are finished but not yet charged should be left where they are. Files on jobs completed, charged and which have not produced any queries after a lapse of six months could be condensed by throwing out all non-essential papers and leaving only letters about fees, policy decisions, contractors, suppliers and suchlike. These could then be bundled together and put in storage boxes with a contents label on the outside. After seven years you can throw away the lot. If any of them relate to jobs which are unlikely to recur, like exhibition stands, temporary exhibitions, printed matter for a limited dated purpose (a programme or invitation card) you could safely throw away your bundled files after two years. But not sooner, because the 'annual' jobs may come back to you again and again (stands at the same exhibitions, programmes, Christmas cards, company reports, year-books) and then it is very useful to be able to look back and see how the job went on the previous occasion. Do not forget also that some exhibitions only recur every other year. How long to keep artwork and drawings depends upon who owns the copyright of them. As we saw in Chapter Three, preliminary designs not proceeded with by your clients remain your property. Keep them if you feel that the client might change his mind in the nearish future or if they might ever be useful as references for other jobs. Otherwise they are as dead as mutton and can be thrown away. Finished artwork for jobs where the copyright passes to your client on completion and payment can always be sent to him for safekeeping. This practice is often not appreciated and even then very seldom followed by designers, who clutter up their files and provide rent-free space to their clients for what is no longer, in fact, their property. Drawings of interior design work are another matter. Whether or not you have decided to retain the copyright (see Chapter Three) drawings of this kind are much more likely to be referred to again after a considerable lapse of time, when some structural alteration or extension may be required. It would be advisable to keep sets of such drawings for as long as you could possibly find space for them.

Paying bills
As bills come in they should be checked against estimates and orders. If they are correct they can be ticked as such and put aside in a file ready for paying-out day. If they appear to be incorrect, they should be queried at once with the supplier, not left for weeks before anything is done about them. If they are directly connected with a job the supplier should have quoted your order number and job number on his bill. You can thus easily identify the charge and after checking it, enter it on the relevant job sheet.

Don't forget the advantages of a 'standing order' as it is called, to your bank to pay certain bills for you—your rent instalments, subscriptions and anything else where the regular amounts do not fluctuate, at least within a twelve-month period.

Book-keeping and accounts
Now we come to the most important of all jobs in running your office—your accounts. To a free-lance designer planning to set up on his own they may seem to be a terrible worry to contemplate. And well they may be if he tries any amateur solution to the problem. The simple and, in fact, only answer is to employ the services of a professional accountant. He has been looming in the distance several times in this book so far and now he is right on the doorstep of your office, waiting to be of essential service to you.

But first—why keep accounts? After all you are on your own, you have (presumably) money in the bank on which to draw for your personal and office needs and fees come in from time to time to maintain the bank balance. Provided it stays just 'in the black', why should a one-man office worry about the mystical complications of book-keeping and accountancy when nobody else will? There is somebody else who will worry, nevertheless, and that is the Department of Inland Revenue, or in other words the Income Tax man. Just as you are required to send in an annual return of your personal income so also must you send in a return of the profits, if any, from your business. Failure to do this will not bring any legal penalities but it will, after a lapse of time, cause the Income Tax authorities to assess what they think your profits might be in the absence of any evidence to the contrary. They will assess them pretty high and tax you accordingly. Then you can appeal but only with success if you can produce accounts to show what your profits or losses actually were.

Apart from all this you can have no idea at all how your business is progressing unless you keep accounts according to an established pattern; no idea whether you are making a net profit or a loss or how much money you owe or are owed at any given time. Your bank balance is absolutely no indication at all as to how you are doing. It might be deeply in the red and yet a statement of your accounts drawn up at that moment might show that you were making a profit because you were owed a lot of money and vice versa.

There is one more rather dismal situation in which properly kept accounts will help you: that is if you are ever unfortunate enough to go bankrupt. If your books are in good order for the three years previous to your bankruptcy you may be discharged at once. Otherwise your financial difficulties will be much greater and more prolonged. So open the door forthwith to your chosen accountant and invite him into the most secret recesses of your practice. The first thing he will do is to buy for you a set of the necessary 'books'—a cash book, and two ledgers. They do not need to be weighty leather-bound tomes. Woolworths can provide all that is necessary.

The next thing he will do is to agree with you on the minimum amount of work which you *must* do in order to give him the necessary basic facts for his accounts. At its very least this would mean, as we have seen, a written record somewhere of the money you draw out of the bank and what you spend it on and of the money you pay into the bank and who it has come from. The former needs details on the 'cheques drawn' slip and petty cash chits. The latter, details in the paying-in book. In addition he would want copies of all your invoices to your clients (these are dealt with in Chapters Eight and Seventeen) and he would want to see the bills, whether paid or unpaid, for everything you buy. No more than that and he will do all the rest, keep your books entered and up-to-date and give you a monthly or quarterly balance sheet, whichever you prefer, an annual balance sheet and profit and loss account and look after all your income tax problems for you.

For these valuable services your accountant will charge you fees based on the time he spends on your accounts, probably an hourly rate in fact. We saw in Chapter Eleven that when you are drawing up a budget for your first year, your accountant could probably assess approximately what his total fees would be for that year. He might even do a deal with you and agree a small lump-sum fee for his first year's work for you and stick to it, win or lose, while you are getting your feet on to the bottom rung of the ladder. Many chartered accountants take on a simple set of books, as yours would be, as private work to be done in their spare time. If, however, you are paying an hourly rate fee for your accountancy there is a way in which you could save yourself a few pounds by going a step further beyond the minimum records which your accountant will require you to keep. That is to write up the cash book yourself. Your accountant could show you how simply this can be done, provided it is done regularly and often, even in a cheap notebook. Between the covers of it you would give him all that he needed to carry on from there and 'do' your books. This would save his time and fees spent in collating all your petty cash chits, 'cheques drawn' and paying-in slips and entering them into the cash book himself.

Revenue and expenditure budget

Your accountant will be able to show you with actual figures and at regular intervals how you have done during the previous month, quarter or year. In doing this, he will also automatically show you your financial position *at that moment* so that if you closed down your office there and then you could know if you would be left with an eventual profit or loss after everything had been settled up. So much for the past and the present. But just as important is the future. About this he can tell you nothing from the books or the balance sheets. It lies in the fees you know you are going to earn, when you are likely to have earned them and what it is going to cost you to earn them. In other words, a budget.

In Chapter Eleven, your budget for the first year, after a lot of initial hard work, was summarized in three or four total figures, nearly all of them based on careful estimating and inspired guesswork. It was worked out thus to help you to decide whether or not to set up on your own. But once started and after the first six months, you will find it extremely useful, even essential, to budget ahead again at regular intervals. Only by doing this will you know if you are going to earn enough over the next six months to pay the overheads and keep on an even keel. The picture might even be rosy enough for you to start considering taking on a secretary and an assistant.

Here is a very simple way of putting down a revenue and expenditure budget and keeping it going. Let us assume that you have been in private practice for six months and during that time you have acquired six clients. On a large sheet of paper rule a narrow column for the job numbers, a wide column for client and job, and six columns for the six calendar months. Having done this you will need to have by you a note of all the fees which have been agreed with your six clients and particularly the stage-payments likely to fall due for invoicing. Enter them under the appropriate month by which you are reasonably sure you will have completed the stage of the work, will have allowed a decent interval to elapse (not less than a week) and could send out an invoice soon after the end of that month. If any of the jobs involve development work to be done at hourly rates you will have to make a careful guess at fees and when they can be invoiced. With your fees all filled in you can then add up the budget column for each month and this will be your gross estimated revenue. Below this you have to put your outgoings—your 'salary' and your overheads. The total of these two, which is your expenditure, subtracted from your revenue will give you your profit for the month. If expenditure is more than revenue, there will be a loss for that month and if too many months show a loss, the overall picture might be considered a bit grim. By carrying forward your profit or loss each month, you will get an accumulated nett total at the end of the six months period which may show that the profits of some of the months will have outweighed the losses of others and you can breathe again. On the following page there is a hypothetical budget to show you how it might look. In preparing your own, the only safe thing to do is to be pessimistically *low* about estimated revenue and pessimistically *high* about estimated expenses. Then you are much more likely to come out on the right side. Far, far too many budgets are worked out with optimism replacing pessimism and 'low' and 'high' changing places.

There are several things to notice about this invented budget which you will need to remember when you are compiling your own. First those losses at the end of August and September need not cause alarm and despondency because the budget shows that by the end of December the situation will have righted itself quite satisfactorily. That fact alone is sufficient to show how valuable to

Budget for July to December inclusive

A Estimated Revenue

Job No.	Client and job	July	Aug	Sept	Oct	Nov	Dec
1	Smith & Brown stand	£100 (p/d)	—	—	£100 (on a/c)	—	£150 (on a/c)
2	Jones' letterheadings	—	£ 25 (p/d)	—	£ 25 (f/d)	—	£ 50 (f/d)
3	Green cutlery	—	£ 75 (p/d)	—	£ 55 (dev)	£ 35 (dev)	£ 50 (f/d)
4	Robinson booklet	—	—	£ 35 (p/d)	—	£ 40 (f/d)	—
5 .	White trademark	£ 50 (rep)	—	—	—	£ 50 (p/d)	£ 60 (f/d)
6	King's packaging	—	—	£100 (p/d)	£ 20 (dev)	£ 15 (dev)	£ 50 (dev)
		£150	£100	£135	£200	£140	£360

B Estimated Expenses
'Salary' per month £65

Overheads " " £75	£140	£140	£140	£140	£140	£140

		July	Aug	Sept	Oct	Nov	Dec
C	Profit or loss per month	+£ 10	−£ 40	−£ 5	+£ 60	—	+£220
D	Profit or loss c/f	—	+£ 10	−£ 30	−£ 35	+£ 25	+£ 25
E	Accumulative profit or loss	£ 10	−£ 30	−£ 35	+£ 25	+£ 25	+£245

p/d=preliminary designs   f/d=finished drawings
on a/c=on account   dev=development work
c/f=carried forward   rep=report

you a budget will be. Secondly this budget assumes that by the end of the previous six months, ie 30 June, you were all square, and that there was neither profit nor loss to carry forward at D under July. Thirdly this simple form of budget does not take into account any expenses to be charged out to clients. That is because while they are on a fairly small scale, they make little or no difference either to revenue or expenditure. If, however, you undertake later on to contract for a client on a larger scale, in which case you may be entitled to a handling charge on the monies you pay out for him (see Chapter Seven), then the total of the handling charges (possibly 2½% or 5% on costs) should be added to your estimated revenue. But *only* the handling charges, not the costs themselves. Another important thing to remember is that the fees revenue is your estimate of when the work stages will be finished and ready to invoice.

But some jobs may run late, others be finished ahead of time. It is a good idea to leave room under each month to put in the actual figures you invoice and to carry over those which were not ready. Then you can keep a watch on how the one situation is balancing the other. Six months is about as far as it is safe to budget ahead with reasonable accuracy for a small design practice unless you are doing only interior design when the time between fee stages is much longer. Even so, the whole thing should be revised every three months, again for the next six months ahead. This means that the budget shown here would be recast at the end of September to show the anticipated revenue and expenditure for October to March inclusive and then again at the end of December, and so on. Fees not invoiced because jobs had lagged behind would be put in again under revised months, new jobs would be added and the monthly overhead figure checked with your accountant to see if it should be put up or down.

You will find that your budget, once you have got it running, will serve two useful purposes. The first is as a budget to show you what the future looks like. The second is to help you when you come to do your invoicing. All your jobs will be listed on it and all their various stages. You can see at a glance what is ready for invoicing, what must be carried over to another month. It should prevent you ever forgetting to render an invoice for some small job or intermediate stage of a job, which is otherwise quite easy to do.

Staff

As your practice grows, the moment will inevitably come when you decide that you must have and can afford some help. A secretary's salary will add to your overheads but she will if she is a good one, relieve you of all the office chores and enable you to give far more time to your creative work and to finding clients. The time of a good design assistant should nearly all be 'sold' against fees and so enable you to take on more work and increase your turnover without unduly increasing your overheads.

Choosing a design assistant is fairly easy—the applicants for your vacancy can show you their work. Choosing a secretary is much more difficult. Glowingly written references are really not enough and if you can get the name of a recent employer who can be rung up, an informal talk about your applicant with someone for whom she has worked is much more useful.

When you have selected your applicant, whether secretary or design assistant, it is a legal obligation for you to confirm the appointment in writing, referring to the agreed salary, deductions for Income Tax and National Insurance, hours of work, whether Saturday mornings are worked, length of paid annual holiday, whether overtime is paid for and at what rate (time or time-and-a-half or . . . ?), whether the appointment is on a trial basis, and what notice is required on either side to terminate the appointment. You should also ask for a written acceptance of the job and its terms and make sure that you get it. These exchanged letters are the contract between you and your employee.

The first thing you have to arrange for your new staff is payment of their salaries—weekly or monthly, usually the latter. Weekly salaries are usually paid in cash, monthly salaries by cheque. But in either case you *must* first deduct Income Tax and the employees' contributions towards the weekly National Insurance rate. In the Bibliography on page 229 are the titles of one or two books and pamphlets which will give you useful advice about Income Tax in relation to staff but your accountant is your best guide through these mysteries.

Disabled staff

If your full-time salaried staff ever reaches a total of twenty then you have to take account of the Disabled Persons (Employment) Acts of 1944 and 1958. These require you by law to employ a quota of disabled persons on your staff—3% being the applicable quota when you have reached the twenty mark, which means in fact, one person. But of course you do not have to take the first disabled person who comes along. Instead of taking the usual steps to fill a vacancy in the open market, you must first notify it to the nearest office of the Department of Employment which deals with disabled persons. If they have any suitable applicants they will send them along. Again, unless they are entirely suitable, you are not compelled to employ them. You then ask the Department for a permit to go into the open market and this is always readily forthcoming. But until you have your quota, you must go through this drill for every vacancy.

National Insurance

Every *employee* must make the appropriate contribution to National Insurance and this is done by the *employer* making a compulsory deduction from each salary payment. Every *self-employed* person must also make the appropriate contributions but this is done by having a special card, buying the necessary NI Stamps and sticking them on the card. The stamps are bought from the Post Office, the card and all information about this can be had from your nearest Social Security Office. The same office will tell you what the appropriate amounts are (they are different for men and women and for self-employed people) and can also give you a booklet with all the necessary information in it about claiming sick benefits. This is another office chore which must not be overlooked or allowed to accumulate, as that might mean suddenly having to pay out an unexpectedly large sum of money to buy stamps in arrears. On the other hand, there are ways in which you can arrange in advance with the local office to do exactly that—either buy stamps of much larger value for much less frequent stamping or even to pay regularly by cheque.

Maintenance

If you have started your practice with a newly-decorated room and mostly new furniture and equipment, it is worth spending a little money frequently to keep it all in good order rather than to let deterioration set in for so long that large sums are needed to restore respectability and usefulness.

You will find, for instance, that an annual washing down by a good office cleaning firm of your walls, paintwork and any painted furniture or fittings will be comparatively inexpensive and will probably produce a surprisingly good result if the original finishes were of good quality. Then you would only need a complete redecoration every three years or so. As your practice grows and more of your clients come to see you, the more important it is to keep your office impressively spick and span, apart from the fact that to do so will always save you money in the long run.

You can also add greatly to the life of your typewriter, which may have been one of the most expensive items in your initial outlay, if you keep its dust cover on when you are not using it and pay out the few pounds a year necessary to have it regularly serviced. There are specialist firms which do this, calling several times a year to clean and oil it and make any adjustments or minor replacements.

In the first part of this book in Chapter Four you will find information about how to estimate fees. Although intended primarily for students it gives I think all the basic facts for fairly straightforward fee estimating for practising designers as well. You might find it useful to skim through it again to refresh your memory and to remind yourself of other smaller problems dealt with there: reducing fees, 'sprats', progress payments and introductory commissions. There are however two important fee problems not dealt with in that Chapter, because their complexity makes them more appropriate to this second part of the book. These are: how to calculate your own hourly rate and how to quote fees for retainers and consultancies.

The cost of your time
I am going to repeat here what I said in that previous Chapter:
The secret of all successful fee estimating is to know the selling cost of an hour of your own time (and of each of your assistants as soon as you have any).
If that is accepted and the first calculations worked out, you will then only have to adjust them from time to time, usually upwards as costs inevitably increase. By the way, be sure to keep all the bits of paper when you make the first calculations. They will be very useful to refer back to when you have to do the subsequent adjustments, which is usually once a year.
The *basic* cost of your time is in fact your personal budget or more explicitly the 'salary' you are proposing to pay yourself out of the business if you are working as a free-lance or in a small partnership. If you are a salaried designer, then it is obviously your actual salary. I am still going to stick to the fictitious designer John Brown whom we used in Chapter Eleven, and his ludicrously fictitious figures, in order to avoid the slightest risk that you might adopt the figures I shall use here. I am going to give you the formula for you to work out your own.
We saw that John Brown was going to give himself a 'salary' of £1560 for his first year in private practice. Assuming an 8-hour day and a 5- day week, there will be 2080 hours in his working year. Dividing his 'salary' of £1560 by 2080 means that his basic time is going to cost his business 75p an hour.

The cost of time off

But he is not going to be able to sell every hour of his working time to his clients. He must allow first for annual and public holidays and for the risk of some sick leave. So the following sum gives a more realistic picture of his saleable time:

Total working hours a year		2080 hours
Less seven public holidays*	56 hours	
Less three weeks annual holiday	120 ,,	
Less say one week's sick leave	40 ,,	216 ,,
Balance of possible saleable hours		1864 ,,

Even if you decided with praiseworthy but probably misguided enthusiasm that for your first year you would take no public or annual holidays and that you were tough enough not to anticipate any sick leave, it would be foolish to work out this calculation in any other way, for two reasons.

The calculation is a normal, almost statutory one for any design office and allows for the time off which any hard-working designer should expect to take and would certainly get in a salaried job.

Secondly and more important, the more hours you calculate as being saleable, the lower will be the selling price of an hour of your time. This may seem on the face of it a good thing and certainly would be for your clients. But in a small design office in the first years of its existence, it would leave you with dangerously low margins for contingencies. You might work yourself to a standstill or a breakdown and have to take that sick leave and then most likely that three weeks holiday. You might after all have a domestic obligation to take mum and dad or wife and kids for Bank Holiday outings. So my advice is stick to the calculation and then you are covered for the time off even if you don't make use of it.

Now back to John Brown's basic rate of 75p an hour. This is not the rate at which he is going to sell it to his clients. There are his overheads to be taken into account as well and to these must be added the cost of his 'time off' hours referred to above and another portion of unsaleable time, as you will see further on.

The overhead percentage

John Brown's overheads represent all the money he has to spend to enable him to sell his time. His fictitious overhead figure came to an annual total of £1000 as we saw in Chapter Four. But none of these overheads can be sold to a client. They can and must be sold indirectly by spreading out the total as a percentage over every hour of time he plans to sell.

But before we do this calculation, we must return to that extra portion of unsaleable time which I mentioned above. If you look back to the 'cost of

* New Year's Day, Good Friday, Easter Monday, Spring and Summer Bank Holidays, Christmas and Boxing Days.

171

time-off' calculation given there, you will realize that the resultant total of 1864 hours implies that you are going to sell every one of these to clients. It could never be so in any design office however well organized. Even junior assistants will have to log up a few weekly hours of their time spent quite legitimately in general matters—tidying up, filing drawings, fetching and delivering and so on. The more senior the designer, the larger will be the proportion of his unsaleable time which must be given to administrative responsibilities and nowhere will this proportion be higher than in the one-man-first-year design office. Such a free-lance will have to spend a great deal of time looking for clients, entertaining possible ones, following up enquiries, going on wild goose chases after tenuous contacts and, just as important, in running his office and its finances and keeping the daily chores under control. This will probably amount to *at least* one third of his net working hours for the first year and none of it can be sold to anybody. With this very important fact in mind, all too often overlooked by small young design offices, we can now do the overheads calculation:

John Brown's overheads budget from page 152 say			£1000
Public holidays 56 hours	at 75p	£42	
Annual holiday 120 hours	at 75p	90	
Allow for sick leave 40 hours	at 75p	30	
			162
Allow for one-third of the saleable hours to be spent on general administration, ie, one-third of 1864 hours—620 hours at 75p an hour			465
Therefore total overheads budget allowing for all estimated unsaleable time			£1627

Now we can work out that overhead percentage or mark-up as it is sometimes called. John Brown now knows that he will have for sale about two-thirds of the possible saleable hours given at the end of the first calculation above, that is two-thirds of 1864 = 1243 hours (the other third has gone into overheads). This number of hours at the basic rate of 75p amounts to £932.

John Brown also knows that his overheads are likely to total £1627 for the first year, including the cost of all the time he has estimated he will not be able to sell. The following little sums give him his overhead percentage:

$$\frac{100 \times £1627}{£932} = 174.5\%$$

That result can be rounded off to 175% quite acceptably and for easier calculation; also to provide a bit of safety margin in case you have underestimated your overheads at any point.

John Brown must now apply his overhead percentage to his basic hourly rate of 75p:

$$\frac{75\text{p} \times 175\%}{100} = £1.31$$

Therefore the basic cost of an hour of his time plus 175% for overheads together give £2.06.

The profit margin
Now if John Brown were to sell all his saleable working hours at this rate for a year, he would 'break even', that is he would have earned enough to have paid his basic 'salary' and to have paid all his overheads but financially he would be just where he was when he started because he would have made no profit. Naturally he looks forward to making a profit and he must now decide what profit margin he is going to add as a further percentage to the cost-plus-overheads of his time. A minimum should be 10% but he may be bolder and aim at 20%. Using the latter, here is his final percentage sum:

$$\frac{£2.06 \times 20\%}{100} = £0.41$$

This profit percentage added to the cost-plus-overheads figures gives us the final total—£2.47. We could round off this figure again for ease of calculation and to provide another margin for contingencies to £2.50.

Work out your own
Now work out your own following that pattern right through and you will have something of inestimable value to every designer, the selling price of an hour of your time. When the problem of quoting a lump-sum fee comes up, you are only faced with the task of assessing how long the work will take (probably the first stage of preparing preliminary design proposals). Say one week for research and meetings, two weeks on the drawing board, one week for preparing it for presentation and the presentation meeting, say four weeks in all. The rest is simple arithmetic: four weeks = 20 working days = 160 hours at say John Brown's hourly rate of £2.50 and you arrive at a lump-sum fee of £400. To this would need to be added an allowance for special costs in connection with the job itself but not chargeable separately—special materials, present-ation folder, entertainment, etc. say £30. John Brown would then have arrived at a safe and probably quite reasonable fee of £430 knowing that it should be sufficient to cover the cost of his time and the built-in overhead and profit percentages.
But don't forget that when you have worked out your own hourly rate it will only apply to your *current* financial circumstances and is unlikely to be valid for

much more than a year or even less. It is wise to do a twice-yearly check to see whether the figures on which you based it still stand. This is particularly important when you quote hourly rate fees for a long term job. You should always cover yourself against the real possibility of having to increase them in the middle of a job by a clause in your original fee letter to the effect that 'these rates are current in my office at the moment (or for this year) but may have to be increased to keep in line with increased costs. We should of course notify you of any such increases, etc.'

Retaining fees

These are difficult fees to estimate since the amount of time you are going to be required to give is often a very unknown quantity. Also it is probable that, by the time a client wishes to retain your services as a designer your reputation will have grown to a point where it has a value of its own and this you must also allow for in trying to assess your fees.

In the case of an annual retainer, there is probably a sizeable programme of actual design work to be gone through during the first year, as well as regular meetings to be attended and a great deal of *ad hoc* consultation by discussion, telephone and correspondence. In addition, there may be all sorts of ancillary activities to be allowed for—finding and briefing contractors and suppliers, research of all kinds, supervising the making of models and prototypes, checking proofs, liaison with advertising, sales and publicity staff and so on. All of this will take x hours of your time at £x per hour and a real effort must first of all be made to try and compute what the hours will be. You will, of course, have worked out with your client as definitely as possible what the design programme is going to be for the first year and what is to be the incidence of regular progress meetings with him. All of this can then be computed at your hourly rates with a *very* generous margin for contingencies. For all the rest you will have to allow, after very careful consideration, for an average number of hours or days per week, knowing that a succession of busy weeks will probably balance a succession of slack ones, for a particular client, over a year. Your weekly average can then be worked out at an hourly rate total for the first year and added to your design work total.

Exclusive services

The next thing you may have to allow for is the understanding that while you are retained to design for Client A, you will not undertake any design work for competitive Clients B or C without A's written permission (and subsequently the agreement of B or C as well). This means that you may have to turn down any offers of work from his competitors, to your own financial loss and you should therefore increase your retaining fee accordingly. This increase might vary from a fifth to a third or a half, according to the competitiveness of the field in which you are going to work. Much-advertised consumer products are likely to be more competitive than capital goods and equipment advertised and sold only in specialized and limited markets.

While on the subject of exclusive services it should be pointed out that this

174

clause may not necessarily prevent you from working for an apparent competitor. If during the period of your retainer, you are approached by a client whose products appear to be in the same field, first consult the client who retains you. He may invoke the 'exclusive services' clause absolutely and then you must say 'no' to your enquirer, telling him why. But your client may just possibly say that your enquirer's products are not directly competitive. They may be in a quite different price range or marketed in different areas or countries, in which case he may tell you that it is in order to negotiate with your enquirer. *Confirm this in writing to your client* and then see what your enquirer feels about it. He may be a more militantly suspicious character and not feel so happy about it, in which case you will not get the second job. But you will at least have gone the right way about it, making your position quite clear to both sides and then letting each, in the proper order, decide what to do about it. Any other way of working, in this highly competitive world, will never do your reputation any good. In these days of more and more mergers into larger and larger groups of companies this question of exclusive services needs watching rather carefully by the designer. If say your contract with the A to Z Group of Companies is to provide them with your exclusive services under your retainer you may unwarily assume that this only applies to the immediate job on hand, say designing fan heaters for Company A. But as well as mergers, diversification is also the order of the day now and the Group may include Company B which makes furniture and Company C which sells soap and so on. And your office may already be designing furniture and soap packs for clients directly competitive to Companies B and C.

If the group were a tough one, it might hold you to the clause, which could be disastrous for you. But if you take some care to investigate the possible difficulties before your fees are finally tied up, you could negotiate the inclusion of a clause which said in effect: 'This fee includes my exclusive services only in the fields of electrical fan heater design and production and in the fields of other electrical space-heating appliances.' You would have conceded something quite reasonably in that clause by extending it to cover all electrical space-heating appliances. But electrical only, mark you. Not gas or oil or solid fuel.

It will be obvious from this warning note that the wider the fields of design and services over which you are required and agree to provide your exclusive services, the larger must be your retaining fee. This could reach the ultimate whereby the A to Z Group wanted to have you entirely to themselves as a designer, not only for their current products but for those of any other company with which they might merge in the future. This would mean an annual fee large enough to obviate the necessity for you to have any other clients at all. Although this might seem a very rosy prospect with all financial worries over, consider first before you enter into it the possible lack of the stimulation you get from dealing with a wide variety of clients and their problems and be sure to consult your solicitor before you sign anything. It is a situation which would call for a proper legal agreement between you and the group with a fairly massive compensation clause in case the group itself were merged into a yet bigger group with its own designers. Then you might be out of a job overnight and would probably need at least six months to a year to re-establish yourself in the open market.

The value of your reputation

Now back to the final rounding off of your retaining fee assessment. The growth and extent of your practice and reputation, the size and importance of your client's business and the circumstances in which the enquiry came to you, must all be considered. They are too often left out of account altogether when assessing a retaining fee. But if you can answer 'yes' to the following questions: 'Are both my practice and reputation growing steadily? Has this client a well-established business which my design services are likely to improve? Has he sought me out apparently unprompted?' then you can justifiably increase still further the amount of the retainer you have assessed so far, adding perhaps another fifth and a bit more to reach a tidy round sum per annum.

One way of checking any misgivings you may have that your total figure is too high or too low is to assess if you can what sort of annual salary your client might have to pay an experienced specialist designer of your calibre if you were going to join his staff. The result is often surprising and nearly always encouraging.

Consultancy fees

If someone enquires for your services as a consultant, it is important to find out first whether you both attach the same meaning to the word in this context. In fact, it should mean exactly what it says—a designer who is consulted about design problems and who thereby advises as to how they might be solved but who does not illustrate his advice with designs of any sort. Some clients will, however, mistakenly expect a consultancy fee to include a certain amount of original design work as well and it is important to clarify this from the beginning when you are negotiating fees.

There is, of course, no reason at all why a consultancy should not include, or lead to, designing but the extent to which it may do so is usually, at the fee negotiating stage, an unknown quantity. It is essential therefore to keep the two activities quite separate in assessing fees. Suppose for instance a big printer, who runs his own studio of designers and typographers, invites you to act as a consultant by criticizing and advising on the creative side of his business in order to raise the overall design standards of his print. This might mean a regular visit to his works, as well as frequent *ad hoc* consultations by exchanged visits, telephoning and correspondence. You would work out your suggested annual fee for such a consultancy by assessing, with generous margins, how much time you might be required to give per week or per month and round it off to a total which allowed for your exclusive services, if required, and the value of your reputation and experience in being invited to act in such a capacity. None of this would cover any original design work by you. But the occasion might easily arise when your printer landed an important contract and his own design staff found themselves unable to cope with it. He would almost certainly ask you to take it on; or more frequently he might ask you to take over and complete those design problems which the more limited abilities of his studio could not seem to solve successfully.

At such times it might be difficult and embarrassing to start negotiating *ad hoc* fees, particularly if your client had not expected to be charged any, over and above the consultancy fee.

Make it quite clear, therefore, when you write about your consultancy fee that it covers a specified number of regular visits *for consultation*; that it allows for a reasonable amount of *ad hoc* exchanges; that it does not include any original design work by you and that if the necessity for this should arise, you would either do such work for hourly rate fees or quote lump-sum fees at the time of being asked to take it on, whichever your client preferred.

Fees for special meetings

It may happen that your services as a consultant are likely to be required at very irregular intervals, to sit in on a design committee or progress meeting or to inspect work or prototypes in a long-term production programme. This makes it very difficult to assess an annual fee which is fair to both sides and the best thing to do is to quote a day or half-day fee, chargeable only when you are called upon. It should be adequate to cover your time and travelling time (but not your expenses, which are always charged extra) and, as before, should reflect your reputation and experience. It should be made tactfully clear that anything less than half a day would still be charged as such, and that the *pro rata* fees would still apply if your client found it more expedient to bring his meeting to your office.

Travelling time

If it is proposed to charge fees for travelling time, which as we saw in Chapter Three could quite reasonably be done on occasion, it would be essential to agree them first with your client, unless long journeys were not foreseen at the beginning of the collaboration. Even so, when they do arise, and you find that you are being involved in an 'exceptional expenditure of time' in travelling, the problem should be discussed with your client before it goes too far and a reasonable extra fee amicably agreed. It will be more difficult to come to terms if you wait until the job is finished and then make your claim out of the blue. Apart from the inherent and understandable dislike of most clients for being presented with extra fees for which they had not bargained, they could begrudge the missed opportunity of sometimes having come to you instead of having expected you always to go to them, so saving your extra charges.

It is not very easy to define precisely when and how to suggest fees for travelling time. It depends not so much on the length of the journey as on the nature of the job and its basic fee. Sometimes, when a reasonable number of journeys can be foreseen in connection with a lump-sum fee job, a large enough fee can be quoted to cover them so that the travelling time seldom arises as a separate issue. On a percentage fee job, which usually means exhibition or interior design, a really generous budget and consequently a possibly lucrative fee may also be considered sufficient to cover day-long journeys for site supervision. But a very tight budget, and thereby a very tight fee for, say, a small overseas exhibition job, could lose you a lot of time, and therefore money, in journeying to and fro, however bedazzled you may feel at the prospect of trips abroad at someone else's expense. This could be overcome by quoting a slightly higher percentage fee than you would normally do and explaining at the time why you had done so. The extra money which this would bring in would cover the time spent in two or three journeys to the site to supervise construction and installation.

When the circumstances are such that you know with certainty that the basic fee will be too meagre to cover a number of site visits and that there is little hope of negotiating any extra fees, it is a good idea to try and find a local designer or architect practising near your site, who for a suitable share of your own fee, would take on site supervision for you. You may not be any better off financially in the long run, but at least you will have been saved some of the journey-time to get on with other jobs on your home ground.

When lengthy travelling time is involved on jobs, or stages of jobs, for which you are charging hourly rate fees, there is no problem since the hours spent in transit can be charged with the hours spent on the drawing board or in meetings and are usually quite acceptable as such. But when a separate fee really has to be negotiated for travelling time, your hourly rate can still serve as a basis for this, either just as it stands, or used to arrive at a lump-sum fee. You may feel, however, that the total arrived at by multiplying your hourly rate by the duration of your journey may be reduced somewhat before putting it to your client, since you can usefully occupy some of the time at any rate in dealing with papers, drafting a report or catching up on reading your technical magazines.

In Chapter Six the techniques of simple report drafting were dealt with. These presupposed a fairly straightforward assignment where major policy problems were not involved. The technique suggested there would nevertheless apply basically to any design report and practising designers might think it a good idea to read that chapter first as a refresher before tackling the more complicated type of design report which I am going to deal with here.

Suppose a client says to you 'We are an old-established firm with a number of offices and factories all over the country making and marketing a wide range of products with a generous advertising and publicity budget to promote them. And yet our sales are not increasing, our image is perhaps a bit out-of-date and we know that our competitors are pulling ahead of us. Can a designer tell us what is wrong and how to put it right?'

What a question and how flattering to be asked it! But how wildly rash it would be to answer promptly that obviously everything needed redesigning and that they had better commission you to start doing that right away. They would rightly be suspicious of such a facile solution arrived at in such a superficial way. What do you know of their production methods and difficulties, the capacity of their factories, their competitors, their image (if any) to the world? Little if anything but you have got to find out and they have to be persuaded to commission you to do the finding out. (There is advice about fees for these survey reports in Chapter Three.)

This means making a wide and detailed survey of all their activities, researching into suitable new techniques and materials which they may not be using, acquainting yourself with the work of their competitors, scrutinizing every aspect of their visual image and at the end of what may be three to six months concentrated study, reporting to them in considerable detail with your conclusions and written recommendations as to what could and should be done. Some design reports end there because that is as far as you have been commissioned to go. Your client wants to browse over your report and decide whether to accept any or all of your recommendations before commissioning you to translate them into visual form. Other reports may by prior negotiation and agreement lead straight on from the written recommendations to their implementation in visual form as preliminary design proposals.

The survey programme

I am not going to tell you how to do the survey itself nor how to draw your conclusions from it. By the time you are commissioned to carry out such an assignment your training, experience and increasing reputation should enable you to take it on with confidence and expertise. Nor am I going to repeat here the advice given in Chapter Three about how to draft a basic framework for the report before you start on the survey. But I am going to enlarge on some aspects of the survey-in-depth type of report. It is almost certain to fall into the basic pattern of brief/survey/conclusions/recommendations but the section dealing with the survey would have to be more elaborate.

Design surveys and reports are not commissioned lightly. They are usually the subject of much internal worry, argument and soul-searching by the senior executives of the firm. The big surveys covering a wide field of activities often entail big fees and heavy expenses by the client to the designer. Which is nice for the latter but may be an additional worry for the former. When the finished and anxiously-awaited report arrives on the managing director's desk, it will probably contain recommendations for quite drastic action entailing further heavy production expenditure for the firm. It's advice may even affect people in the firm as well as things: the inadequacy of staff in existing design, advertising and promotion departments for instance.

The report will almost certainly have to be considered by the firm's whole board of directors and they have got to take what may be serious and far-reaching decisions based on your advice. This puts a very considerable responsibility on you and you need to demonstrate that you have been equal to it. The best and only way to do that is to build up your case on a precise and logical sequence of investigation which proves that you have really immersed yourself in the firm's visual and production activities and problems.

Now back to the framework. After you have put down the draft section on the brief, according to my suggestions in Chapter Three, then take your sheet headed 'Section 2 The Survey' and under that title put down the subheadings which will summarize your already agreed activities. For a survey in depth such as we are presupposing it would be usual for the firm to arrange a programme of visits for you to all its departments and branches with the names of people to meet and facilities to probe into all its secrets. It will sometimes even provide you with a guide from its head office staff who will make all the necessary appointments for you, accompany you on all the visits and see that you get all the information you need. This is very desirable as it saves you endless correspondence and phoning and, more important, helps to dilute the possible suspicion with which you may be met by some departmental managers who may regard you as an assailant of their little private empires.

Your first sub-heading therefore would almost certainly be Visits and this, according to the brief and what you also decide to do, would be broken down again into at least three parts. For instance:

Visits—throughout your Organization
    —to other places to inspect your competitor's products
    —to trade exhibitions
    —etc.

Those would probably be the three basic sub-sub-headings but there might be more to add according to the subject of your survey. For an air-line's corporate identity you would certainly have to fly to airports at home and overseas. For a consumer product or packaging problem, you would need to visit retail shops and showrooms to see their display techniques.

Under 'Visits throughout your organization' you could write into your draft the already agreed dates, places to be visited and names of people to meet. Then leave a space for the names of anyone else you met and talked to by chance and anything else you saw or visited which was not on the programme. At the bottom of your draft under this heading leave space to fill in extra visits which the client might suggest that you make after the original programme has been agreed. Warning note here: If such extra visits are numerous and time-consuming, say a week in Europe on a conducted tour to meet their overseas agents, consider whether this would affect your already agreed fee for an agreed programme. If so, negotiate the extra fee there and then, not after you have completed the work and submitted the report.

Now turn to the next Visits sub-head: 'to other places etc.' This part of the programme may have been left entirely to you so it will be a useful preliminary exercise to decide just what you are going to do and put down a check list with tentative dates. Then you can eventually get them into your diary suitably related to the rest of the programme and begin to make the necessary travel arrangements.

Visits to trade exhibitions are easy or may not apply. If they do, the dates and places of the relevant ones must be discovered (the Board of Trade Journal gives all the important ones, both at home and overseas, at regular intervals) and then integrated into your programme.

If there are any more categories under Visits add them to your draft with as much advance detail as you can.

Now you will realize that when you have finished such a draft of the second section, you have almost written it as well. All you have to do when you return to base after each visit is to fill in dates, places and names of people met, which probably only means looking back through your pocket diary and the notes you will have made throughout the course of the survey.

Conclusions

The next section, Conclusions, is always more difficult to write and particularly for a design policy survey but again a draft framework prepared in advance will be a great help to the final writing. Suppose you are going to survey a firm's whole corporate identity or lack of it in any coherent form. It may have at least .the three usual ingredients of an image—symbol or trademark, logotype and house colour or colours. Those would give you the first three sub-headings for your framework and under the first 'Symbol' you might put down a check list such as

How and where it is used
Its adaptability for size
Its suitability for different production methods—print, mouldings, castings, three-dimensional, illuminated signs, transfers, etc.

Its impact and memorability
Its comparison with competitors' symbols
The value of its long-standing acceptance by customers and so on.

You could then frame comparable lists under 'logotype' and under 'house colours.'
Remembering that for this hypothetical case you are going to survey the whole visual image of the firm as it exists, further sub-headings suitably broken down might be

Packaging of		Factories	—external appearance
your products	—home trade		—signposting
	—export		—reception
Print	—stationery	Staff	—uniforms
	—technical literature		—overalls
	—promotional literature		—badges
Shops and showrooms		Transport fleet	
Displays and exhibitions			

Then you might have to bring in the wider issue of technology, such as

New materials and processes—already in use
                                        —suitable for consideration
Plant and machinery

I hope that is sufficient to show you how to construct the framework of Section 3. The headings and sub-headings will depend entirely on the subject of your survey but to spend an hour or two drafting then will prove to be a most useful preliminary to the survey itself. During it you will of course take copious notes so that when you actually sit down to write this section you should be able to extract from them and put in the proper place and order what you saw, what you were told (and by whom) in considerable detail with appropriate critical comment, comparisons and cross-references.
The reaction you will hope to get from readers of this section is 'Well he certainly has looked at everything we do in great detail and although he has some fairly harsh things to say here and there, he is able to justify his reasons for saying them'.

Recommendations
Now comes Section 4 Recommendations and this is where I am afraid you are right out on your own. Only you can decide what you are going to advise your client to do. The only thing I can suggest is that your recommendations should each be well-considered and as short and positive as possible. For instance:
'I find your symbol somewhat old-fashioned in appearance and of a complexity which makes it unsuitable for reproduction by modern techniques. Nevertheless it has an important recognition value due to its very long life. I

RECOMMEND therefore that your symbol should be retained but re-designed in a simplified and more contemporary way.' The use of caps. for the word 'recommend' is a gimmick often used in this part of a report. It enables a busy director or executive to pick out almost on sight the actual recommend-ations themselves if he has not had time to read the whole report before a meeting when it is going to be discussed. There is another way given below in which one can helpfully anticipate this difficulty.

A contents page
When you have got to the end of your recommendations, there remain only the supporting pages to draft: cover and title page and for these see page 87. But for long-ish to very long reports, a contents page is a good idea. This will consist of sections, main headings and sub-headings taking the latter down as far as you think is appropriate. Every item which you decide to put on the contents page should of course have the correct page number alongside it and for this reason it must be the last proof to check.

I mentioned above another method of providing a busy man with an at-a-glance summary of the whole report. This would be to précis the whole thing into just that—a short sharp summary in paragraphs to fill not more than a single page. For instance:

1 Thirteen of your offices, factories, shops etc. were visited between (date) and (date).
2 Discussions were held with twenty-five of your Managers, Senior Executives, specialists and technicians.
3 Your overseas agents were visited in three countries during (month).
4 Relevant trade exhibitions were visited and your competitors' goods and services studied.
5 We found that your house style has become very diluted and makes little impact; thortant competitors.
6 We recommend that your trademark be retained but re-designed; that a new logotype and house colours be adopted and that, after rationalization of your print, packaging, displays, etc. the three elements in a new corporate identity should be applied to all visual aspects of your Company's activities.
7 We further recommend that on completion of this implementation, a design manual should be prepared, to ensure that the new high standards set will not again be eroded in use.

That could be all that our busy director needed basically to know if he had to rush from a plane to a board meeting where your report was to be discussed and important decisions taken. It might even give him time to record gratefully a mental 'full marks' to the foresight and efficiency of the designer who provided the summary.

It could go either at the front of the report after the title page or at the end. The first is preferable.

Illustrations
Even if a report of this type is not going to finish up with visual design

proposals, it is almost certain to be illustrated. You will be able to press home a point much more forcefully if you can include photographs to record the way things look to a designer's critical eye compared perhaps with what the competitors are doing more efficiently. Such illustrations as you use should be numbered or lettered, using a different system to the one you are using for the text of the report to avoid possible confusion. Figure 1, Figure 2 might be an idea. They should also of course be cross-referenced in the text (see Figure 1) and unless they are completely self-explanatory, should also have brief captions, either individual or grouped. This is particularly important when, for cost reasons in the production of your report, you cannot afford to mount and bind them into the body of the report itself. In this event you would probably choose a folder with half pockets each side. The text pages with individual cover and suitably bound together could tuck into the left pocket and the illustrations into the right.

Production and quantities
The way your report looks when it arrives on the directors' desks is a design job in itself and very important—the designer's image this time. When you have produced several such reports you will probably have established a design style and production techniques which form part of your own 'house style'. But there are two other points to bear in mind at this point.
If your own report production budget is tight, spend as much of it as you can on a really good binding system. There is nothing more infuriating to a report reader than such a tight binding that the pages will not turn over easily or lie flat, or such a loose one that pages fall out all over the place. A spiral binding is much the best.
The other point is to a certain extent to tailor the production of your report to the type of client to whom you are submitting it. It could probably be as impressive as you like and could afford, for the big corporations and groups of companies. But for a smallish conservative firm, worried about money and commissioning a designer for the first time a lavishly-produced report could provoke the wrong reaction. 'This is what we are spending our money on (ie the fees they are paying) is it?' If you suspect the possibility of such a reaction, a simple workaday production method would probably make a better impact. When your report is nearly ready to go into production, check back to your fee letter and see how many copies of it you were to provide (see also Chapter Three) as an additional reminder about this. It is then a good idea to ask your clients if they still only need the agreed number of copies. More often than not they will have changed their minds over the intervening months and find that as your submission date approaches, they will want extra copies, sometimes several dozen extra. You will already have agreed in your fee letter that copies over and above the agreed number will be charged extra. With their definite request for extras, you can cost the production, order the additional quantities of everything at the same time—covers, paper, folders, photoprints etc. and know how much to charge for the extra copies when you invoice your fees.

Strictly confidential

One last reminder: allow at least two copies for yourself and more if you can afford them. One would be your working copy and the other would go into a cellophane wrapping to be kept as a specimen. Although most design reports are highly confidential and should *never* be sent out as specimens to other clients, they could be shown across the table to an interested client who was considering commissioning you to do likewise and wanted to see what he might get for his money. Even this should not be done if the would-be client's activities were in any way competitive to the content of the report you wanted to show him.

For the same reasons of confidentiality, the covering letter you will write when you are ready to deliver or post your report and all the copies of it, *must* always be headed 'Private and confidential' and so must the envelope, packing or labelling of the outer wrapping. Most of these kind of reports have to be fairly critical of both things and people and what you have said in this respect is for the eyes of the firm's top executives only.

Chapter Sixteen   **Interior design and exhibition contracting for a client**

This chapter is meant both for practising and student designers in the fields of interior, exhibition, shop-fitting design and the like. But because I have already covered the ground of general contracting procedure fairly thoroughly in the first part of this book, I am not going to repeat any of it here. A look back at Chapter Seven might be a good idea and particularly at the two relevant Clauses 13 and 14 of the SIAD Code of Professional Conduct on page 239. Here I am going to enlarge on the special aspect of contracting in these fields. The first important thing is the specification which for any structures which human beings are to be in or on poses special problems and responsibilities. They must present no danger to life or limb either from instability, overcrowding or fire risk. There are officials whose job it is to see that you and your contractor comply with all the statutory safety regulations. Their word is law and they should be asked to check and clear all relevant points before you finalize your working drawings and specification. In the Greater London Area, it would be the District Surveyor and the Fire Officers. Outside London, ring the Borough or County Council to find the right man or men.

Exhibition specifications
In the case of exhibitions there are the added complications of site requirements, particularly in the case of stands at trade or public exhibitions. The organizers issue printed rules and regulations which govern very precisely what the exhibitor (your client) and consequently his designer and contractor may do with and on the site which he has rented. As we saw in Chapter Two, one of the questions you would ask at your initial briefing on the design of an exhibition stand would be about the organizers' rules and regulations and you would study a copy of these before you even began to design at all. In addition to those rules which would affect your design—height, set-back, shell-stand, fascia colours and lettering and so on, there would be others equally important concerning fireproofing, first access to the site for display contractors, floor loadings and a host of others. The mere fact that towards the end of the job your contractors are going to be working in somebody else's premises gives rise to many problems which have to be covered contractually—insurance, trade union labour, making good, transport, etc. For any but the simplest exhibitions there are likely to be other contractors and sub-contractors involved and this too presents problems of integration and planning which have to be allowed for.

However the consolation about all this seemingly complicated activity is that it follows a very similar pattern from one such job to another. It is therefore a time-saving idea to draft a set of your own general 'preliminaries' to an exhibition specification and to have plenty of copies made. You will find that when you are faced with the usual last-minute rush job of writing your 'spec' from the design construction angle, you will be able to add your standard preliminary clauses with perhaps only minor adaptations here and there.

Here then are some suggestions for preliminary clauses which cover most general points though not necessarily all. As your experience in this field practice increases, you will know how to adapt them to individual jobs and to your own way of working.

Some standard clauses for the preliminaries of an exhibition specification

1 *General* This specification shall be read in conjunction with drawings Nos. . . . and all work is to be carried out according to the drawings and specification taken together. Figured dimensions are to be followed in preference to scaled.

2 *Regulations* The Contractor shall conform to all regulations, including those regarding the fire-proofing of materials used in the construction of the work, etc., as laid down by the Exhibition Authorities and other interested bodies. The Contractor shall, before making variation from the drawings or specification that may be necessitated by conforming to the fireproofing or any other regulations, consult the Designer. The Contractor will be deemed to have visited the site to obtain correct dimensions and his own information on all matters affecting the work.

3 *Use of premises* If the execution of the work requires that areas, properties or services which are part of the exhibition premises should be used in any way other than those indicated as available for the purpose, permission must first be obtained by the Contractor from the responsible authority, or he must ask the Designer to do so for him. The Contractor must allow for making good any such amendments or for any damage to the exhibition premises after the exhibition has been cleared away.

4 *Insurance* The Contractor shall provide full insurance coverage of the works as included in this specification, against all risks and including third party, Workmen's Compensation Act, etc., for the period from the commencement of the works to the final date of demolition. This shall not include insurance of exhibits or other items supplied by the Specialist Contractors, the Designer or the Client.

5 *Labour* The Contractor is reminded that he must observe the requirements in the Factories Acts, and the regulations made thereunder, wherever they may be applicable to the work; also the requirements of the Exhibition Authorities regarding the use of Trade Union Labour.

6 *Overtime* If the Contractor considers that any overtime or week-end work will be necessary in order to complete the contract by the required date, he must allow for it in his tender. No extras for overtime or week-end work will be allowed unless prior approval has been given in writing by the Designer.

7 *Sub-contractors*   If any work, except those parts specifically mentioned, be sub-contracted, the Designer's prior approval of the Sub-contractor is to be obtained. The Contractor must allow for attendance upon and making good after all Sub-contractors.

8 *Specialist contractors*   The Contractor shall grant all facilities to any Specialist Contractors who may be employed direct by the Designer's Client.

9 *Transport*   The Contractor must allow for all transport of his own materials to and from the site, during erection and dismantling and afford full protection and insurance of such materials in transit.

10 *Hire or sale*   All materials supplied by the Contractor, including those supplied by provisional sums are to be on hire for the specified period, unless otherwise stated.

11 *Finishes*   The Contractor is required to provide the most careful workmanship and best quality materials and finishes. (Here you should follow with your requirements concerning type of hardwood (if any) and finish; type of metalwork (if any) and finish; finish of softwood, ie, painted three coats, gloss, or emulsion, or eggshell etc.; varnished, sealed, etc. and any other *general* points on materials and finishes that can better be covered under these preliminary clauses than later in the design construction clauses.)

The Contractor must provide adequate protection to finished work, particularly floor finishes, as the work proceeds; remove all such protection, plant, gear etc. on completion and hand over the whole work in clean and perfect condition.

12 *Prime cost and provisional sums*   Where provisional sums are included for work not specified in detail, the Contractor will be required to submit with his final invoice a detailed account in respect of each item so covered, priced in accordance with the provisions for payment on variations contained in this Specification.

The amount to be allowed to the Contractor for work covered by a PC (Prime Cost) or provisional sum, in this Specification shall be the net cost to the Contractor after trade and other discounts have been deducted (except cash discounts when allowed by merchants and others up to a maximum of 5% in the case of materials or goods to be fixed by the Contractor and of 2½% in all other cases).

13 *Variations, errors and extras*   If any work instructed by the Designer be extra, in the opinion of the Contractor, to that on which his estimate was based, he shall inform the Designer before proceeding with the work and no allowance for an extra will be made unless previously agreed by the Designer. The Contractor shall be responsible for all errors and defective workmanship whether executed by him or by Sub-contractors employed by him and shall remedy them as directed by the Designer unless otherwise agreed by the Designer.

14 *Maintenance*   Any defects which may appear during the period of the exhibition arising, in the opinion of the Designer, from materials or workmanship not in accordance with the drawings and Specification, shall be made good by the Contractor at his own expense.

15 *Completion*   All work is to be completed by (time) on (date).

16 *Dismantling*   The Contractor must allow for dismantling the work and clearing away to the satisfaction, and in accordance with the regulations, of the exhibition organizers.

17 *Contingencies*   The Contractor is to allow the sum of £ . . . in his tender, for General Contingencies.

18 *Tendering procedure*   Tenders are to be received by not later than (time) on (date) and delivered in a sealed envelope clearly marked with the name of the works. It is understood that the lowest of any tender will not necessarily be accepted. (Here you should add, if appropriate: The Contractor is to state a separate price for the following items: . . .)

Most of these clauses are self-explanatory but some need enlarging upon if you are dealing with exhibition contractors for the first time.

The Hire or Sale Clause 10 may seem unusual to you and even more so to your client if he also is new to the field. But it is accepted practice in the exhibition contracting world, *unless otherwise specified*, for the general contractor's materials for exhibition stands to be on hire and the contractors' prices take this into account. Their prices will naturally be higher if they are asked to quote for the 'sale outright' of the whole job. It sometimes happens that you know in advance that your client will wish to retain certain items in your design—an enquiry counter, perhaps, a plinth or showcase for a model, a panel with a specially drawn diagram, map or mural on it. In this case you should indicate clearly in the design clauses of your specification those items for which you want the contractor to quote a separate sale outright price.

In Clause 5, reference is made to Trade Union labour and in Clause 8 to specialists. There is an important link between these two. The exhibition organizers' rules and regulations will most certainly require that no non-union labour whatsoever be employed to work on the site. Otherwise lightning strikes may follow. You must therefore be meticulously careful in respect of any specialists who are to be employed direct by you or your client to work on the site. If they do not already belong to an appropriate union they must be persuaded to join. Otherwise they can only supervise the execution of their work by union labour. They must not even knock in a nail or pick up a screwdriver. It is worth paying considerable attention to this important detail in the early stages to avoid disastrous trouble later on.

Clause 9 deals with general transport. But into the appropriate design clauses of your specification should also go special instructions about extra transport. You may be going to have a model made, a mural painted, a map carried out on a specially treated panel. In such cases you may have to specify that the Contractor must provide, and allow for the cost of, transport to collect such completed items and take them to his workshops or to the site for fixing; or must deliver a panel to a specialist for special treatment and then collect it again when it is ready.

It will be seen that the Maintenance Clause No. 14 deals only with defects which the contractor must remedy at his own expense. It does not cover the repairing of damage due to fair wear and tear. At a crowded and popular exhibition running for more than a week or two such damage can be considerable and if your client agrees to the extra cost, it is a good idea to specify a daily visit for running repairs and touching up.

Under the dismantling Clause 6, you may have to specify extra transport for the delivery of special displays and exhibits to your client at the end of the exhibition.

Now for the provisional sums, prime costs, or PC sums, as they are often called, referred to at Clause 12. The terms 'provisional sum' and 'prime cost or PC sum' in a specification are used either together, separately or interchangeably, according to individual preference. They either make financial provision for an unknown quantity or for services or materials to be supplied to the main contractor by a sub-contractor or supplier but which the former will be required to fix or handle or deal with in one way or another.

Suppose you know that a display unit to take a special exhibit will be required for an exhibition stand for which you are writing the specification. You have not been able yet to design it as you still have no details from your client about the exhibit itself. But you do know where it will go and therefore you have a pretty good idea of its approximate dimensions and of the form it will take. So you make a careful guess-estimate of its probable total cost and, in the design sections of your specification you instruct that 'the contractor shall allow a provisional sum of £x for such-and-such'. When the contractor who wins the tender eventually gets your working drawings for the item in question, he can go right ahead with the work and need only refer back to you for instructions if the provisional sum is not going to be sufficient. Otherwise he will show any savings on this sum on his final account.

You can also use the provisional or PC sum method for anything like a floor covering, a textile or a wallpaper when you have an idea of the quality you want but have not yet been able to make a final selection. If you instruct your contractor to allow a provisional or PC sum per metre or per piece, that will enable him to measure up for the total lengths required and include the total estimated cost in his tender. Then when you go shopping for your carpet or curtain material or whatever it may be, you will have in mind your provisional sum per metre as a ceiling figure not to be exceeded if possible. In all such cases there may be certain discounts which the contractor is permitted to retain and others which he must pass on for the client's benefit. The second paragraph of Clause 12 covers this point.

Interior design specifications

An interior, unlike most exhibitions, is permanent or at any rate semi-permanent. Your specification must therefore be more stringent about materials and workmanship. Also unlike exhibitions, there are no organizers' rules and regulations to control your contractor on the site so you must make them for him. The preliminary clauses to a specification of works involving interior design both for public and private premises are therefore lengthier and more legal in their phraseology than for an exhibition. The suggestions which follow will guide you towards gradually compiling your own. You will also find the most detailed advice and instructions about the writing of specifications in *Architectural Practice and Procedure* by Hamilton H. Turner, which has been a classic in its field for many years. (See *Bibliography*)*

Some standard clauses for the preliminaries for an interior design specification
1 *General*   This specification shall be read in conjunction with Drawings Nos. . . . and all work is to be carried out according to the drawings and specification taken together. Figured dimensions are to be followed in preference to scaled. The Contractor is to check all dimensions on site.
2 *Insurance*   The structure, the contents, the works and all unfixed materials and goods (except plant, tools and equipment) shall be at the sole risk of the Employer as regards loss or damage by fire and the Employer shall maintain a proper policy of insurance against that risk.
3 *Injury to persons and property*   The Contractor shall be responsible for all structural and decorative damage to property (except for loss or damage by fire) and for death, injury or loss caused by the works or workmen to persons, animals or things and shall indemnify the Employer against all claims and proceedings whatsoever, arising from any statute or at Common Law, unless due to any act or neglect of the Employer or of any person for whom the Employer is responsible. The Contractor shall secure the due performance of these indemnities by entering into proper and sufficient policies of insurance.
4 *Overtime*   The Contractor must allow in his tender for all overtime which he considers will be necessary to complete the work within the time stipulated and no claim in this respect will be considered, unless written permission has been given by the Designer.
5 *Sub-contractors*   The Contractor is to enter into contracts with the various sub-contractors, making such conditions as those under which he has himself contracted and is to impose no conditions more arduous. Such contracts to fix a time for completion; such time must be a reasonable one for the due and proper execution of the works. The Contractor is to attend upon and afford facilities to all sub-contractors and to provide them with such scaffold and ladders as they may require.
6 *Specialist contractors*   The Contractor shall grant all facilities to any Specialist Contractors who may be employed direct by the Designer's client.
7 *Transport*   The Contractor must allow for all transport of his own materials to the site and afford full protection and insurance of such materials in transit.
8 *Finishes*   The whole of the materials (except where described) and workmanship to be provided by the Contractor to be the best of their respective kinds and the Contractor is to be responsible for the proper and efficient carrying out of the whole of the work. Samples of all materials to be used must be submitted to the Designer. All work is to be carried out to the entire satisfaction of the District Surveyor and all other authorities having jurisdiction over the work.
9 *Scaffold, plant, etc*   The Contractor must provide all necessary plant,

* See also *The Architect in Practice*, Arthur J. Willis and W. N. B. George, Crosby Lockwood.

scaffolding, tackle, cartage, labour and materials necessary for the prompt and efficient execution of the works and is to remove the same at completion.

10 *Watching*   The Contractor must take all necessary precautions to secure the safety of his materials and completed work, and for the safety of the remainder of the building.

11 *Protection*   The Contractor must cover up and protect from injury, from any cause, all new work and all existing work which is liable to damage from his materials and workmen. Any damage caused by his failure to do so must be made good at his expense. The Contractor must hand over the whole work on completion in clean and perfect condition.

12 *Prime cost and provisional sums*   Where provisional sums are included for work not specified in detail, the Contractor will be required to submit with his final invoice a detailed account in respect of each item so covered, priced in accordance with the provisions for payment on variations contained in this Specification. The amount to be allowed to the Contractor for work covered by a PC or provisional sum in this Specification shall be the net cost to the Contractor after trade and other discounts have been deducted (except cash discounts when allowed by merchants and others up to a maximum of 5% in the case of materials or goods to be fixed by the Contractor and of 2½% in all other cases).

13 *Variations, errors and extras*   If any work instructed by the Designer be extra, in the opinion of the Contractor, to that on which his estimate was based, he shall inform the Designer before proceeding with the work and no allowance for an extra will be made unless previously agreed by the Designer.

14 *Bad workmanship*   Material and workmanship which, in the opinion of the Designer, do not conform with the Specification shall be removed from the site and shall be replaced with proper materials and workmanship at the Contractor's expense. If the Contractor fails to do so, the Employer shall have the power to employ and pay other persons to carry out the work and to recover the cost and the incidental expenses from the Contractor, or deduct the cost from money due to the Contractor.

15 *Defects after completion*   Any shrinkage or other defects which may appear within six months from the completion of the works arising, in the opinion of the Designer, from materials or workmanship not in accordance with the drawings, Specification and other instructions issued by the Designer, shall upon direction in writing from the Designer be amended and made good by the Contractor at his own cost. If the Contractor fails to do the work, the Employer shall have the same powers as under 'Bad workmanship'. Should any defective work have been done or materials supplied by any Sub-contractor employed on the works, whether nominated by the Designer or not, the Contractor shall be liable in the same manner as if the work or materials have been done or supplied by the Contractor. A sum amounting to 5% of the contract sum will be retained by the Employer until the expiration of the period mentioned above.

16 *Access to the site*   The Contractor will be able to take dimensions on the site by (date) and will have access to the site at all time after (date). He must

acquaint himself with the times when he will be allowed to unload materials and make full allowance in his estimate for any restrictions there may be.

17 *Tenders* Tenders are required to reach this office not later than noon on (date).

18 *Time schedule* Instructions to proceed will be given to the successful contractor by not later than (date) and the work is to be completed in every detail by (date).

19 *Damages for non-completion* If the Contractor fails to complete the work by the date specified or within any extended time allowed by the Designer, he shall pay or allow to the Employer the sum of £x per week as liquidated and ascertained damages for every week beyond the said or extended time, as the case may be, during which the works shall remain unfinished.

20 *Contingencies* The Contractor shall allow the sum of £x in his estimate for general contingencies, this sum to be used only as the Designer may direct and which is to be deducted in part or in full if not required.

21 *Payment* Payment will be made at the rate of 90% of the value of the work actually done and fixed in the building. The balance of 10% will be retained until the works are certified as complete, when one half of this sum will be paid; the other half, together with any further sum due to the Contractor at the final adjustment of accounts, will be paid on the expiration of the period of maintenance. Applications for interim payments are to be accompanied by detailed approximate statements showing the amount of work executed.

Tenders—competitive and single

The procedure for inviting competitive tenders has already been given in detail in Chapter Seven as well as some of the reasons why single tendering can be appropriate—specialist firms and so on. The latter are equally applicable to the work we are considering in this chapter but there is often a further overriding reason why single tendering is resorted to and that is lack of time.

If this is the trouble you will wonder why a single tender will save any time since it takes no longer for three firms to tender than for one. But the answer is that your single selected contractor would not tender at all. You would explain the job to him and then start passing the working drawings and specifications to him as they came off your drawing board instead of waiting until they were all complete. The contractor would price the work in sections and for the time being you would have to accept his prices. For a small job you would have to accept them in the long run as well. For a large job you would have been wise to make it part of the initial contract with him that his accounts at the end of the job should be submitted to a quantity surveyor. It would then become what is known as a 'cost plus' contract; that is, he would charge you for labour and materials at cost, plus an agreed profit margin.

The quantity surveyor

According to Hamilton J. Turner's *Architectural Practice and Procedure* referred to above, a quantity surveyor 'is a man who has received a thorough and severely practical training in all matters relating to building . . .' He stands midway between the architect, exhibition or interior designer and the builder. He is able to understand the practical problems of both and in addition, and most importantly for you, it is his job always to be *au fait* with the current prices of materials and labour in the building industry and to know how much (what quantities in fact) of both would be reasonably required to fulfil your specifications. His fees will be a small percentage of the value of the work which he surveys and his decisions are held to be acceptable to both sides, as would be those of an arbitrator.

If therefore you have agreed with your client that a single tender only shall be invited, you should at the same time suggest and agree with him that the services of a quantity surveyor should be employed to check the contractor's draft accounts and that his percentage fee should be a charge against the budget. Equally you should get the contractor's agreement in advance to this kind of contract and confirm it to both parties in writing.

Firm estimates and guess estimates

The kind of work we have considered so far, for the purpose of writing specifications and inviting tenders, is usually that part of an exhibition or interior design job known as the main contract. It usually includes all the structures, decoration and installation. It *may* also include the electrical work and light fittings, the furniture and soft furnishings and specialist display work. Or all of these and other similar things may be the subject of separate single estimates, not competitive tenders. At big public and trade exhibitions the organizers usually nominate electrical contractors whose services must be used for all wiring, connecting to mains and for the supplying and fixing of all standard light fittings. They provide printed order forms for this work with fixed prices which also usually include the value of the electric current which will be consumed.

While, therefore, you are waiting for the tenders to come in for your main contract, you must be urgently busy about getting estimates for all other aspects of the job not already in it. These may include furniture, carpets, curtains, models, art-work, photographs, maps, diagrams, murals, flowers and plants, ashtrays, wastepaper baskets, captions, titles, text and so on. Very few of these would be suitable for competitive tender: a single estimate would do. But each would need a carefully worded specification on which to give a firm estimate. Don't forget to ask that VAT, packing and delivery charges should always be included where applicable. For some of them it might be difficult to get even a single firm estimate. This usually applies to graphic work—titles, text, captions, photoprints, photostats and the like—which may not have been finalized at the time of getting in tenders and estimates. This is where you will have to learn to guess-estimate and Chapter Eighteen will give you some guidance about this.

Collating tenders and estimates

With all your tenders and estimates in and carefully checked to see that there are no holes in them anywhere nor any qualifying clauses which would make them unacceptable, they must now be collated into a concise summary for submitting to your client. But in the case of exhibitions and interior design first add up all your figures and see how the total relates to your budget, remembering to include your fees if it has been agreed that the budget must be an all-in figure. If your total is inside the budget, all is well and in that case your client will probably not need a very detailed summary. If it is not very much over the budget, say not more than 2% or 3%, your summary will have to be fairly detailed to show where cuts could be made if your client is adamant. If it is seriously over then it would be foolish to submit it as such to your client. You will have to call in the contractor who has submitted the most acceptable tender, go over it with him and see what economies you and he suggest. You will have to give him a day or two to re-price the job and in the meantime you must go through all your other estimates to see how they can be pruned or what can be left out altogether without spoiling the job. If, after this painful process, your total is still too high and yet it seems that there is nothing left that can be cut, then you must present the figures in great detail to your client and get his reactions.

Here is how you might present the tenders and estimates for an exhibition stand, where the total was on the right side. Remember to round off each figure to the nearest pound.

SMITH & JONES LIMITED (*Job Reference No.*)
Estimated cost of design and construction of stand (No. R. 15, *xx* metres × *xx* metres = *xxx* sq metres) at (title of exhibition, place and opening date).

1 *Construction*
Including all structural work in connection with the platform, partition walls and ceiling; three double-sided showcases; office fittings and free standing panels; all decoration, mounting of photostats and fixing of transparencies; cutting, sewing and laying of haircord carpet overall; supplying material for, making and hanging curtain; supply of fire extinguisher; insurance of all structures from commencement of work on site to final date of demolition; transport; maintenance and final dismantling and clearing away at the close of the Exhibition, ALL MATERIAL ON HIRE from (Contractor's name)   £1,191

2 *Electrical*
(a) Display lighting generally, supplying and connecting three fans; wiring and fixing special light fittings to be provided; connecting up to mains,
ALL MATERIAL ON HIRE from (Contractor's name)   £90
(b) Special light fittings and animated display, ON SALE OUT- RIGHT from (suppliers' names)   £157

195

3 Display
Including the supply and maintenance of flowers in specially constructed flower boxes on the display cases; supplying and fixing of cut-out lettering; all typesetting, copy negatives, photoprints and photostats, say £176

4 Miscellaneous
Cost of drawing office prints, hire of eight chairs, and two coffee tables, supplying one wastepaper basket and six ashtrays and other minor out-of-pocket expenses, say £55

£1,669

5 Fees
For taking your instructions, preparing preliminary design in the form of a perspective drawing, plans and elevations and submitting to you; preparing working drawings, obtaining estimates, placing contracts and supervising all construction, installation and completion @ 20% of total estimated costs £334

6 Reserve
For unforeseen contingencies £50

£2,053

Notes
(i) The above estimates do not include insurance of your exhibits, installation of a Post Office telephone, daily cleaning, electric current consumed or record photography.

(ii) While the above estimates have been prepared as carefully as possible, variations may be made to cover savings, or extra work found advisable during the progress of the work. A detailed account will be rendered when invoices from contractors are received and collated and the percentage fee adjusted accordingly.

(iii) The normal contract clauses covering increases in the cost of labour and/ or materials during the execution of the contract, release of responsibility in the case of strikes, lock-outs, go-slow or working-to-rule movements, postponement or cancellation of the exhibition, or Acts of God, apply.

(iv) Other tenders received for Item 1 above, were as follows:
(Contractor's name) £1,250
(Contractor's name) £1,500

(Designer's name, address and telephone number)
(date)

There are several points in that collated estimate which need explanation. The inclusion at the top of exact data about the stand—its number, dimensions, and the place and date of the exhibition are not only useful as a record at the time for both you and your client but useful to you later on as reference material for guess-estimating and budgets for other jobs, for working out square-metre costs and so on, as you will see in Chapter Eighteen. You will realize that the first three items are only a summary of the work allowed for. This is usually quite sufficient unless, as I have said, you have to present an estimate which is over the budget. Then it would be advisable to break up each item as much as you can and as far as your contractor's and suppliers' prices allow.

Under 'Fees' it is important to state that your percentage fee, whatever it is, is 'of total *estimated* costs'. The figure which results in this case, £334, is not of course a fixed and firm fee. When you are able to apply the percentage to actual *final* costs the resultant fee may well be less, if you have been able to make savings; or more, if there have been a number of agreed extras. Note (ii) at the end of the estimates makes this clear to your client.

Item 6, the reserve for unforeseen contingencies is very important. *Every* job is likely to have its totally unforeseen contingency, however careful your planning and this applies particularly to exhibitions where you have to rely on so many things and people who are quite outside your control. If you have a contingency sum within your budget you can by agreement with your client use it without further reference to him at that moment of crisis, usually at a weekend, when he may not be available for consultation. From his point of view it helps his own budget problems to know that there is an allowance for a contingency within the total estimate for the job, which may be part of a total annual appropriation for advertising, sales or public relations and consequently just as tight a budget for him as for you.

Now about the Notes at the end of the estimates. We have already seen the reason for Note (ii), and Note (iv) is self-explanatory. But Note (i) may vary considerably according to how much of the ancillary chores in connection with a stand your client has asked you to look after for him. They should all be either in your estimates under Miscellaneous or referred to in Note (i). In this way the actual as well as the financial, responsibility is established. 'Electric current consumed' refers to those public or trade exhibitions where the supply of electricity is separately metered to each stand and a bill for the current consumed follows at a later date. The alternative method is where an electrical contractor is nominated by the organziers and his prices for fititngs include the current they will consume during the exhibition period. In which case, the reference to 'current consumed' should be included under the 'Electrical' item.

Finally, Note (iii): This is a purely legal formula which is very important to you in the case of the client who might refuse to see reason when he finds his stand incomplete on the opening day because of any of the disasters it lists. It is even more important to you if you have accepted the responsibility of paying all the contractors yourself and then re-invoicing your client, about which there is more below.

For interior design jobs, the method of setting out collated estimates would be much the same, but as it would be likely that furniture and furnishings would be a much larger proportion of the budget, these would need to be separately listed and priced. The fees item too would probably need to be shown under two headings, one percentage against the main contractual items and one against furniture and furnishings selected from stock, as we saw in Chapter Three. It would still be wise to include a contingency, if the budget allowed, and Notes (i), (ii) and (iv) would apply. Note (iii) would only be included if you were working to a very rigid completion date.

Agent or principal?

Your collated estimates should as we have already seen in Chapter Seven go to your client with a covering letter from you. At this point I beseech you to turn to page 99 in that chapter and read from 'The covering letter' sub-heading to the end of 'Paying bills for your client'. If you are reading this part of the book as a practising designer you may know it all already and be well aware of the danger point but because the sums of money involved in the production of an interior, shop-fitting or exhibition job are usually so much larger than in any other design field it is very important for you to know what the risks would be if you agreed with your client to finance any such job. In spite of what might look a quite attractive sum of money to be earned as a handling charge my strongest possible advice would be—don't do it. Stick to the much more suitable and safer role of being your client's 'agent'.

You will find advice about a suitable covering letter, getting your client's written acceptance of the collated estimates and the method of placing the contracts all in the same part of Chapter Seven as well.

Interim payments

Just as you, the designer, are entitled to interim or progress payments of your fees, as we saw in Chapter Three, so your main contractors on an exhibition or interior design job will almost certainly have included as a clause in their side of the contracts that they should receive interim or progress payments as the work proceeds. The amounts and the incidence of these may vary but they must be dealt with as soon as they are received. If your client is paying the bills, the interim accounts from contractors will be made out to him but sent to you. If you feel that the sum requested is reasonably related to the amount of work done, you should type or write on the invoice 'certified correct for payment,' sign it with the date and send it to your client asking him to pay it direct. Always refer in your covering letter to the date, reference number and amount of the contractor's invoice and send a copy of it to the contractor. Your copy of the letter will then be a useful record of the proceeding and a reference for checking final invoices.

If you are going to pay the bills for your client, you also can ask him for interim payments, not only for fees, but to meet contracting costs as well. You will have to pay the contractors' interim accounts and your client could not reasonably expect you to finance these transactions for long. The amounts for which you would ask might vary from a half to two thirds of the total collated estimates as a first instalment, probably at the time of placing the contracts; the balance less a retention of 10% on completion of the job and then a final account showing all the costs in full, less the amounts you have received on account, leaving a final balance due, which is likely to be in the region of the 10% retention unless you have seriously exceeded the budget.

Final accounts and the QS
Under 'Final accounts' in Chapter Seven you will find general advice about your professional responsibilities in arriving at an agreed final account with your contractor. For the more elaborate and costly kind of work we are considering in this chapter this can often be a very protracted business, taking many months to complete. If you have agreed with your client to bring in a quantity surveyor from the beginning he will do all this for you but if not, you have got to do it yourself.

The defects liability period
I have already touched on this on page 92 and you will have read the formal wording of the clause at (15) in the specification for interior design. But perhaps a little more explanation is needed here.

Although the contractor, like you, is entitled to ask for stage payments as his work proceeds, he must wait for six months, sometimes twelve, after the job is complete before the final balance of his bill is paid in order that any defects in his workmanship or materials will have had time to show themselves. Then they must be put right by him at no extra cost. The percentage retention of his final account can be either 5% or 10% according to the size and complexity of the job. As it will be your responsibility to draw up the list of defects which he must remedy and see that he does the work, you also must wait the necessary months, plus the time taken to do the remedial work, before you can invoice the final 5% or 10% of your fee.

In Chapter Eight in the first part of this book you will find information about how to invoice the three basic types of fees—lump sum, hourly rates and percentage. But when you are running your own office invoicing will be a vitally important activity in your monthly programme. This chapter is therefore to tell you more about the problems which may arise and also how to be sure that you get paid the fees which are rightfully due to you.

Regularity of invoicing

Like so many other office chores, invoicing should be done regularly. You will find that those firms with which you have credit accounts will send you their invoices monthly, about a week or ten days after the last day of the month and dated on that day. So that on or about 10 August, say, you might get your regular monthly account from your typesetters. It would be dated 31 July or perhaps even just 'July'. It would consist of all the work you had ordered and received from 1 to 31 July but not beyond that, not up to 10 August when you might have received the bill.

If you had not paid such an account by 31 August you would soon after that date receive a statement, which would give only the total of the July bill and the totals of any previous bills from the firm which you had not yet paid. You would continue to get these statements each month until you had paid the whole account. Single invoices for single items, however large or small, will also probably come in just after the end of a calendar month and be followed at monthly intervals thereafter by their relevant statements.

There is thus a monthly rhythm to invoicing and statement-sending which you would do well to adopt. If you have ordered various things in connection with a job, some of which may be chargeable to your client, you will need to wait until you get all the bills for them in, checked and agreed before you send out your own. The bills you receive are called, in accountancy jargon, purchase invoices and those you send out, sales invoices.

Another and even more important reason for sticking to the monthly rhythm of accountancy is that it has a quite definite effect on how soon you will get paid. When the accounts department of one of your clients receives an invoice from you in the middle of a month, actually dated, say, 15 June, they will probably put it aside until they have received all their June invoices by early July and then start work on the whole batch together. But if they receive your invoice, still on or about 15 June but back-dated to 31 May, the chances are that they will start work on it immediately because at that time they will be dealing with all their incoming invoices dated May. It may thus have saved two or three weeks' delay when nothing happens to it at all. Even so, it still has a long way to go before it is ready for payment to you.

Your 31 May invoice sent in about 15 June must first be checked against the order issued to you or the file copy of the letter which commissioned you and agreed your fees. Even if these tally exactly with your invoice, it will probably go before the actual person who employed your services, to ensure that he approves what he has received from you. With his OK on it, it will then go back to the accounts department who will enter it with all their other May invoices in their ledgers. This has all taken time and it may well be the end of June before your May invoice arrives at this point. It may, alas, be even longer with some firms whose accounts departments are understaffed or inefficient or whose executives are tardy and forgetful about giving the final OK on invoices. However, even assuming that all is going smoothly with your sales invoice, the chances are that when it has become a ledger entry it will still not be paid. Many big firms nowadays 'pay on statements'. That is, they file away the actual invoice they have received from you after it has been checked and agreed because it contains all the details of the job in question and is therefore very useful for a later reference, and wait until they receive your statement. This is a bare reiteration of the total amount which you are owed. You would send out early in July a statement dated 30 June in respect of your 31 May invoice. On receiving this, it would be checked against the ledger entry and then in due course a cheque would be made out to you, signed, counter-signed and posted to you. If, therefore, your invoice dated 31 May had followed a smooth and uninterrupted course you might expect to get paid by about the middle of July.

This has been explained at some length in order to show why it is not reasonable to render your invoice one day and expect to get paid the next. But this unfortunately is what free-lance designers often do. They neglect altogether to send out any invoices for some weeks or even months. Then the exchequer suddenly and inevitably runs dry. Invoices are hastily rushed out and the cheques are waited for in daily desperation. When a crisis seems unavoidable they have to start ringing up their clients' accounts departments and even the clients themselves, to plead for immediate payment. Which is embarrassing and a pity since it tends to spoil the picture the designer will be trying to create of an efficient and steadily expanding organization.

There are two ways of helping to prevent this situation. One is to attend to your invoicing with rigid regularity every month. The other is to make sure that your invoices themselves are as accurate and explanatory as you can possibly make them to prevent them being held up in the pipeline by queries. Of course you cannot avoid the lapse of time before you get paid for the very first invoice you ever send out. But your budget for the first year should have allowed for this. As we have seen above, you may have to wait up to two months before you receive your first payment. But if you had followed your first month's invoicing with some more the following month and the next and so on regularly, the money would start flowing in equally regularly and the gap would close.

Extra fees

In Chapter Three 'Writing letters about fees' we saw how you should refer in your own fee letters to the eventualities which would justifiably earn you extra fees—for changes to your brief, for extra work not in the original brief and so on. With these agreed in principle before you start work on the job there is no problem at invoicing time particularly when you have agreed to charge at hourly rates.

But that rather vague phrase '*quantum meruit*' can sometimes be worrying. It can be translated variously as 'as much as it is worth' or 'as much as is deserved' or 'the extent of the work entailed'.

This does not get you out of the difficulty since only you can decide what fee you think you deserve and how much work has been entailed. The one thing which makes the decision easier is if you have kept time sheets and know the selling value of your time. Then you can produce what should be convincing evidence to your client as a basis for your fee. Without time sheets you will have to arrive at a figure which seems reasonable and see if your client will accept it. The same procedure would apply if the change of brief happened during the preparation of working drawings, if they were only affected to a minor extent. But if the change of brief were so radical as to entail virtually starting again, you would be justified in charging as an extra the full fee agreed for all the stages which had had to be abandoned. You might decide to reduce the full fee by, say, 10%, 15% or 25% according to whether you did not again have to visit a factory or a site, make a survey or select exhibits before re-starting design work on the new brief. Such a reduction would strengthen your client's goodwill in what usually tends to be an irritating situation for everybody concerned.

Extra work which your client may ask you to do during the progress of an exhibition or interior design job is usually automatically covered by the percentage fee which will have been negotiated. Just one point needs watching, however, in this situation. It can happen, particularly with exhibitions, that after you have handed over the completed job and left the site, the client may instruct the general contractors direct regarding some small extras. If these are shown on the contractor's final account, you should not of course include them in the total amount against which you will compute your percentage fee since you have presumably not been involved at all.

Invoicing retainers and consultancies

Although a retainer is in fact a lump-sum fee it differs from the method of invoicing for this type of fee already described in Chapter Eight. A retainer is seldom less than an annual arrangement and as such is usually payable in regular instalments, usually quarterly, sometimes monthly and always 'in arrears' that is at the end of each agreed period, not the beginning. Monthly instalments mean that you will have to render twelve invoices instead of four but the regular and frequent revenue coming in can be very useful to small young offices and therefore well worth the trouble if the client agrees to it. The starting date of the retainer and the periodicity of invoicing the instalments should always be agreed in writing between you and the client. It can then be helpfully referred to in each invoice. The wording of a quarterly retainer instalment might be as follows:

Ref 000 General design programme
1 Retaining fee for design consultancy services from (date) to (date) as agreed in Mr J. Smith's letter of (date) at £1000 per annum   £250
2 Expenses incurred to date etc

Each subsequent quarterly invoice would be worded in exactly the same way except for changing the two dates at Item 1. In Item 2 the 'to date' means the date of the invoice itself. If you were dating it 31 March you would charge all the expenses on your books up to that date, not up to the date when you were actually drafting the invoice.

If you are going to receive a large lump-sum fee, not a retainer, for a big long-term job and have agreed that it should be invoiced in instalments at fairly regular intervals, it is again useful to number the instalments, thus
1 First instalment of fee as agreed etc.

Your last invoice of the series would then say 'Sixth and final instalment of fee etc.'

For a consultancy on an annual basis, the invoicing procedure would be just the same as for a retainer.

Renewals
Don't forget that each renewal of retainers and consultancies has to be negotiated with your client. The time to do this is not necessarily after you have invoiced the last instalment of the current arrangement. If you are continuing to do urgent work you will be doing it without the protective cover of a renewed fee arrangement and your client may need some weeks to get the financial authority of his firm to renew it. If it seems almost certain to you that the arrangement will be renewed you could send a covering letter with your last invoice (probably a fourth quarterly one) in which you could point out the fact that it has run out and ask tactfully if it is to be renewed because your agreed programme of work continues etc. etc. If the programme of work for the second year looked like being consistently larger than for the first this would also be the moment to make a case for an increase in the annual fee. You should follow this reminder procedure at the end of each year of a retainer or consultancy arrangement. There are however retainer and consultancy arrangements which have run for a year or more and then the volume of work or collaboration begins to tail right off. This may be because you seem to have done for the time being all you were required to do or equally that the collaboration does not seem to have been a very useful one on either side. In either of these cases you would be wise to write your reminder letter about renewal when you send your penultimate invoice instead of the final one. You might even find it preferable yourself to suggest that the arrangement should not be renewed if you felt that this would get you both out of an embarrassing

situation and would therefore be good for your continuing relations with the client. It can cause you considerable worry and guilt complexes to continue to receive retaining or consultancy fees when you do not seem to be earning them, even through no fault of your own. The relief when they are ended by mutual consent is almost worth the hole they may make in your budget.

Invoicing for interiors
In Chapter Eight under 'Invoicing percentage fees' on page 107 I gave you the basic pattern for invoicing percentage fees related to the stages of the work. Here I am going into this pattern in much greater detail. When you are involved in contracting for a client on a sizeable interior job (or equally a shop-fitting or any comparable assignment) the invoicing sequence is complicated, as I have already said. It involves the gathering together of a lot of data from your records, making accurate calculations and all in a meticulously correct sequence. If these activities go wrong anywhere you will get into a terrible tangle.

The simplest way to explain all the detail will be to invent a small showroom job for the XYZ Company Limited for which your client's budget was to be about £5000 and for which you had agreed a design fee of 15% and 5% on all new furniture and furnishings chosen by you from stock. In addition, you had agreed an initial (*fictitious!*) fee of £20 for making a measured survey of the site since your client could not provide you with any accurately-dimensioned plans of it.

Your first invoice would be for the survey fee and for your Stage One fee. In presenting your preliminary design proposals, let us assume that you would have told your client that it looked as if your designs could be carried out within his budget, breaking it down into £4500 for the main contract and £500 for standard furniture. This would give you an estimated fee of £675 on the main contract price and £25 on the furniture budget, £700 in all. As we saw in Chapter Eight, your fee for Stage One can be one-fifth of the total estimated fee. In this case therefore it will be £140. Now for your first invoice:

XYZ Company Limited
(address)   (date)
Ref (your job number)—New showroom at 12 Main Street, Westchester

(1) Fee as agreed for making a measured
     survey of the ground floor at the above
     premises and preparing a set of accurately
     dimensioned plans and elevations   £20
(2) Fee for the preparation of preliminary design
     proposals in the form of plans, elevations
     and coloured perspective sketches, with
     samples of proposed floor and wall
     finishes, and photographs of suggested
     standard furniture, with guide to approximate

total cost, ie, one-fifth of 15% of estimated
contract price of £4500 and at 5% on
£500 for standard furniture   £140   £160

(3)   Expenses incurred to date etc.

If for any reason you were not asked to go ahead with the job after submitting your preliminary design proposals (client didn't like them, lease of premises fell through, firm's change of policy and so on) your first invoice, which would also sadly be your last in these circumstances, would be exactly as above but it would be wise to add at the end '. . . excluding copyright in my designs'. Admittedly this would already have been covered in your fee letter and its acceptance but when a job folds up at this stage it is an added precaution to reiterate the copyright position.

Now for your second invoice: remembering to put in the name and address, date and same heading:

(1)   Further fees on account for the preparation
       and submission of final designs, incorporating
       agreed amendments to preliminary design
       proposals, including approximate estimate
       of costs, programme and negotiations in
       progress with (relevant Authorities) for
       approvals, ie one-third of estimated fee of £700   £233
(2)   Further expenses to date etc.

Although one-third of £700 is actually £233.33 it is quite in order at this stage of invoicing to round it off to the nearest pound. Next comes your stage three invoice which for the sake of this example we will assume is up to the point of being ready to invite tenders. Incidentally one of the reasons why Stages Three and Four in fee letter structure C are sometimes moved down one is because the job is going through so quickly that when the time comes they have caught up with each other and there is little point in invoicing yet again on an estimated cost when the actual contract price is imminent. But here we will assume that the job is a slow and steady one and that the stages of work and of invoicing are following the more usual pattern.

Notice that expenses are nothing to do with fees and are merely added to each invoice you render according to whatever you have spent up to that date. They are never 'on account.'

(Name, address, date and heading as usual)

(1)   Further fees on account for the prepar-
       ation of finished working drawings, full-
       size details and specifications, obtaining
       estimates from sub-contractors and sup-
       pliers, and completing negotiations with

relevant Authorities for approvals, ready
for inviting tenders ie, one-third of esti-
mated fee of £700   £233
(2)   Further expenses to date etc.
(3)   Purchase on your behalf of ashtrays and
desk lamp   £25

Your fourth invoice will be your final one (except for the agreed percentage
retention of fees while you cope with the defects liability period (see page 199)
and this is the really complicated one. What you would send finally to your
client would be never less than two and sometimes three pieces of paper:

(1)   an invoice from you to him re-charging him with any small production
      purchases you had made for him for the job and which were still
      uncharged on your job sheets.
(2)   a complete schedule of all final production costs, in which your invoice at
      (1) above would be listed as one of the items.
(3)   another invoice from you giving your final percentage fees on the total
      cost of the job, less the instalments you have already had on account,
      with any final expenses chargeable extra to fees, such as travel, phone
      calls, etc.

The first item above is the piece of paper which might not be needed at final
account stage, either because you had not made any purchases yourself or
because you had and had recharged them earlier, perhaps with one of your 'on
account' fee invoices. If the latter applies you must still remember to bring
them into your Final Schedule of Costs so that you can get your percentage fees
on them.
First we must assume that as each final account from contractors and suppliers
came to you, you checked it carefully, certified it and sent it on with a covering
letter referring to the essential details (see page 103). You will see below why
this is important. Now look back through your previous 'on account' invoices
to see whether you have in fact already charged any production purchases. If
so, extract a list of the date and reference number of your invoices, your item
numbers in those invoices and the total amount on each invoice of the
purchases recharged. In the case of the small showroom we are using as an
example, the only thing in this category would be item (3) of your third invoice,
the ashtrays and desk lamp which you bought yourself and recharged to your
client at £25.
Next look carefully through your order books, job sheets, petty cash chits,
receipts etc. to see whether there remain any more production purchases not
yet charged. If there are, draft a separate invoice for them. That deals with
Item 1 above. Now you should be able, if you have done your homework, to
turn to a waiting file of copy letters giving you the necessary detail for each item
of the final schedule of costs, so:

The XYZ Company Limited
Final Schedule of all production costs for your new Showroom at 12 Main Street, Westchester.

1 *Main contract*
  Certified invoice No. xx dated x.x.x. from (contractors'
  name) sent to you with my letter of (date)   £4344

2 *Soft furnishings*
(a) Carpets – certified invoice no. xx dated
    x.x.x. from (supplier's name) sent to you
    with my letter of (date)   £226
(b) Curtains – certified invoice no. xx dated
    x.x.x. from (contractors name) sent to
    you with my letter of (date)   £193
                                               ─────   419

3 *Special display cabinet*
  Certified invoice no. xx dated x.x.x. from
  (contractor's name) sent to you with my
  letter of (date)   85
                                                            ─────
4 *Furniture etc. from stock*   4848
(a) Settees – certified invoice no. xx dated
    x.x.x. from (supplier's name) sent to you
    with my letter of (date)   224
(b) Armchairs – certified invoice no. xx
    dated x.x.x. from (supplier's name) sent
    to you with my letter of (date)   85
                                               ─────
                                    (c/f) 309   4848
                                    (b/f) 309   4848
(c) Coffee tables – certified invoice no. xx
    dated x.x.x. from (supplier's name) sent
    to you with my letter of (date)   38
(d) Ashtrays and desk lamp – already
    charged to you with my invoice Ref. xxx
    dated x.x.x.   25
(e) Waste paper bins – my invoice Ref. xxx,
    dated x.x.x. for the purchase of these on
    your behalf is attached (Note: this would
    be your first piece of paper referred to
    above)   4
                                               ─────
                                                            376
                                                           5224
                                                          ─────

Just two points about that imaginary schedule: I have invented figures in round pounds for the simplicity of this exercise but of course in 'real life' you must never round off actual *final* costs such as these. If the main contractor's account at Item 1 above had been £4344.90 that is the amount you would have to put in, which can make your percentage calculations a bit complicated. Secondly the reason for grouping and totalling Items 1 to 3 inclusive (the part of the job you have designed) and Item 4 with a total (the part of the job where you have selected only) is because this obviously makes your final fee calculations easier and clearer as you will soon see.

When you have got it all drafted and totalled like that, add your full name and address, the date and your job reference number and have it typed. You will need not less than three copies, the top copy for the client, one to be attached to the copy of your fees invoice and one for the job file. An extra copy will be a good idea because these final schedules of cost are very useful for later reference when you may have to do some advance guess-estimating on a comparable job. That completes your second piece of paper.

Now you prepare the third piece of paper, your final fees and expenses invoice and it is usual in this field of design to summarize all the services you have given, so:

(Name, address, date and heading as before)

(1)	Fees for taking your instructions, preparing and submitting preliminary and final designs, negotiating with (relevant authorities) for the necessary approvals; preparing full set of working drawings, full-size details and specifications, inviting tenders and estimates, receiving these and submitting to you as a collated cost budget; receiving your instructions to place contracts and orders on your behalf; supervising all work in workshops and studios, and installation and completion on site; checking all final accounts and certifying them for payment, at 15% on total final production costs and 5% on furniture etc. selected from stock, ie, 15% of £4848 (See attached Schedule Items 1 to 3 inclusive)	£727.20
	5% of £376 (See attached Schedule Item 4)	18.80
		£745.00

                                less amounts invoiced on account*
                                        (date)   £140
                                        (date)   £233
                                        (date)   £233
                                                   ———   £606.00

                                                              £139.00
                Less 5% retention for supervision of
                remedial work at end of six months defects
                liability period   6.95
                                                              ————
                Fees now due   £132.05
(2)   Further expenses to date etc.

The Schedule should be stapled to the fees invoice (because it is an essential part of it) and your separate purchases invoice should be paper-clipped to the covering letter you will probably write.

And there you have to leave it until the six months are up and the contractor has put right any defects under your supervision. Then you can render what is positively your final invoice on the job, that 5% retention of your fee—£6.95 plus any further and final expenses.

(1)   Final balance of fee after 6 months defects
        liability inspection and supervision of con-
        tractor's remedial work   £6.95
(2)   Final expenses incurred, etc.

Watch out during that inspection. It can happen that your client will take the opportunity to ask for additions and alterations which have little or nothing to do with remedying defects on the original work. It is quite reasonable that he should but equally reasonable that you should receive extra fees if it involved you in work on the drawing board and supervision of the contractor to carry it out.

I have used a simple showroom job as an example but the procedure would be exactly the same for a big interior or shop-fitting job.

In the (to me unhappy) event of your being the principal in this type of work and financing the whole job you would not need any final schedule of costs, just one large long invoice from you to the client for all production costs, fees and expenses, less of course any interim payments. All the production costs should come first and be totalled; then should follow the agreed handling charge; then the total percentage fees based on the total production costs *excluding* the handling charge item, then your final expenses. Against the grand total of all that you would show the deductions for all interim payments and then the 'final balance due.'

* Your £20 fee for the initial survey is quite separate and extra to your percentage fees and therefore does not have to be absorbed by them.

A client's own materials and labour
I referred in Chapter Four under 'Fees based on a percentage of costs' to the action you must take at the beginning of a job if it is clear that a client's own materials are going to be used as part of the production of an exhibition, shop, show-room or suchlike. If you were able to get a priced value of them from your client then and there and preferably in writing, this price must be included as a separate item in your final schedule of costs, referring to the date of the relevant letter, because you are entitled to get your percentage fee on their value. If you assess that in the long run larger or smaller quantities were used, or materials of different quality and value than originally priced, this should be checked with your client and an up-to-date valuation asked for, for inclusion in your final schedule. The same procedure would apply if the client had provided any of his own labour on some specialist aspect of the job done under your supervision.
You will need to be careful to differentiate between a client's materials used as a production item and for display purposes. In a showroom for a carpet manufacturer, say, there needs to be a floor finish to cover a rough concrete floor. If the client decides that his own carpeting should be used throughout, then that would be a production item on which you should earn your percentage fee. But if in the same showroom you are providing wall units on which carpet lengths are to be displayed then such carpet should not rate for your percentage fee. In the borderline cases which can often arise in these circumstances you can usually get round the difficulty by suggesting a reduced percentage fee on such materials.

Invoicing for exhibitions
Invoicing for exhibition work, which is normally done on a percentage fee basis, follows much the same pattern as for interior design. But the proportion of the Stage One fee, already agreed as a breaking clause, could by agreement be higher than one-fifth if you had to be involved in a considerable amount of research and inspection of your client's exhibits and production processes.
For a large long-term project, as we saw on page 198, it is quite acceptable to negotiate for interim fees to be invoiced between the normal stage payment fees.
The defects liability clause and consequent retention of fees from your final invoice would not arise in the case of temporary exhibitions but would apply to permanent exhibitions in museums, showrooms, etc.

Records are vital
Dealing with the final accounts of an exhibition or interior design job is a fairly complicated operation. It is made infinitely easier if you have been able to keep your records in order and up-to-date as you worked through the job with a work file of copy orders and contract letters, job sheets, copy invoices, diary notes and petty cash expenses ready at your elbow to give you all the facts and figures.

Statements

I have already mentioned statements at the beginning of this chapter on page 200. Now here is what to do about them. At regular monthly intervals after the date of your invoice, your statements should follow relentlessly until you get paid. A statement is really a copy of the page in your ledger showing your client's account with you, a 'statement' of how it stands. Supposing you had sent out two invoices dated 31 January to Smith and Robinson, one for fees and expenses totalling £75.50, the other for production costs of £7.75, and suppose that by 28 February neither had been paid. On 1 March you would send a statement on your letter-heading, making a carbon copy for your accountant, thus:

STATEMENT

31 January (year)	To invoice Ref. ?	£75.50
31 January (year)	To invoice Ref. ?	£ 7.75
		————
		£83.25

Now suppose that during February you had sent in another fees and expenses invoice to Smith and Robinson, for £50.25, and that by the end of March they still had not paid you. The statement you would send on 31 March would show:

31 January (year)	To invoice Ref. ?	£75.50	
31 January (year)	To invoice Ref. ?	£ 7.75	
		————	£83.25
28 February (year)	To invoice Ref.?		£50.25
			————
			£134.50

So they now owe you £134.50 in all, but during April they settle up the first account by cheque. Your statement on 30 April would then show:

31 January (year)	To invoice Ref. ?	£75.50	
31 January (year)	To invoice Ref. ?	£ 7.75	
		————	£83.25
28 February (year)	To invoice Ref. ?		£50.25
			————
			£134.50
		By cheque	£ 75.50
			————
			£59.00

Now they only owe you £59.00 but in the meantime they have queried your January invoice for £7.75 and have convinced you that this has been charged to them in error. So you will have sent them a credit note (see below) and your May statement will read:

31 January (year)	To invoice Ref. ?	£ 7.75
28 February (year)	To invoice Ref. ?	£50.25
		————
		£58.00
20 May (year)	By credit note Ref. ?	£ 7.75
		————
		£50.25

And so on. The total of every unpaid invoice must go on appearing on your statements until you can show the receipt of payment for it to cancel it out. Then both disappear from your next statement, leaving only the ones still unpaid and any which have been added since. It is really not at all complicated and since you will constantly be receiving statements from your own suppliers which you will be checking and paying, you will soon see the principle involved.

Credit notes

I have twice mentioned credit notes in this chapter. The words have a rather ominous ring, as the need for you to send one out means either that you have made a factual error in the figures on your invoice; that you have charged something altogether by mistake or that your client has proved unshakeably convinced that you have charged him too much for what he has received and you have decided to placate him.

All of these things can happen in even the most efficiently run office but obviously the less they happen the better for your reputation and your pocket. When a credit note is inevitable it should be worded as follows:

(For an error in figures:)

> CREDIT NOTE
> *Ref. ?—(Heading)*
> Credit in respect of error in addition at
> Item 2 of my invoice of (date)   £2.50

(Or for a wrong charge:)

> Credit in respect of Item 3 of my invoice of
> (date) charged in error   £3.75

(Or for a reduction in fees:)

> Rebate as agreed in respect of fees at item
> 4 of my invoice of (date)   £10.50

Commercial credit note forms are nearly always printed and often typed as well, in red. This is for quick identification by accounts clerks who may be thumbing through sheaves of invoices. If you can type your own few credit notes on the red ribbon of your typewriter or even just the words 'credit note' in red, it will be appreciated and look efficient. You will always need your own carbon copies of credit notes for your accountant.

Receipts

Since the Cheques Act of 1958 it has not been necessary to issue receipts. This is a great saving of time and postage stamps but needs a little care in recording what you have paid and been paid. A rubber date stamp that says 'Paid' with adjustable dates is a very useful way of doing this. When you *receive* a cheque from a client, date stamp the file copy of your invoice right away so that you will not make the mistake of sending out another statement to him and also for your accountant's information. The cheque is then endorsed and paid in by you, cancelled by the bank and eventually returned to your client, which is his form of receipt. When you *pay* a bill, again use your date stamp on the invoice, send your cheque with the statement and eventually your own cancelled cheque will come back to you as a receipt. Of course, if anyone specifically asks for a receipt, which still happens sometimes, then you must send one.

Debtors

What does one do when, for no apparent reasons, a client does not pay his bills? It happens frequently to all designers and is particularly unfortunate when it represents hard-earned and much-needed revenue to a young designer trying to build up his practice and his bank balance. Under any circumstances it is a situation which must be dealt with according to an accepted 'drill' which starts with infinite tact, patience and kid gloves and ends, in the very last resort, with the mailed fist of the law. There are probably three reasons why a client does not pay your bill. He may be genuinely dissatisfied with your work or your charges; he, or more likely his accounts department, may be hopelessly slow and inefficient in dealing with accounts; or for reasons varying from temporary financial difficulties to near-bankruptcy, he just may not have the money with which to pay you.

Let us assume that you had rendered an invoice for fees on 31 December and had followed it with a statement at the ends of January, February and March without getting paid. However much you needed the money, it would not really be reasonable to start imposing any pressure to get paid until a clear three months were up. Then with your April statement, you might send a polite covering letter to the Secretary or Chief Accountant . . . 'account now four months overdue . . . very grateful if it could be settled without further delay, etc.' No response to that means another letter with your May statement, this time being just a little firmer . . . 'surprised not to have received a reply to my letter of . . . or settlement of my outstanding account, now five months overdue . . . must ask for settlement by return, etc.' If this and even a telephone call to the Chief Accountant still produce no result, you may then have to try a tactful and apologetic approach direct to your client. This usually works if non-payment has been due to the first or second reasons given above. You can deal with the queries which have been holding up your invoice and he can immediately instruct his accounts department to mend their ways, at any rate as far as you are concerned. But if you find yourself put off with vague excuses and promises and if still no payment comes in, then you must consider very carefully your next step perhaps after having first discussed it with your accountant and solicitor. This is to send yet another statement—either June or July by now—with a covering letter to the Secretary on these lines:

'I very much regret that, unless I receive payment of the enclosed outstanding account, now *x* months overdue, within seven days (or fourteen days) of the date of this letter, I shall have to pass the matter over to my solicitor. I hope that you will not make it necessary for me to take this unpleasant action, etc. . . .'

The chances are high that this letter will produce a cheque within the appointed time. But if it does not you must, repeat, *must* pass all the papers to your solicitor for him to go into action. It is absolutely pointless to have threatened to do so and then not to do it, whether from half-heartedness or soft-heartedness. And if the situation ever arose again, as well it might with some firms, it would soon be realized that your threats had no substance.

Your solicitor will then write a suitable legal letter and the chances are even higher that he will receive payment. But if he does not then the law must take its course and the end of its course will bring your client to court. It may be a consolation to know that this happens very seldom indeed, except when a firm goes bankrupt or is downright dishonest. It is also a consolation to know that it is possible to insure against the legal costs involved in getting your fees paid by a reluctant client. Your insurance broker could advise you about this.

There are two further points to remember about your debtors. As your clients multiply and come back for more, you will gradually get to know which are the good payers and the bad payers. If the latter are valuable in other ways as clients and if they always pay up in the end, it is much better, if you can afford to wait, not to nag or threaten them but to accept them philosophically as slow payers.

But it has always been my experience that, during the summer holiday months, roughly July to September, good payers become slow payers, and slow payers become even slower payers. This is obviously because accounts departments are short-staffed due to holiday-making and there seems to be, as a consequence, an all-round slowing up of the normal rhythm of paying and being paid. There is absolutely nothing one can do about this except to remember it at the beginning of each year and try to invoice out as much as possible during the first three or four months in order to fill your financial reservoirs before the summer drought sets in.

References

We saw above that a debtor might eventually be brought to court for failing to pay your bills because he was either bankrupt or dishonest. In either case, all you might get out of the situation would be a bill for your solicitor's fees so it is obviously desirable to do everything possible to prevent it happening. If you are negotiating fees with a possible new client whose firm is quite unknown to you and about whom you feel uneasy, try to find out more about his set-up before you commit yourself to working for him. Your accountant and your solicitor might be able to make very discreet enquiries as to his standing and how long he has been operating. Anyone in the same kind of business whose judgment and discretion you could trust might give you a line on him. And your bank manager, if asked formally to do so, will obtain a confidential report for you as to his ability to pay your fees. It is just as reasonable for you to take these private but necessary steps to get 'references' about his financial status as it is for him to ring up another client for whom you have worked to find out about your efficiency. A disturbing report and a polite withdrawal at the beginning may save you a court case at the end.

There will come a time, many times, when a client will say to you 'Give me an idea of what it is likely to cost me before I decide to go ahead with your design'. Also it will be necessary, as we saw in Chapter Three, to do some guess-estimating when you are preparing a schedule of costs for an exhibition or interior design job; when you have to put a provisional sum into a specification or when a client asks your advice about a budget before you have begun to design at all.

First, never make a guess off the cuff. However much you try to impress upon your client that it is only a rough guess and however much he promises not to hold you to the figure you give him, it will nevertheless stick in his mind and emerge in his conversations with his colleagues until it will seem to have established itself as a fact. Since all such estimates are usually far too low there will be a nasty shock for everybody when your firm estimates turn out to be twice or three times as much.

To be able to guess-estimate production costs and not be wildly wrong is something you can learn to do only with considerable experience, based on a constant and vigilant collection of useful data.

Print
But in the case of print, it is wise never to guess-estimate at all however experienced you may be. There are too many variables—size, number of colours, method of printing and quantities. Fortunately most printers are very long-suffering and helpful about this. They are nearly always prepared to give you an estimate on an approximate specification for something which does not yet exist, 'subject' as they always say 'to a sight of the final artwork'.

Naturally it is no use saying to even the most helpful printer 'What would a booklet cost?' But if you are able to say 'What would, say, 5,000 copies of an A4 size sixteen-page-plus-cover booklet, printed litho in four colours, cost?' he will be able to give you an approximate price sufficient to enable your client to make up his mind as to what he can afford. If this process takes place when you can show a printer your preliminary design, his approximate estimate is likely to be even more accurate.

Price lists, catalogues and samples
Price lists of every kind for all the sort of things you are likely to use on a job should be collected assiduously, date-stamped when they arrive (manu-facturers all too often do not date their own lists) and filed. Labelled and priced

samples of carpets, textiles, wallpapers, wall and floor finishes should also be date-stamped and filed. Lists of charges from photographers, process engravers, photographic processors, firms who supply cut-out letters, lettering sign-writers—all these and many more like them will be invaluable in your files provided you do not let them get out of date. One important item cannot be price-listed and that is typesetting, since it is charged on a time basis. Fortunately most typesetters have the custom of supplying with their invoices a rough pull of the settings for which they are charging. After checking the invoices you will not need to keep these pulls in your accounts files but with the individual cost of each setting pencilled on to the pulls from the invoices, you will be able to build up a file of very useful information about the sort of prices charged. If you use them as a guide sufficiently often, you will be able in time to guess-estimate the cost of typesettings with reasonable accuracy and eventually be able to do without them. For a thematic exhibition, typesetting can be a very big item in your budget. Do not forget, too, that foreign language settings for an overseas job are rather more expensive than English ones.

Costs per square metre
But all these are ingredients. What about a single total for a guess-estimate or a budget such as you will often be asked for by a client who wants an interior or an exhibition designed? Or conversely, what about the client who says flatly that he cannot spend a farthing more than £x? How are you to know whether in fact it can be done or whether he is setting you an impossible task which you ought not to attempt? The only answer to these problems is to learn, by experience again, the square-metre method of estimating based on comparable jobs.

In the previous chapter it was suggested that you should always put dimensions at the head of your estimates for an exhibition or interior design job. It is then quite easy to divide the estimated total cost by the area to give you an *estimated* cost per square metre. When you send in your final schedule of all costs and fees at the end of the job, check it against your estimates and then work out the actual square metre price. These sets of figures should be entered up somewhere where they can always be found and referred to quickly—perhaps even your pocket diary? Add to them whenever you can, not only your own jobs but other people's. If a fellow designer can be persuaded to tell you the total cost of one of his jobs, add it to your records with a brief description as a reminder. After a time with such records as a practical guide, you will begin to be able to assess the cut-price job at £x a square metre; an average job at £x xx a square metre; and a really luxurious one at £x xx a square metre. You will learn from such experience how to push the square metre price up for a thematic exhibition involving a lot of typesetting and photographic work or a lot of specially-made models; to push it up for an interior where much of the furniture is to be specially designed and made; to push it down where a client's exhibits will occupy a lot of space, or for an interior where little more than painting or decorating is needed. To compile such a record of costs in relation to areas will be invaluable to you—much safer than trying to rely on your memory.

Wage awards and price increases

From time to time in the building, printing and other industries with which you will be concerned, there will be wage awards which will increase contractor's costs. As well as in press announcements, they will probably be notified to you by circular letters from those firms with which you deal most frequently. These letters should be kept in sight and in mind so that when you are guess-estimating, say, for a sizeable amount of typesetting on a job, you will not forget to increase what would be your normal assessment of its cost by the percentage increase of the wage award.

On a long-term job a wage award in the building industry or a sudden increase in the cost of a basic structural material in the middle of the work can make a considerable increase on the original contract price. This increase will have to be met, since there will inevitably have been a clause in the contractor's tender or estimate whereby such increases are passed on to customers. That is why it is so important for you to include a clause to this effect in *your* collated estimates to your client, where it has been agreed that you will accept financial responsibility as the principal and pay all the bills before re-invoicing your client. This point was referred to in Chapter Sixteen and a suitable wording for such a clause was given at Note (iv), at the end of the specimen estimates. Here is the wording again as a reminder: 'The normal contract clauses covering increases in the cost of labour and/or materials during the execution of the contract . . . apply'.

The quantity surveyor again

You may have prepared preliminary designs for a large and very complex job for an exhibition or interior where your experience of the usual rules-of-thumb are not sufficient for you to produce an approximate estimate of cost. Your client may, however, require this before he decides whether or not to go ahead. In such cases, the help of a quantity surveyor will be necessary. If you go over with him, in as much detail as you can, your perspectives, plans and elevations, he will be able to give you eventually an approximate assessment of costs in round figures which will be a safe *guide* to the necessary expenditure. His fees for providing this useful information will probably be a very modest percentage of the estimated cost.

If your client really respects and admires the quality of the work you do for him, he may be prepared to endure for quite a time the constant repetition of firm costs proving to be alarmingly higher than guessed-estimates. But it is a situation which is unlikely to last for ever. Sooner or later his patience and his pocket may be exhausted and he may go elsewhere. That is why it really is worth your while to take a lot of trouble with your estimating. His respect for you will be greatly increased if your final costs, more often than not, are within a few pounds of the budget.

'. . . result happiness'

As Mr Micawber said in *David Copperfield* 'Annual income twenty pounds, annual expenditure nineteen nineteen six, result happiness. Annual income twenty pounds, annual expenditure twenty pounds ought and six, result misery.'

The figures are somewhat out of date and the context is different but the underlying thought applies, nevertheless!

Throughout this book there have been references to the ways in which a designer in private practice must comply with the law in general. Apart from stressing once more how essential it will be for you to engage the services of a solicitor to advise and act for you in all legal matters, it may be useful to recapitulate, before dealing with the legal aspects of design itself, the points touched on so far.

Tenancy of premises
There are no laws which insist that you must have a tenancy agreement or lease for any premises which you may rent, but the obvious desirability of having a proper legal agreement drawn up, assuming that one had not previously existed, was explained in Chapter Ten.

Registration of a name
If you decide to practice as a free-lance under anything but your 'true surname', you are required by law to register the alternative as a business name. How to do this was also explained in Chapter Ten.

The Offices Bill
The Offices Shops and Railway Premises Act 1963 lays down certain minimum requirements for premises where employed people are to work. Some of its basic requirements are outlined in Chapter Ten under 'Amenities for your staff' but they will only apply to you as an employer of labour, not if you work quite on your own.

Disabled staff
When your staff reaches a total of twenty, you are required to notify all further vacancies to the relevant office of the Department of Employment and Productivity to give them the opportunity of sending you disabled persons as applicants before you advertise on the open market. This applies until you have a 3% quota of disabled persons on your staff.

Insurances
The only thing which is compulsory in this respect (unless you also drive a car) is the payment of National Insurance. In Chapter Eleven under 'Your overheads', what you must do about stamping National Insurance Cards is

referred to. Chapter Thirteen, under 'National Insurance' explained how to do it.

Income Tax

While there are no legal penalties for failing to send in an annual return of income tax, it was explained in Chapter Thirteen under 'Book-keeping and accounts' what the outcome of this omission would be in terms of heavy financial penalties. It is, however, a breach of the law not to pay your income tax when it has been assessed.

Annual audit of accounts

As explained in Chapter Thirteen, under 'Book-keeping and accounts', you are only required to have your books audited if you have formed yourself into a limited company. In this case, your accountant will explain what must be done.

Retention of correspondence, etc.

It is a requirement of Company Law that all records of financial transactions should be kept for seven years, that is, again, if you have formed yourself into a limited company. In this case also, correspondence is usually kept for the same length of time. This is enlarged upon in Chapter Thirteen under 'Retention of letters and drawings'. The question of retention of drawings is referred to below under 'Copyright'.

Paying bills

It is hardly necessary to point out that the law will sooner or later catch up with you, through creditors who will take you to court, if you do not pay your bills. If you fail to send in your own bills for seven years your clients are not legally required to pay you after that lapse of time.

Financial responsibility

In Chapter Seven it is made clear that if you agree to act as the Principal in respect of placing a contract, instead of as your client's Agent, then you become legally and financially responsible for paying the bill, whether your client reimburses you or not.

All of the above would apply to anybody in business or in a profession. Now we come to those aspects of the law which are of particular significance to a designer.

Safety regulations

In an interior design job, where structural alterations are required, or in any job, interior or exhibition, where the safety of the public is involved — staircases, fire risks, floor loadings, etc., we saw in Chapter Sixteen that there were certain important officials who would be concerned to see that your design complied with the safety regulations. It is essential not to run any risks about this but to submit your drawings in the early stages and get written approvals. You must not start any work on site until you have them.

Planning approvals
In the case of almost any alterations to a building, even the addition of a sign, the approval of the local Planning Officer is also required. His approval must also be obtained if you propose to convert what is scheduled as living or factory accommodation to offices or vice-versa, 'change of use' as it is called.

Patent agents
Before we come to those aspects of design itself which may be affected by the law, another reminder is necessary about the usefulness of including a patent agent in your team of professional and technical advisers. This suggestion was touched on in Chapter Ten and you will see now, as we go further into the problems of copyright and registration, how essential his services will be in certain circumstances. If you need to seek out a patent agent and do not know how to go about it, your solicitor or bank manager could help you or you could write to H.M. Patent Office, (address in the London Telephone Directory). They would send you a free official pamphlet 'Applying for a Patent'. This sets out in great detail what you must do if you intend to apply for a patent yourself but it advises further that 'An application for a patent has to be accompanied by a specification. This is a specialized document which is both legal and technical. Unless he has experience of such documents, the applicant is usually well-advised to employ a patent agent.' You can get a list of registered patent agents by writing to the Secretary of the Chartered Institute of Patent Agents, (address in the London Telephone Directory). Alternatively, if you find a patent agent in your locality by personal recommendation, so much the better.

Types of industrial property
There are four types of 'industrial property' as they are called, with any of which you may be concerned as a designer. These are:
Patents
Registered Designs
Trade Marks
Copyright
Protection for each of these types of industrial property is provided under a separate Act of Parliament, the Acts being:
The Patent Act 1949
The Registered Designs Act 1949
The Trade Marks Act 1938
The Trade Mark Rules 1938 (as amended)
The Copyright Act 1956 (with amendments made to it in a further 'Design Copyright Act' of 1968)

New legislation
But before dealing with each of these, I must warn you that, by the time you are reading this, there is likely to have been new legislation about all of them, including the Whitford Report on 'Copyright and Designs Law.

Patents

Patents are granted for inventions and the definition of invention in the Patents Act includes: 'Any manner of new manufacture and any new method or process of testing applicable to the improvement or control of manufacture'. For your purposes as a designer it will probably be sufficient to say that patents are obtainable for inventions which relate to new articles, devices or machines or new methods of making something where the novelty resides not in the appearance of the article but in its construction, operation or function. It is difficult to define briefly what a patentable invention is but if you feel that you may have devised something novel your solicitor or patent agent would be able to advise you as to whether or not it is likely to be patentable.

There is also a very useful SIAD leaflet: 'Protecting your inventions' which includes a section on 'Employee Inventor's Rights.'

Registered designs

A design is defined as meaning 'features of shape, configuration, pattern or ornament applied to an article by any industrial process or means being features which in the finished article appeal to and are judged solely by the eye, but does not include a method or principle of construction or features of shape or configuration which are dictated solely by the function which the article to be made in that shape or configuration has to perform'. Thus you will see that registered design protection is concerned solely with the appearance of the article and in no way with the manner in which it is made or in which it operates.

Both as regards patents and registered designs the law requires that for valid protection the invention or the design must be new at the date when application to protect it is made at the Patent Office. By 'new' is meant that the invention or design must not have been published or commercially used in the United Kingdom either by you or anyone else before the date of application for protection to the Patent Office. It is therefore of vital importance that, if in your work you produce what may be a design or an invention which you feel ought to be protected, before showing it to anyone else outside your own immediate organization you take steps to protect it in the Patent Office either yourself or by consulting your patent agent and then following his advice. The importance of keeping a new invention or a new design confidential until it has been made the subject of an application for protection cannot be stressed too strongly.

From these brief remarks about patents and registered designs, you will see that it can sometimes happen that you may design an article which could be the subject of both a patent application and a registered design application. For instance, you might be working on a food mixer and in the course of your work devise some mechanical improvements in its construction or assembly which could be the subject of a patent application and at the same time you might restyle the mixer as a whole so that its appearance was novel. A patent application could be directed to the mechanical improvements which you have made as applied to all food mixers of any shape or appearance, whilst a design application could be made for the particular appearance of your restyled food mixer either with or without the mechanical improvements which you had also evolved.

If you do wish to protect the appearance of one of your designs, it would be best for you to seek professional advice so that you can be sure of taking the proper steps in accordance with whatever the law requires.

Again there is a very useful SIAD leaflet: 'Protecting your inventions' which includes a section on 'Employee Inventor's Rights.'

Trade marks

A trade mark may be either a word or words or a device or symbol or possibly both, the purpose of which is to indicate to the public a connection in the course of trade between goods in relation to which the mark is used and the proprietor of the trade mark. In order to register trade marks an application for registration has to be made and such applications, as for patent applications and registered design applications, are all dealt with by different departments of HM Patent Office.

You may often be commissioned by a client either to re-design or restyle an existing 'device trade mark' or to produce an entirely new device trade mark for him. If you are concerned with restyling an existing trade mark it is possible that your client will wish to re-register it in its new form and he will probably arrange to do this himself. You would then submit your design to him before preparing the final art work so that he or his patent agent can consider whether any new registration is necessary and can tell you whether any change or re-design is necessary.

If, however, he has asked you to design for him an entirely new device or symbol as a trade mark for subsequent registration, how are you to know whether the device which you will invent will be acceptable for registration or whether you may unconsciously get dangerously near to someone else's mark? The answer is that you cannot know, nor can anybody else. You must go through the recognized but somewhat tedious and expensive drill of preparing designs, having your client make his choice, having your, or his, patent agent make a search to see if the selected device would be acceptable for registration and then if so, preparing the finished art work, with meticulous attention to any registration requirements which may have been indicated as a result of the search. But if not acceptable, then you will have to start all over again and for this you would have to earn further fees.

To a client who had never previously had a registered trade mark or any mark at all, it would be necessary for you to explain this procedure to him at the time of quoting fees and to indicate that there would, of course, be patent agents' fees to be paid as well as your own design fees. He would probably appreciate your offer to look after all this for him through your patent agent, if he had not one of his own. The search could be instigated by you, and the fees for it paid by you on your client's behalf and re-charged to him; but the final registration of a successful mark would have to be in the name of your client.

And up comes our old friend and ally again: the Patent Office issues a pamphlet entitled 'Applying for a Trade Mark' (1975) to complete a trilogy which every designer should have on file. (Again see Bibliography on page 229.)

Copyright

Copyright is a form of protection available to writers and artists which allows them to prevent others from copying their own work. Copyright applies to the whole of the field of literature and the arts and includes books, articles, poems, music, painting, drawings, etching, photographs, sculpture, architectural designs, maps and other forms of artistic creation. The Copyright Law permits the author or artist to prevent others from copying his work, but it does not give the artist or author any monopoly in the particular work so that if two artists quite independently of one another paint precisely the same picture or design the same chair, neither can prevent the other from publishing his own work, although both would have copyright in their own work as against any third parties who wished to copy it.

The most important question in all forms of industrial property is of course to know to whom the invention, design, trade mark device or copyright work belongs. Fundamentally all the rights will belong to the author, artist, designer or inventor who by his own brain and hand has produced the original work. This fundamental right, however, is subjected to any contractual obligations which you may have entered into before executing the work or which you may enter into afterwards. If you are employed as a salaried designer or inventor the rights in your work may well belong to your employer in consideration of the salary which he pays you, whether you are producing valuable work or not. The law relating to the property in an invention, design, or copyright is quite complex and the ownership of the rights in your work can be effected by a written or verbal agreement and by terms in such an agreement which are either expressed precisely or are only implied. If you are in any doubt as to whether the rights in your work belong to you or to your employer or to your client you should always seek professional advice.

If you are a free-lance designer all the rights in the work which you do will automatically belong to you subject to any arrangement which there may be with the client who commissions you. This being the case it is essential for you to reach prior agreement with the client who commissions you *before you start work* so that both he and you know precisely what he is paying you to do and to whom the result of your work will belong.

It is really quite simple—either you retain the copyright completely, or you assign it completely or in part. Which of these alternatives you adopt will vary, if you are going to follow established practice, according to the type of job.

On page 51 in Chapter Three 'Writing letters about fees' I have dealt at some length with the way in which the ownership and conveyance of copyright must be dealt with in your fee letters and the various alternatives normally applicable in different fields of design. There is no point therefore in repeating the information here.

In spite of all this excellent advice, the basic facts remain—the copyright of your original designs as a free-lance designer remains your own, to do what you like with. But of course, unless you are going to produce and market yourself everything you design, you will almost invariably assign your copyright to your client.

When you have assigned your copyright for a single or restricted use only, you are entitled to receive back your original artwork if you wish. If you have made over the full copyright, then of course your client retains your originals and can use them in any way he chooses. He can even alter them, provided he does not do so to the detriment of your reputation. If this should happen, you can sue him for damages. If you are interested to know much more about this complex subject than I have room for here or the sufficiently detailed knowledge even to include it, try reading the excellent book *Copyright in Industrial Designs* by A. D. Russell-Clarke (see *Bibliography*). It is written by a barrister who has specialized in the subject for years and is the standard text-book. In spite of its excellence however I hope it will serve to strengthen my plea that you should seek expert advice as soon as you are faced with a copyright problem.

The copyright of photographs
Since it is assumed that you, as a reader of this book, are a designer and not a photographer, it may be useful to outline the copyright pitfalls which you must avoid in using other people's photographs, which you may often have to do in designing exhibitions, displays and all sorts of things for reproduction in print. The photographer, amateur or professional, who takes a photograph with his own camera, using plate or film which he has bought himself and because he wants to and not because he is being paid by someone else, is the absolute owner of both the negative and the copyright. If you want to reproduce a print from his negative you *must* pay him his quoted reproduction or copyright fee. This will be for one use only and may vary according to whether the photograph is to appear once in a short-term exhibition or to be reproduced many times in a locally, nationally or internationally distributed publication. It is fatally easy, in the pressure of photograph selection for say, a big thematic exhibition or illustrated publication, when you or your client may have assembled dozens of photoprints from agencies, libraries and museums, to rush through into production with the finally chosen pictures and forget to clear the copyright on each. Watch out too, for the prints which will inevitably come in, probably from private sources, without any identification on the back. One mixed in with the rest of the batch all hope of knowing where they came from is lost until, if you reproduce one and the owner recognizes it, you are threatened with an action for infringement of copyright.

So as your batches of prints come in, check their identities on the backs and add what may be necessary. When your final choice is made agree with your client whether you or he should clear the copyright position on each. If you are to do it, ask the owner of each print in writing if you may reproduce it, telling him in what form, asking what his fee will be and if there are any other stipulations. Some photographers insist on a credit caption as well as a reproduction fee. Some insist on themselves providing whatever enlargement you require. All these conditions must be met otherwise you will be in trouble. On the other hand there are a number of people and organizations whose photography of their work is only a side-line and not a revenue-earning activity. They are often content to allow the free use of a photograph in return for a credit caption. In such circumstances it would be a considerable discourtesy to omit the credit line.

If you commission a photographer to take a photograph for you, even of your own work, he still retains the ownership of the negative even though you own the copyright. However, he may not supply a print from the negative to anybody except you, without first getting your permission. Photographs of your work, which you have commissioned, could earn you a copyright fee from any publication wishing to reproduce them. It would be foolish to insist on this however since to get them published suitably is the best publicity you can hope for. You can however insist on a credit caption if you know they are to be used rather indirectly as far as your work is concerned. Someone who is going to write an illustrated article on 'The Design of Tea-Pots' can reasonably be expected to credit designers' names with the photographs since design is the subject of the article. But for an article on 'Tea drinking down the ages' a photograph of your tea-pot might well go unacknowledged since it is being used to illustrate a different theme. You can prevent this happening by rubber-stamping on the back of every photograph of your own which you send out 'No reproduction fee provided this photograph is credited to . . .' and add your name or title as you would wish it to be printed, with that of your client too, if necessary.

Plagiarism

According to the *Concise Oxford Dictionary*, to plagiarize is to take and use another person's thoughts, writings, or inventions as one's own. The word derives, very suitably, from the Latin *plagiare*, to kidnap. In the SIAD's Code of Professional Conduct, Clause 18 states that 'The Society regards copying or plagiarism as wholly unprofessional.' It does not seem necessary to enlarge upon that quite definite directive.

Arbitration

If you find yourself in dispute with a client about your contract with him whereby both of you seem convinced of the validity of your claims, it is possible, after discussion with your solicitor, to 'take the matter to arbitration'. This is a process covered by the Arbitration Act of 1950 whereby both sides agree on an arbitrator, sit round the table with him (accompanied by the relevant solicitors if desired) and state their cases and their points of view. There will have been prior mutual agreement to abide by the judgment of the arbitrator.

The process is usually quicker and sometimes less expensive than taking the dispute to court.

Summary

This Chapter has only touched on the problems of registration, patents and copyright and contract disputes, all extremely complex subjects needing the advice of legal experts in case of difficulty. A layman's book which advises you how to try and keep healthy may be a good thing; one which aims to tell you how to cure yourself if you are ill is to be deplored: that is the job of a qualified doctor.

I have only tried to show you how to start off at any rate with a healthy copyright situation by agreeing and confirming before you start work who is to be the copyright owner of the work you will produce. Ninety-nine times there will be no problem. The hundredth time there may be. Then you should go straight to your patent agent or solicitor.

Bibliography

Annuals, magazines, etc
The Advertisers' Annual, Business Publications Limited
Crafts, published by the Design Council for the Crafts Advisory Committee
Design, Design Council, monthly
Designer, Society of Industrial Artists and Designers, monthly
Engineering, Design Council, monthly
Writers' and Artists' Year Book, Adam and Charles Black

Books
The Architect in Practice, Arthur J. Willis and W. N. B. George, Crosby Lockwood, fourth edition (metric) 1970
Architectural Practice and Procedure, Hamilton H. Turner, B. T. Batsford 1960
The Complete Plain Words, Sir Ernest Gowers, Penguin Books 1962
Copyright in Industrial Designs, A. D. Russell-Clarke, 1968 Tiranti
Group Practice in Design, Michael Middleton, The Architectural Press 1967
Reports and how to write them, H. A. Shearing and B. C. Christian, George Allen and Unwin Limited 1967
Writing Technical Reports, Bruce M. Cooper, Penguin Books, 1964
Your Business Matters, Frederick A. J. Coundrey, ACA, AACCA, ACCS and Allen J. G. Sheppard, Bsc(Econ), FREconS, ACCS, John Murray 1958

Official Pamphlets (many of these are free)
Applying for a Trade Mark, the Patent Office 1975
Applying for a Patent, The Patent Office 1969
The Copyright Act 1956, Her Majesty's Stationery Office
The Design Copyright Act 1968, Her Majesty's Stationery Office
The Employer's Guide to Pay-as-you-earn, issued by the Board of Inland Revenue
The Protection of Industrial Designs, The Patent Office 1975
The Registered Designs Act 1949, Her Majesty's Stationery Office
Registration of Business Names—Notes for guidance on, Department of Trade, Registry of Business Names

SIAD pamphlets
Prospectus 1982
Protecting your inventions 1981
Protecting your designs 1980
Code of Professional Conduct 1976
Protecting your designs 1980
Code of Professional Conduct 1976

229

RSA   The Royal Society of Arts
Address   John Adam Street   Adelphi   London WC2
Telephone   01-839-2366
'The Society for the Encouragement of Arts, Manufactures and Commerce' (the prefix 'Royal' was granted in 1908) was founded in 1754 by William Shipley, a Northamptonshire drawing master with the object of stimulating industry and invention by means of prize competitions. These were applied as a spur to progress in Britain and her possessions overseas for nearly 100 years, but since the 1840s the Society's mission has been predominantly educative— the increase of knowledge, the refinement of taste, and the advancement of skills. The Society was responsible for the first exhibitions of art in industry to be held in this country, and for initiating the Great Exhibition of 1851.

The Society is third in seniority amongst the learned Societies of England.

The aims of the Society are the advancement, development, and application of every department of Science in connection with arts, manufactures, and commerce. It serves as a liaison between the various practical arts and sciences, and provides a medium for the announcement by leading authorities of recent developments of more than specialized interest.

The Society also exists as a potential agent for the inception of tasks of public service which do not fall very definitely within the scope of any more specialized body. Its function in such cases, however, is purely that of a pioneer, its policy being to hand over schemes requiring permanent superintendence to some other appropriate institution.

Ordinary Meetings for the reading of papers are held regularly on Wednesdays from November to May. A wide range of subjects—artistic, scientific and technical—is dealt with in the course of each session. The papers are followed by a discussion.

Courses of Lectures of an expository and semi-technical character are delivered on Mondays. Normally, three courses of three lectures each are given during the Session.

Commonwealth Section   The Commonwealth Section holds meetings during each Session at which papers are read on subjects covering a variety of Commonwealth problems and developments.

Royal Designers for Industry   The Society in 1936 established the exclusive distinction known as 'Royal Designer for Industry' (Designer for Industry of the Royal Society of Arts), and designated by the letters RDI. This honour, conferred by the Council of the Society, is strictly limited, and is recognized as the highest distinction to be obtained in the field of industrial design.

Examinations The Society was the originator of commercial and technological examinations in this country, and still holds a foremost position in connection with the former, which, instituted in 1856, are now held periodically throughout the British Isles, mainly in commercial/office skills and languages at levels ranging from elementary to postgraduate.

Industrial Design Bursaries An annual Competition is held for the award of Bursaries and Attachment Awards to enable young British designers, primarily in colleges, either to travel abroad to study foreign design at first hand or to spend a period of working experience with the sponsoring body.

Presidential Awards for Design Management—These awards were instituted in 1964 to recognize every two years outstanding examples of design policy in British firms and public undertakings in this country, under British control.

Environment The Society usually organizes at least two major conferences and several smaller seminars annually on issues, trends and developments affecting the environment.

Music A scheme of awards to young professional singers and string players, holding British or Commonwealth citizenship, provides financial assistance for advanced studies.

Improvement of Navigation To assist the Science of Navigation and to promote the educational interests of the British Merchant Navy, the Council offers annual prizes, and makes numerous awards, under the Thomas Gray Memorial Trust.

Fellowship The privileges enjoyed by Fellows of the Society include the receipt of the monthly Journal, the use of the Society's House, the loan of books from the Library, the right of attending all Meetings and Lectures, and of taking part in the government of the Society. Fellows may also introduce visitors to meetings of the Society.

Candidates for election to Fellowship of the Society must ordinarily be proposed by three Fellows, one of whom, at least, must sign on personal knowledge.

Associate membership is open, under the same conditions of election as for Fellows, to persons not over the age of 25.

Trading companies may be admitted into association with the Society.

Associated Institutions Schools, colleges, libraries, literary and scientific institutions or other organizations whose primary object is the promotion of arts, manufactures and commerce, may be admitted into union with the Society and enjoy most of the privileges of individual membership.

DIA The Design and Industries Association
National headquarters 17 Lawn Crescent   Kew Gardens   Surrey
Telephone 01-940-4925
The DIA was founded in 1915. It is a free and independent society of companies, institutions and individuals which exists to promote functional and pleasing design. It is concerned with all aspects of the human environment, whether public or domestic, including buildings and landscape, transport and

household appliances, shops and their merchandise and visual communications of all kinds.

As well as conferences, exhibitions and overseas study tours, the DIA holds more than 100 meetings a year throughout the country.

SIAD   The Society of Industrial Artists and Designers
From February 1987 **The Chartered Society of Designers**
Address   29 Bedford Square, London WC1B 3EG
Telephone   01-631 1510

Introduction
The Society of Industrial Artists and Designers, founded in 1930, was the first society of its kind in the world. It is today the world's largest and most comprehensive association of designers with a membership of over 6000, concerned with consumer products, textiles, engineering design, fashion, visual communications, exhibitions and interior design. The Society's standing as the leading professional design organization in Britain was recognized by the grant of a Royal Charter in 1976.

In private practice or salaried employment the Society's members are working in industry and commerce, for local and national government and in the fields of entertainment. They are united in their concern for the visual aspects of design, in applying their creative faculties to the solution of design problems and in their attention to the details involved in translating conceptions into actuality. They are not only concerned with designing but also with design management, planning and education.

The Society is concerned with standards of competence, professional conduct and integrity. It makes a significant contribution to the establishment of good standards in the field of design education. The Society represents the interests and views of professional designers on other bodies and with government authorities. It promotes the cause of high standards of design for the benefit of the public, industry and commerce.

A professional society
Professionalism means competence and integrity in practice, with an overriding concern for the quality of the environment in which we live and for the needs of the individual: a responsibility not just to the client or employer, but to the user and to society as a whole.

All Corporate Members of the Society will have submitted to the appropriate assessment board, evidence of work of a high standard successfully carried through to the production stage. Applications are also accepted for noncorporate Diploma membership principally through assessment at college under the Society's Direct Admission Scheme for students taking SIAD approved vocational courses and the Direct Nomination Scheme for BA and MA graduates who are accepted with assessment on the recommendation of their colleges. Associate members are those working at a high level in management or education, making a valuable contribution to the design profession while not being practising designers.

233

High standards of behaviour are axiomatic and to ensure that the affixes of membership are a meaningful symbol, the Society lays down a code of professional conduct. Observance of this code is a condition of membership, and those who infringe it may be reprimanded, suspended or expelled. In the widest sense, behaviour includes a concern for the continuing development of knowledge and skills which future generations of industrial designers must acquire.

Organization of the Society

The Society is incorporated by Royal Charter. Its Bye-Laws provide for the management of the Society by a Council, elected annually by and from the membership; this is supported by a series of Boards, standing committees and Groups, covering the sectional interests of the members and the six geographical regions. A small team of salaried staff, which is responsible to Council through the Director, co-ordinates the voluntary work of the members.

The Boards cover matters concerning membership, professional practice, international relations, education and training, information, the regional groups and the SIAD Trust. Seven specialist Groups look after the particular interests of the categories of practice in which the members are registered. Through its regional groups, the Society spreads its activities throughout the country. The Council's committees and working parties ensure that the Society's members at all levels have the opportunity to fulfil an active role in formulating policies and initiating action.

Activities of the Society

In all fields the Society has established high standards of admission. Successful applicants are elected to the grades of Diploma membership, Membership, Associateship or Fellowship; details of the application procedures are given elsewhere in this prospectus. Responsibility for the review of admission requirement and the administration of the various procedures for entry to the Society is vested in the Membership Board, which organizes the regular Assessment Boards and the student assessments, calling on the body of the membership to provide assessors with the expert knowledge necessary to assist adjudication in the many specialized fields in which applicants work.

To foster a mutually satisfactory relationship between members and their clients or employers, the Society publishes a code of conduct that is binding on all members. This aspect of the Society's work is the responsibility of the Professional Practice Board and on behalf of Council it investigates any alleged infringement of the code and recommends any necessary action that Council should take. The Board also deals with such matters as industrial relations and trade union questions, registration, methods of charging, salaries and competitions.

The Society will, when requested, recommend qualified adjudicators for design competitions and assist organizers in the drafting of regulations to ensure that they are mutually acceptable.

One of the Society's aims is to ensure that an adequate number of graduates come from the schools and colleges of art and design and that they are sufficiently well trained to complete their later development into practising designers of competence and skill. The responsibility for this rests with the Education and Training Board. The membership provides a reservoir from which are drawn many of the full-time and part-time teaching staff and governors of colleges and polytechnics. The Society is also called upon to assist in the deliberations of official committees and panels concerned with design education.

The promotion of the understanding and use of good design is encouraged through the independent magazine published by the Society—*Designer*—sent monthly to all members, and through the publication of specialized literature. The SIAD Medal is awarded annually for particular distinction in design and focuses attention on outstanding achievement which can stand for the aspirations of the whole profession. Honorary Fellowships are awarded to individuals who have made a significant contribution to the design profession, though not as practising designers. Lectures, open to members of the public, are arranged from time to time on topics relevant to designers and the profession. There are annual lectures for schoolchildren covering careers in art and design and the Society also stages design conventions and exhibitions in the regions where there is local demand.

These regional events are directed by elected regional Councils under the overall co-ordination of the Regional Board.

The Society's International Relations Board co-ordinates activities with the international design bodies. The SIAD is a founder member of the International Council of Societies of Industrial Design (ICSID) and the International Council of Graphic Design Associations (ICOGRADA) and is the British representative member of the International Federation of Interior Designers (IFI). It plays an active part in the work of the Bureau of European Designers' Associations (BEDA) and the European Committee of Interior Architects (ECIA), the liaison bodies for designers within the EEC.

Through its Designers' Register, the Society provides the names of members suitable for freelance commissions or salaried employment. A visible record of members' work is available to assist those seeking the services of a designer.

The SIAD Colour Group was formed to bring together people from all sectors of industry to promote the more effective use of colour as a vital factor in the profitable marketing of products and services. Members of the Group are drawn from both outside and within the SIAD.

Grades of membership

Membership of the SIAD is open to all who can satisfy its entry requirements. The SIAD provides a professional not an academic qualification for designers. There are two classes of membership: Corporate and non-corporate. Corporate Membership which carries with it the full rights of a Chartered Designer, including an affix and a vote at general meetings, comprises the grades of Fellow (FSIAD) and Member (MSIAD). The non-corporate grades

(Associate and Diploma member) do not carry with them an affix or vote at general meetings, but in all other respects these members are expected to play a full part in the Society's affairs. Entry may be by assessment or sponsorship as appropriate.

Applications should be made in one or more of the categories of practice recognised by the Society, from product design, through fashion, textiles, interiors, exhibitions, graphics, photography and engineering, to design management and education. Appropriate application forms may be obtained from the Membership Secretary. Application, entrance and yearly sub- scription fees are payable as prescribed by the Society's Bye-Laws.

Diploma membership

This is a grade of membership, replacing the previous Licentiateship (LSIAD), for young designers who have the potential to become professional designers of a high standard, though they are as yet unable to furnish evidence of the reproduced work required for full Membership. Applicants must have a good standard of general education (usually five GCE 'O' levels) and be 21 years of age or over when they take up membership. Diploma membership may be held for not more than seven years, before the end of which period full Membership must be applied for.

Applicants may seek election:

1 Through the SIAD Direct Admission Scheme for students successfully completing a vocational course or courses totalling four year's full-time design study; or the Direct Nomination Scheme for BA and MA graduates. Application may be made in the candidate's final year, through the college concerned.

2 Through the Society's twice-yearly Assessment Boards. Practising de- signers with more than eighteen months' professional experience and who are less than 30 years of age may make application by presentation of work. The requirements are the same as for full Membership except that the submission need not refer to finished work.

Membership

This grade of membership is open to designers in industry and commerce, aged over 24 and with a good standard of general education (usually five GCE 'O' levels) who have been in practice for a minimum of five years and who have attained the necessary standard of professional competence in one or more of the categories of practice recognised by the Society. Application is made by presentation of work. Election gives rights to the affix MSIAD, to be called a Chartered Designer and to vote in general meetings.

Associateship

Associateship is a class of membership for those who, though working at a high level in design management or design education, are not and have not been practising designers. (It should be noted that practising designers who also

236

work in these fields may be eligible for full Membership or Fellowship in either of these two categories.) They must be at least 26 years of age, have a good standard of general education (usually five GCE 'O' levels) and have held a position of responsibility in design management or design education for at least five years.

The applicant in design management should have been continuously engaged for not less than five years in a position of responsibility for, and control of, the work of designers employed or retained by a design office, industrial or commercial organization or Government Department.

The applicant in design education should have been continuously engaged for not less than five years in a position of substantial responsibility in Further or Higher Education.

Application is by sponsorship from three existing Members/Fellows or, in the case of design education applications, two Members/Fellows and an Associate. The Fellowship and Associateship Committee may also wish to interview applicants.

Fellowship

Fellowship is granted to designers, aged at least 26 and with a minimum of seven years' professional experience, whose standards of performance and professional behaviour have demonstrated their eminence.

Existing Members may be sponsored by three Fellows of three years' standing or, alternatively, Members who have been in practice for at least ten years may apply for interview with the Fellowship and Associateship Committee.

Similarly qualified non-members may also be eligible for Fellowship. They may not make application themselves, but may be sponsored by three existing Fellows. From time to time the Assessment Board may also recommend an outstanding candidate for direct election to Fellowship.

Categories

Each member of the Society is registered in one or more of the following categories. These are grouped under a number of Sections, each of which has a committee to safeguard the interests of its members. The categories are intended primarily as an aid to administration and as an indication of the scope of the Society. They help in matching assessor to applicant, ensure that specialist literature reaches interested members and identify possible helpers in new Society projects.

Section A: product design
A1   Engineering-based products
A2   Furniture
A3   Craft-based products
A4   Automotive design

Section B: fashion and textile design
B1   Fashion and clothing

B2   Surface pattern
B3   Textiles

Section C: inscape design
C1   Exhibition and display
C2   Domestic, commercial and industrial interiors
C3   Television, film and theatre design

Section D: graphic design
D1   Typography, lettering and calligraphy
D2   Illustration
D3   Design for advertising and for print
D4   Corporate identity and signing systems
D5   Photography, audio-visual and tv/film graphics

Section E: engineering design
Section F: design education
Section G: design management

The SIAD Code of Professional Conduct
Introduction
1 This Code issued by the Society of Industrial Artists and Designers
    establishes a workable pattern of professional conduct for the benefit of its
    members and of those who employ their services.
2 All Members of the Society undertake as a condition of membership that
    they will abide by this Code.
    (*Note: This Code applies to all members, whether they are working on their
    own, are principals in private practice employing both member and non-
    member staff, are employed by a member or non-member in private practice
    or are employed in industry, commerce or the public service. It also applies
    to all members who may also be manufacturers, retailers or agents.
    Members should ensure that their non-member staff observe this Code.*)
3 The Council of the Society has empowered its Conduct Committee to
    question any member thought to be behaving in a manner contrary to this
    Code and may, as a result of the Committee's Report, reprimand, suspend
    or expel that member.
    (*Note: A member has the right to appeal direct to Council through the
    Executive Secretary, should he be dissatisfied with the Committee's
    findings.*)
4 When members are working or seeking work abroad they will observe the
    rules of professional conduct currently in use in that country.

The Designer's Professional Responsibilities
5 Designers work primarily for the benefit of their clients or their employers.
    Like everyone engaged in professional activities, designers have re-
    sponsibilities not only to their clients or employers but also to their fellow

practitioners and to society at large. It follows therefore that designers who are members of the Society accept certain obligations specifically in regard to these responsibilities.

The Designer's Responsibilities to his Client or Employer

6 Good professional relations between a designer and his employer or client depend on the designer's acceptance of the need to be professionally and technically competent and on his ability to provide honourable and efficient advice and performance.

7 They will also depend on the reliance which the employer or client can place on a designer's integrity in all confidential matters relating to his business.

8 No member may work simultaneously for more than one employer or client known to be in competition, without their knowledge and approval. Similarly no member, or his associates or staff, may divulge information confidential to his client or employer without their consent, subject to any requirement under law.

(*Note: Nor should a member have an interest in any business which might breach this principle.*)

9 The Society believes that it is in the interest of the design profession and of industry that the employment of qualified designers should be increased. Members may therefore promote their own services and those of their profession in a manner appropriate to the various fields of practice in which they work. It is essential however, that any claims made by them or by those acting for them, are factually correct, honourable and clear as to their origin and that the effect shall not be at variance with this Code nor cause harm to their fellow members.

10 It is normal for designers to be paid for their professional services, whether executive or advisory. But whether members work for a fee, a salary or an honorarium must ultimately depend upon the circumstances provided always that members shall not use the offer of reduced charges to gain an advantage over their fellow members to obtain work or some other professional benefit.

(*Note: In certain circumstances a member may make no charge to a charitable or non-profit-making organization, provided that by doing so he gains no advantage over a fellow member.*)

11 The Society recommends methods of charging which it considers appropriate for various types of work but members will use their own judgment in agreeing fees with their clients.

12 The Society recommends conditions of engagement to enable proper working relationships to be established between members and their clients.

13 Whereas a member will make for his client the best possible trading arrangements with contractors, manufacturers and suppliers, his responsibility to contractors or suppliers is as professionally important as is his responsibility to his client. He must therefore be prepared to act as

impartial arbitrator, if need be, to ensure fair dealing on both sides.

14 Whilst acting for his client, a member may not divert to his own advantage any discounts, reductions or other financial benefits offered as inducement by contractors, manufacturers or suppliers. Similarly a member must disclose any financial involvement which he may have with contractors or suppliers he may recommend.

    (*Note: Members should avoid putting themselves under an obligation to contractors or suppliers by the acceptance of lifts or other benefits if by so doing they could prejudice the impartial nature of their professional advice to their client.*)

15 On the other hand, if a member is also a manufacturer, retailer or agent in his own right, he may accept those financial terms which are normally honourably offered within the trade, provided they accrue to his company or his organization and not to himself privately.

    (*Note: It is common practice for graphic designers, whilst acting as print buyers for their clients, to benefit from discounts offered by the trade. The Society regards such a practice as permissible but members should keep their clients fully informed on any arrangements they may make with the trade. Where a member does not enjoy such a discount, he may invoice his client for a print-handling charge, in addition to his design fee. In all such cases it is advisable that matters of this kind are agreed between members and their clients at the commencement of each job.*)

16 Although the relationship between a staff designer and his employer may well differ from that between consultant and client, the employed designer who is a member of the Society, shall accept a responsibility to his employer on the same terms of professional integrity and confidentiality.

The Designer's Responsibility to his Fellow Designers

17 From time to time members may find themselves called upon to comment on other designers' work and in a consultative capacity may reasonably be expected to do so. Personal opinion must play a significant part in any criticism but members should be aware of the fine dividing line between objective and destructive criticism. Personal denigration amongst members is regarded as intolerable and the Society will support any member who is shown to have been so affronted.

    (*Note: Members should beware of the dangers of denigration inherent in the act of swearing an affidavit, honourably undertaken on behalf of a client or another. Under no circumstances should a member agree a legalistic form of words, set down by a legal adviser, unless the member is wholly satisfied that they properly represent his professional judgment. The Society possesses evidence of the effect of just such a situation. Should a member be in the slightest doubt that his professional judgment may be misinterpreted in writing, he should seek the advice of the Executive Secretary before committing himself.*)

18 Similarly the Society regards copying or plagiarism with intent as wholly unprofessional.

19 There are occasions when more than one designer may be engaged on the same project. Where, however, a member suspects that his engagement may supplant rather than augment the service of another, he shall seek an assurance from the client that any previous association with another designer has been terminated. Similarly no member shall knowingly seek to supplant another designer currently working on a project whether satisfactorily or not.

20 Neither shall a member charge or receive a fee, neither make nor receive a gift or other benefit, from a fellow member in recognition of a recommendation to a post or an assignment.
    (*Note: the giving and receiving of gifts are difficult acts on which to give advice and therefore the Code makes no specific judgment other than that set out in this Clause. In general terms, the Society advises its members, if indeed that is necessary, to be aware of the motives behind such acts. Where there is the slightest risk that the result of accepting a gift or benefit could place a member in a position of unprofessional obligation to the donor, then that gift should be refused.*)

21 Members should assure themselves that competitions they may be invited to assess or may wish to enter are in accordance with the Society's regulations for holding of design competitions.
    (*Note: Under certain circumstances the Society may find the published rules of a competition acceptable in principle even though they may not conform in every detail to the Society's own regulations. This may well happen when the sponsors are unaware of the Society's interest in design competitions. It is essential therefore that members should confirm with the Executive Secretary the standing of a competition, in the Society's view, before becoming involved in it. There are occasions when, in the interest of informed design judgment, it is better for the Society to be represented by a member on a judging panel, than to have no say in the judgment, even though the Society may not have been able to give the competition its official blessing.*)

The Designer's Responsibility to Society

22 Since design is properly regarded as being a professional activity, a designer's work may be expected to contain a degree of social benefit in addition to client satisfaction. It follows therefore that the Society expects from its members an acceptance of the social responsibility and an understanding that this responsibility accords with the concept of professionalism expressed in this Code.

Notes for members on Clause 9

9 Subject always to the conditions contained in Clause 9 members may for example engage in the following promotional activities.

9.1 They may submit, invited or uninvited, signed articles or features for publication with illustrations on design in general or on their own work in particular. They may also make an appearance at a public meeting, on radio or

TV to talk about design in general or about their own work in particular.

9.2 They may write to existing and potential clients drawing attention to their services.

9.3 They may publish and distribute to existing and potential clients, printed material in leaflet, brochure or book form giving information about their work and their practice.

9.4 They may mount exhibitions of their own work or that of their practice either in a public place hired for the purpose or in their own premises. They may also participate in public exhibitions organized by professional, commercial or charitable organizations.

9.5 Members may take paid space in any medium promoting their services, including local, regional, national and trade press, commercial radio and TV, trade and professional directories including normal listing or semi- and full-display, and films.

9.6 Members may employ the services of an agent to sell their work on their behalf or a public relations consultant to promote their services. It is the established custom for illustrators, graphic designers and textile designers to engage the services of artists' agents, since that is a practice accepted by the trades in which they operate.

9.7 Members should ensure that their agents, or whoever may be acting on their behalf, also observe these conditions and that they act with the same propriety as would the members themselves.

Members should avoid a situation in which they may be seen to be responsible for such promotion although the cost is in fact defrayed by their client or another.

Members should ensure that their clients adhere to the same patterns of behaviour set down in this Code concerning advertising which may involve them or their work. They should not, under any circumstances, agree to their name or professional affiliation being associated with any promotional activities of which they or the Society may disapprove.

Under no circumstances shall members seek to disguise paid advertising as unsolicited editorial comment, nor by employing the services of another to promote their own services, shall they seek to hide the true source of that promotion.

Members are advised to refer to 'The British Code of Advertising Practice' published by the Advertising Standards Authority for guidance on what is regarded as fair and reasonable advertising. They should also consult similar codes published by the Institute of Practitioners in Advertising, the British Board of Television Advertising and the Advertising Association.

9.8 Work produced by members when working as employees or members of an organization is normally attributable to that organization.

Members should not, at any time, claim authorship of work produced in these circumstances without consent from the organization concerned.

The Design Council
London address The Design Centre 28 Haymarket London SW1Y 4SU
Telephone 01-839-8000

Glasgow address   The Scottish Design Centre   72 St Vincent Street
Glasgow G2 5TN
Telephone   041-221-6121

About The Design Council
The Design Council is a Government-sponsored body set up to 'promote by all practicable means the improvement of design in the products of British industry'. It receives through its sponsoring department (the Department of Trade and Industry) a grant-in-aid and earns a substantial proportion of its budget from its services, from the sale of publications, from its programme of marketing assistance, and from sponsored projects.
Policy is determined by the unpaid members of Council appointed by the Secretary of State for Trade and Industry. The Council is advised by various committees and working parties, and employs about 280 staff. It is incorporated by Royal Charter and is a registered charity.

Design Advisory Service
The Design Council helps, through its Design Advisory Service, companies over a wide spectrum of manufacturing industry. The Design Advisory Service is largely concerned with the transfer of up-to-date technology and design skills from where they exist to where they can be applied to produce goods that will compete with the best anywhere in the world. Design Advisory Officers, who are experienced engineers or industrial designers, visit companies throughout the United Kingdom to help in diagnosing design problems, and in finding the right organizations or individuals with the knowledge or experience to solve them.

Design Centre Selection
The Council selects well designed British products as one of the means of providing information for managers, designers and the public. Consumer and contract goods are chosen regularly by independent selection committees to form the Design Centre Selection, an illustrated record of modern British products of above-average design merit. The Selection is continually revised and updated. Before acceptance, products are checked to ensure compliance, where relevant, with British Standards and safety regulations, and to ensure that other functional and user aspects are satisfactory. Such products are then eligible to carry the Design Centre label.

Design Centres
The Design Centres in London and Glasgow provide continuing but changing exhibitions of new developments in design in the consumer, contract and engineering fields. Aimed at the public, trade buyers, industrialists and people professionally interested in design, the programme includes exhibitions on a variety of subjects or themes, and an annual review of all products selected for The Design Centre during the previous year.

Overseas displays

The Design Council co-operates with the Foreign and Commonwealth Office and the Central Office of Information in mounting occasional exhibitions of well designed British goods overseas.

Design Council Awards

The Council also appoints special judging panels to choose the annual Design Council Awards. The awards represent the outstanding design achievements of British industry each year, and seldom are more than 30 products chosen. The majority are for engineering products in various categories, but awards are also given for consumer and contract goods—chosen largely from products already accepted for The Design Centre. After the awards have been decided, the chairmen of the selection panels meet under HRH The Duke of Edinburgh's chairmanship to choose one product of exceptional merit from all the awards—the designer of which receives the coveted Duke of Edinburgh's Designer's Prize.

Education

The Council plays an important role in education by making recommendations on the training of engineering and industrial designers by promoting the study of design in schools for pupils in general, by providing advice on careers in design and by administering a number of prize schemes. It is represented on a number of advisory committees and governing bodies in the educational area.

Publications

The Council produces a number of periodicals and books on design subjects. The monthly magazine DESIGN covers every aspect of industrial design in Britain and abroad and is of considerable interest to overseas readers. *Engineering* magazine, which is also published monthly, concentrates on providing technical information of value to engineering designers. *Designing* is a magazine published termly for pupils in secondary schools. The Council also publishes a range of books on design for professional, technical, educational and general audiences. These, and many other publications concerning design, are available from a comprehensive bookshop in the London Design Centre and by mail order.

Funded Consultancy Scheme

The Design Advisory Service Funded Consultancy Scheme provides specialist help to manufacturing companies wishing to improve their product design. It is operated by The Design Council on behalf of the Department of Trade and Industry.

The assistance available takes the form of a single free design advisory project involving up to 15 man-days' work by a specialist consultant. Subsequently the company may apply for a second project involving 15 man-days' work for which the Design Advisory Service will meet half the cost, the company paying the balance.

ICA   The Institute of Contemporary Arts
Address   Nash House   The Mall   London SW1
Telephone   01-930 0493   Box Office 01-930 3647
Correspondence: 12 Carlton House Terrace   London SW1Y 5AH
The Institute of Contemporary Arts was founded in 1947 to provide a platform for new developments in all the arts. It presents exhibitions, theatre, dance, cinema, concerts, readings, discussions, seminars and lectures. The centre consists of three galleries, two cinemas, a videotheque library, theatre, seminar rooms and a bookshop. The ICA operates a restaurant and bar.

Aims and Activities   The ICA's programme brings together all the arts and encourages experiment in new media. The programme is planned in five sections—Exhibitions; MusICA; Theatre; Lectures, Seminars and Cinema.

Exhibitions   The ICA presents theme exhibitions illuminating central concerns of art and life; group shows of young artists and artists of international standing and one-man shows of artists who have often later been recognized as modern masters. Many of the exhibitions tour Britain and abroad.

Lectures and seminars   Conferences and lecture series are organized around significant issues, often related to other activities in the building. There is also a lunch-time series of literary debate and exploration, where readers and writers can meet.

Performances   As well as performing original experimental works, the theatre programme includes visits by major international companies and mounts several events like Rock Week or The World of Music and Dance.

Cinema   The ICA cinema is an outlet for independently made feature films, often presented in the context of seasons of films spanning the entire history and range of cinema—features, documentaries, silents and the avant-garde in television.

Cinematheque   The First of its kind in Britain, a studio space for showing video, Super' and 16 mm work. An outlet for experimental film and video work. There is also a Video Library with a wide range of interesting and important video work which can be viewed in the cinematheque.

Membership   There are many advantages to be gained by becoming a member of the ICA. Write to the Membership Secretary for information.

ICSID   The International Council of Societies of Industrial Designers
Registered address   45 Avenue Legrand   1050 Brussels   Belgium
Telephone   (2) 648.59.79

The challenge
Industrial designers face increasingly complex problems and opportunities in a world in which dramatic advances are being made in science and technology. Furthermore, economic and social patterns are shifting on a global level that challenges designers to establish networks of communication and co-operation that are committed to the quality of life on this planet.

In response to this challenge the International Council of Societies of Industrial Design (ICSID) was formally established in London in 1957, following earlier meetings that began in Paris in 1953. Since that time ICSID has grown into a global force for design that is directed by an Assembly of 60 professional and promotional societies from 37 countries: Professional organizations defending the interests of professional designers and promotional organizations established and subsidised by the government to devote its efforts to the advancement of industrial design by means of information or promotional activities.

Membership granted to these societies gives participation in ICSID activities and voting rights in the Assembly. In addition, industrial, commercial, research or academic institutions may apply for representation as Associate members. ICSID may also appoint as Patron an individual or organization if such patronage is in accord with the aims of ICSID.

The aims of ICSID

1 To advance the discipline of industrial design as an effective force in meeting the needs and satisfying the aspirations of people throughout the world.
2 To encourage co-operation between individuals, agencies and other related international design organizations that will foster a universal understanding of design.
3 To collect, co-ordinate and disseminate information about industrial design to Council Members as well as to government, industry and the general public.
4 To contribute to the study of international design in theory and practice at academic and research institutions.
5 To stimulate creativity and establish and maintain high standards for quality in design and professional practice.

ICSID activities

Assemblies Council Members send representatives on a biennial basis to an Assembly at which reports are presented describing activities and issues that have been examined by the board of ICSID and its appointed working groups and Commissions. Members of the Assembly review candidates and elect its Board and Officers for the next two years.

Congresses Coincidental with the Assembly the host country stages a Congress based on a theme which is timely and important to designers and society in general. Recent Congresses have been held in Kyoto (1973) 'Soul and Material Things', Moscow (1975), 'Design for Man and Society', Dublin (1977) 'Development and Identity', Mexico City (1977), Industrial Design as a Factor in Human Development' and Helsinki (1981) 'Design Integration.' The Helsinki Congress was co-sponsored by the International Council of Graphic Design Associations (ICOGRADA) and the International Federation of Interior Designers (IFI).

Interdesigns Working Seminars are organized by Council members with endorsement and support from the ICSID Board and Assembly. Each Interdesign is devoted to a general area that deserves unique attention. Participants are mid-career designers gathered from around the world in a host country where they are joined by an equivalent number of designers from that country for a period of two weeks or more to study a problem that is not only of particular interest to the host country but also has international significance. Recent Interdesigns have included Design for Tourism (Ireland), Design for Winter Sports (Austria), Design for Small Industries (Norway), Design for Traffic Safety (Hungary) and Design for the Plastics Industry and Design for the Handicapped (Netherlands). Interdesigns are witnessing an increasing interest among member societies and local authorities and industries for the positive and productive results they bring.

Industrial Design Education ICSID maintains a working group to study issues affecting education and to co-ordinate such studies with other international design organizations. It also organizes international seminars for the purpose of exchanging information on methodology and working toward acceptable international standards in design education.

Competitions, Awards and Exhibitions ICSID will examine and support by endorsement such events as are in the best interest of its Council Members. It also collaborates with ICOGRADA and IFI in developing international standards. From time to time, ICSID develops its own projects in this area.

Publications In addition to a regular newsletter reporting on the activities of its Council Members and other developments affecting industrial design on an international basis, ICSID publishes reports from its Assemblies, Congresses, Interdesigns and working group studies. It also prepares and distributes guidelines on education and professional practices and standards—often in collaboration with other international design organizations.

Additional information about ICSID and its activities, as well as a list of publications, may be obtained from the ICSID Secretariat in Brussels.

ICOGRADA   The International Council of Graphic Design Associations
Secretariat 12 Blendon Terrace Plumstead Common London SE18 7RS   United Kingdom
Telephone   London 01-854-5120

The International Council of Graphic Design Associations was founded in London in April 1963. Its headquarters are in Amsterdam. ICOGRADA is an association of independent Member Associations. Membership is open to societies of professional graphic designers and organizations concerned with the training of designers and/or the raising of graphic design standards.

Member associations are elected at the biennial General Assembly, which elects also the Executive Board, determines policy and over-all activities, and agrees financial arrangements.

The aims of ICOGRADA

1 To raise internationally the standards of graphic design and professional practice by all practicable means.

2 To collect and exchange information on professional, educational and technical matters.

3 To improve graphic design training and to assist the interchange between countries of graphic designers, teachers and students.

4 To organize exhibitions, international assemblies, congresses and symposia, and publish documentation on graphic design and visual communication technology, including a News Bulletin.

5 To act as an international forum for co-operation and exchange of views between designers, organizations representing professionals from allied and other fields and those of commerce and industry.

6 To encourage the better use of graphic design and visual communications as a means to improve understanding between people everywhere.

ICOGRADA has 50 Member Associations in 32 countries.

BEDA   The Bureau of European Designers Associations

Secretariat c/o SIAD, Society of Industrial Artists and Designers   12 Carlton House Terrace   London SW1Y 5AH   United Kingdom

1 Establishment

The Bureau of European Designers Associations (BEDA) unites representative organizations of product designers, graphic designers, environmental designers and interior designers within the EEC countries. BEDA was founded in 1969 by representatives of the professional industrial design societies of Belgium, France, Germany, Italy and the Netherlands, with the British Society of Industrial Artists and Designers as an observer. The increase in membership of the EEC in January 1973 allowed the representative societies in Britain, Denmark and Ireland to become full members. Membership is open to professional societies of all design disciplines within the EEC, subject to the agreement of any existing member societies from the same country.

BEDA societies

Associazione per il Disegno Industriale (ADI), Italy
Bund Deutscher Grafik-Designer (BDG), Federal German Republic
Grafisch Vormgevers Nederland (GVN), Netherlands
Industrielle Designere Danmark (IDD), Denmark
Kring Industriele Ontwerpens (KIO), Netherlands
Society of Designers in Ireland (SI), Ireland
Society of Industrial Artists and Designers (SIAD) United Kingdom
Union des Designers en Belgique (UDB), Belgium
Union Française des Designers Industriels (UFDI), France
Verband Deutscher Industrie-Designer e. V. (VDID), Federal German Republic

A permanent address for BEDA has been provided at the SIAD headquarters in London.

2 The nature of design

The field of activity of design, which includes environmental design, product design and visual communication design, requires exceptional talent and dedication supported by thorough aesthetic, technological and economic analysis, to be devoted to the application of structure, form and colour to systems and materials in the resolution of problems of human needs and environment within the capability of industrial processes.

3 Objects

BEDA was founded with the following objects:

3.1 To ensure permanent liaison between the professional societies of designers within the EEC countries and to act as a liaison committee between them and the authorities of the Community.

3.2 To study the possibility of merging the existing national societies into one European professional organization.

3.3 To undertake together tasks of common interest.

3.4 To exchange information and experience.

4 Aims

The founder members of BEDA recognized the importance of establishing formal coordinating machinery between the design societies in member countries of the Community in view of:

4.1 The need to achieve common conditions of practice throughout the EEC in order to fulfil the requirements of Article 57 of the Treaty of Rome, which provides for the free circulation of services and the right of establishment within the Community.

4.2 The need for collaboration between designers at EEC level to ensure that this relatively new profession can play its proper part in shaping modern European industrial society.

4.3 The opportunity that this would provide for the national societies to benefit from each other's experience, particularly in research projects, studies in professional practice and publications.

5 Organization

BEDA's work is carried out by individual members of the constituent societies or by the societies themselves, alone or in groups. Its tasks are decided on by unanimous agreement between the members at twice yearly meetings, which normally take place in May and November. Chairmanship of the organization rotates annually amongst the members. BEDA has been recognized by the EEC Commission as an official Liaison Committee.

6 Work of BEDA

The need for collaboration described in 3 required a programme for the member societies which included:

6.1 The exchange of publications, information and experiences on a regular basis.

6.2 Surveys being conducted on: i aspects of professionalism; ii entry requirements for professional societies and member societies in particular; iii educational facilities and qualifications.

These were regarded as essential for the foundation for the necessary harmonization of conditions of practice if the requirements of Article 57 of the Treaty of Rome were to be implemented without difficulty and resentment.

6.3 Studies and papers have been produced and discussions held on:

6.3.1 The mutual recognition of education qualifications.

There is a wide range of programmes in the different design disciplines for students within the EEC, at several levels of professional education, resulting in a variety of degrees, diplomas and certificates. For historical reasons, courses are sometimes more closely related to technical and scientific studies, whereas others are mainly based on fine art. In practice the design profession combines both technical and artistic elements. At present there is considerable movement within the EEC, both nationally and at Community level, towards harmonization based on a minimum four-year-programme of full-time study.

6.3.2 Common entry requirements for professional societies.

6.3.3 Study of the problems of intellectual and industrial property rights in connection with design.

6.3.4 A form of Draft Directive which could be proposed by BEDA in response to any initiative by the Community. In this respect the Commission's proposals for the Architectural Directive were examined. **It is to be noted that BEDA views with extreme concern the activities of other professions (architects and engineers generally, and nationally and individually) claiming as their exclusive rights areas where interests could and do overlap.**

6.3.5 Careful consideration has been given to the desire for the **Protection of Title** for the industrial designer together with a form of Certification and Register of Industrial Designers ratified by BEDA based on the **mutual recognition of Diplomas.**

7 Conclusion

7.1 BEDA was created by **professional** societies to tackle the **professional** problems of the designer within the EEC. The initiating societies believed that the best way to advance industrial design is to create the most favourable conditions for the designer to develop his talent and knowledge and therefore his work for the community's benefit. In industrial design competence is vested in the designer.

7.2 The size and the constituent societies of BEDA were determined by the implications of the Treaty of Rome. There is no implied fixed limit to its final size. Its aim is to produce, through the sensible coordination of its individual members, positive results economically and with enhanced efficiency. It is believed that these are the methods by which the qualities of industrial design benefit the community and that through them the professional societies will themselves grow.

7.3 The Association has been gratified that during its ten years of existence common experience and contact have produced a noticeable coming together in thinking and organizational patterns which transcend national boundaries.

IFI   The International Federation of Interior Designers
Address   Keizersgracht 321   Amsterdam 1002   Netherlands
Telephone   Amsterdam 25 49 59
Postal address   PO Box 19610   1000GP   Amsterdam   Netherlands
Secretary General   Leisbeth Hardenberg

What is IFI?
IFI—the International Federation of Interior Architects/Interior Designers, founded in 1963—is a non-political organization of Professional Associations of *Interior Architects/Interior Designers, and Schools and Institutions engaged in the field of Interior Architecture/Interior Design.

> * The term Interior Designer is used in most English-speaking countries, whereas the term Interior Architect, or its equivalent in other languages, is usual in a majority of other countries. Both terms are fully recognized by IFI and by all Member associations as being equivalent and having the same meaning.

What are its aims?
To coordinate all activities relevant to the profession in matters of Professional Codes of Conduct, Professional Practice, Registration and Professional Training, as well as to secure the integrity of the profession and the public confidence in Interior Architects-/Interior Designers.

What is it doing?
IFI organizes meetings, seminars and congresses, sets up working groups, research groups and committees, investigates and enquires into the situation of the profession, its current needs and demands. IFI contacts other international organizations, publishes reports and statements to promote and inform about its activities and points of view.

How is it organized?
IFI's membership is formed by national Associations of Interior Architects/Interior Designers, and of Associations and Institutions otherwise engaged in the field of Interior Architecture/Interior Design.
Individual membership can only be obtained by individual

251

persons specially appointed as Correspondents.

The ultimate authority of IFI is the General Assembly. Each Member association has a delegation to the Assembly. The delegations meet every second year at the General Assembly.

This Assembly takes decisions in all principal matters concerning activities and points of view of IFI.

The General Assembly elects the Executive Committee to organize the IFI activities as responsible body.

Committees and groups can be set up to deal with special matters.

A Secretary General is responsible for the IFI Secretariat.

IFI's aims and purposes

IFI is neutral in respect of politics, creed and trade unions. Its objectives are:

1 to raise the standard of interior architecture/interior design and of professional practice;
2 to improve and expand the contribution of interior architecture/interior design to society both in advanced and developing countries;
3 to initiate or further programs that are concerned with public health, safety and welfare, which apply interior architecture/interior design to the solution of problems affecting the material and psychological well-being of man;
4 to serve the interests of the interior architect/interior designer, in particular to promote the recognition of the professional designation and the professional practice;
5 to support the Member associations where feasible.

IFI does not aim to make a profit.

IFI seeks to attain these objectives in any manner suitable, and in particular by:

1 evolving a common definition of the profession;
2 promoting contacts among the national associations in respect of their codes of professional conduct, regulation of fee structure, and participation in competitions;
3 promoting the achievement of minimum standards in interior design education;
4 issuing IFI bulletins and promoting the exchange of publications;
5 organizing congresses, meetings, study trips, exhibitions and the participation in same;
6 assisting in the exchange of specialized teachers, speakers, trainees and students;
7 working towards collaboration with international institutions having similar objectives;
8 actively supporting, at a request of a Member association, the professional interests of that association within the scope of common interests.

Membership Categories
Members
—Professional Associations of Interior Architects/Interior Designers
—Professional Associations of Architects and/or Designers whose membership includes a Section of Interior Architects/Interior Designers

Associates
—Educational Institutes in the field of Interior Architecture/Interior Design
—Institutions with activities in the field of Interior Architecture/Interior Design
—Associations of interior design educators

Affiliates
—related international non-governmental organizations

Correspondents
—by invitation only

Admission procedure
Prospective Members must meet requirements of representativeness and professional standing. They must further:
—submit documentation (Articles, By-Laws, Constitution, Code of Conduct, Scales of Fees, etc)
—complete a Questionnaire
After examination of the above, the Executive Committee decides upon recommendation for admission at the General Assembly.
Prospective Associates must
—submit documentation.
Educational Institutes must meet the guidelines for admission.
After examination of the above, the Executive Committee decides upon recommendation for admission at the General Assembly.

Membership fees
Members pay an annual fee, based upon the number of their membership. Apply to Secretary General for current rates.

Index

Abandoned work: fees payable for 36, 37, 38, 40, 41, 42, 43, 52
Acceptance of budget: receiving client's 100, 196
Acceptance of fee letter: request for 37, 38, 39, 41, 42, 43; printed orders as 59; verbal 59; first stage only 59
Acceptance of staff job 167
Accounts: your 163
Accountancy 163, 164
Accountant 126, 163; hourly rate fees to 164, 167, 213, 215, 221
Adaptations: for size, range, colour 37, 42, 48; for departmental uses 42; foreign language 42; production costs 57; fees for 65
Additional fees 37, 39, 40, 41, 42, 43, 55, 65, 71
Advertisements: replying to 16; design of 53; fee letter structure for 41; copyright of 51; drawings for 73
Advertisers Annual 152
Advertising 141, 152
Advertising agents: discussions with 42; presentation of specimens to 150
Agent: acting as client's 96, 100, 101, 198, 221
Ancillary work: percentage fee for 68
Annual holiday/s 171
Annual returns 134, 163, 221
Approvals: of designs 82; Planning 222
Arbitrate: designer to 96, 103
Arbitration 227
Arbitration Act 1950 227
Architects: working with 154
Artists' agents 151
Artwork: finished 38, 42, 43, 47; at hourly rate fees 65; for textile design 69; designer entitled to original 225
Assistants 167
Audit 135, 221
Authorities: negotiations with 39
Automotive design: fee letter structure for 37

Bad workmanship 192
Balance sheet: annual 135; monthly or quarterly 134
Bank: accounts 160; balance 163; charges 140; manager 126, 215
Bankruptcy 91, 132, 163
'Before and after' stories 110
'Before' specimens 111
Being briefed 15
Bills: paid or unpaid 164
Blocks: as production costs 58, 94
Boat design 37
Book typography: fee letter structure for 41, 46
Booklet design: fee letter structure for 41
Book-keeping 163, 221
Break even 173
Breaking clauses 37, 38, 40, 42, 52, 68
Brief: contractual aspects of 30; confirmed in writing 30; not fulfilled 30; summary of in fee letter 37, 38, 39, 41, 42, 43; changes to 37, 39, 40, 41, 42, 43, 44; 55, 83, 202; in design report 88, 89
Briefing: asking questions at 31, 52; client's at 33
Budgets: cost 40; collated 48, 97; client's 52; tenders compared with 92 (see also Capital outlay budget; First year budget; Personal budget; Revenue and expenditure budget)
Business correspondence 27
Business letters 16 to 28

Calligraphy: fee letter structure for 41
Capital outlay budget 136
Cancellation by client 52
Captions: advising on 41; drafting 113, 114
Carpet design (see Rugs and carpets)
Cartoons: fees for 70
Case histories 110 (see also Job histories)

255

Cash book 164

Catalogues: fee letter structure for designing 41; filing 161; for reference 216

Categories of Practice (SIAD) 36, 37, 38, 39, 40, 41, 43

Ceramics design: fee letter structure for 37

Change of use 222

Checking: final accounts 40, 50, 102; proofs 42, 49, 86; prototypes 37, 47, 85; at hourly rate fees 66

'Cheques drawn' slips 164

Circulation: fees according to 70

Cleaning: 131; window; equipment 137

Clients: finding 128, 145

Clients' own materials and labour 41, 68, 210

Clients' permission to send out photographs 113; to publicize appointments 155

Code of Professional Conduct (SIAD) 14, 70; all Clauses 238

Colour separations: fees 48

Colourways: alternative 38, 48; additional 69

Commissions: introductory 75; offered by contractor, supplier, agent 75; paid to person or business 75; Codes of Conduct relevant to 75; exchanged with another designer 75

Committees and panels: fees for attendance at 71, 177 (see also Meetings)

Competitions: open and limited 154

Competitive clients 29, 34

Component: specially designed 93

Consultancies 37, 63, 72; fee instalments for 56; fees for 74; meaning of 176; starting date; invoicing 203; renewals of 203; increases to 203

Consumer goods design 37

Contingencies: unforseen 136, 171, 196, 198; contractors' 193, 196

Contracts: placing 92, 198; placing on client's behalf 38, 40, 48, 99, 101; placed direct by client 68, 99; value of, if placed by client 68; legal rules about placing 91; placing in own name 99, 102; placed by clients' purchasing department 101; 'cost plus' 193; main 194

Contracting for a client 48, 91, 186; fees for 71; procedure 91

Contractor/s: remedial work 50, 56; selecting 91; who will pay 92

Contractors' accounts: retentions 50; checking final 40, 50, 92, 102; certifying 40, 50, 56, 92, 103; interim payments 92, 198

Conversion: premises for 41

Copyright: ownership and conveyance of 37, 38, 40, 41, 42, 43, 51, 53, 225; for book illustration 69; identification of drawings for 82; instructions on photographs 115; in invoicing 205; as industrial property 222; salaried designer's rights to 225; of photographs 226

Copyright Act 1956 and 1968; 222, 225

Corporate identity programmes 45; essential components of 45; survey and report for 45; extra work for 57; special presentation of 57; implementation of 66; (see also House styles)

Costs: approximate estimate of 38, 39, 46, 53; firm estimate of 38; guide to probable 39; discussing with TV script writers and technicians 41; allowed for in fees 57, 65, 173; charged separately 57; production 58; against fees 58; non-chargeable 72; invoicing 106 (see also Production costs)

Costs chargeable: special 37, 39, 40, 42, 57, 60

Credits: design 37, 39, 40, 41, 42, 43, 54, 115

Credit accounts 102, 200

Credit notes 105, 212

Creditors 133

Danger points 92, 99, 198

Date schedules 77

Day rate fees 41, 54, 67, 177

Debtors 213, 214

Decisions: verbal 84

Decimal numbering (see Business letters)

Decorations 127, 136

Decorative building materials design: fee letter structure for 39

Defects liability period 92, 199, 209; work at end of 40, 50; six months or twelve months 50; completion of work 56; invoicing at end of 109, 209

Delivery: supervising 38, 49; charges 58; date in specification 94; address in specification 94

Demolition of exhibitions 50

Design administration: anatomy of 15

Design and Industries Association 232
Design Copyright Act 1968 222
Design Council 145, 146, 147, 242; slide
library 113; Designer Selection
Service 145, 147; Design Centres 146;
Record of Designers 147
Design Magazine 146
Design notes 87
Design office: accountancy system 78;
setting up 123; position 123; heating
for 124, 137; lease 125, 127;
decorations 127, 136; light fittings
128, 137; stationery 140; furniture
and shelving for 129, 137; floor
covering for 130, 137; curtains for
130, 137; office, domestic and studio
equipment for 129, 137 (see also
Telephone)
Design registration: 51
Design reports: hourly rate fees for 72,
87; draft framework for 87
Designers: working with other 154
Development work 37, 38, 42, 47, 65;
extra fees for 47; on product design
47; record of modification during 47;
time spent on 65; hourly rate fees for
85; monthly invoices for 85
Diary notes 35, 84
Die/s: as production costs 59
Directory of Designers' Services 153
Disabled staff 168, 220
Discounts 96
Dismantling: clause in exhibition
specifications 189, 190
Displacing another designer 34
Display accessories design: fee letter
structure for 39
Display design: asking questions about
at a briefing 32; fee letter structure
for 39; copyright 52; first multiple use
52; production of multiple 71; lump
sum fee for 71; percentage fee for 71;
reduced fee for 71; contracting
procedure for 91; specification for 95
District Surveyor 186
Domestic equipment design: fees as
royalties for 73
Drawing equipment 137
Drawing materials 140
Drawings: job numbers used on 76;
identification of 81; copyright of 82
Dress accessories design: fee letter
structure for 38
Dress and fashion (see Fashion design)
Dyelines 58

Editorial material: design of 51;
copyright position 51; to the press
116, 155
Editorial notes 113, 115
Editorial publicity 110
Electrical work 68
Electronic goods design: fee letter
structure for 37
Engineering design expertise 147
Engineering product design: fee letter
structure for 37; development work
on 47; record of modifications to 47;
shop drawings for; fixed fees for 64
Engineers: structural 57; heating 57;
ventilating 57
Entertaining 141, 157
Estimates 50; obtaining from contractors
and suppliers 40; making
approximate 46; competitive 48;
approval of 49; fees for cancellation
after obtaining 52; single 93; collated
97; firm and guess 194
Estimating fees 63
Exclusive services: clause in retaining fee
contract 74, 174
Exhibition design: briefing for 32; fee
letter structure for 39; approximate
estimate of cost for 46; copyright in
52; fee instalments for 56; percentage
fees for 67; lump sum fee for 69
Exhibition sites: suitability of 41;
overseas 48, 49; maintenance of 49;
clearing away 49; survey of 61
Exhibitions: tenders and estimates for
48; supervising production and
installation 48; installation overseas
48, 56; maintenance of 49; clearing
away: 49; costs in production budget
58; client's own materials 68; date
schedules for 77; contracting
procedure for 91, 93; specifications
for 186; invoicing for 210; thematic
217
Exhibits: dispersal of 49
Expenditure 142, 165; and revenue 142
Expenses: chargeable 37, 40, 41, 42, 43,
58, 166; subsistence 56, 58; travelling
48, 56, 58; invoiced monthly 56;
out-of-pocket 58; invoicing 104, 106
Extra work (see Fees for extra work)

Fashion design: fee letter structure for
38; fixed fees for 64; fees for 70; fees
as percentage on garments 70; fees as
royalties for 73;

Fashion drawings (see Fees according to circulation)

Fashion designers: commissioned 39, 70; collections prepaid by 39, 70; submission by, to buyers or wholesalers 70

Feasibility study: 41, 60; inspecting alternative properties as 61 (see also Design Reports)

Fee categories 63

Fee contract 15, 36; carbon copy of 16; completed 60; exclusive services clause in 74

Fee instalments 37, 39, 40, 42, 56; for retaining and consultancy fees 56; invoicing 107

Fee letter: writing 15, 16, 36; acceptance of 15, 37, 40, 41, 42, 59; drafting 36; structure of 36; conclusion to 37, 39, 41, 42, 43, 59

Fee negotiations: intermediate 15

Fees: in stages 37, 38, 39, 42, 50; reducing 54, 75, 202, 212; entitlement to 68; nominal 74, 84

Fees according to circulation: 70

Fees for contracting in interior design: 71; in graphic design 71; lump sum 71; hourly rate 71

Fees for surveys (see Measured surveys)

Fees for extra visits (see Visits)

Fees for extra work 30, 42, 43, 55, 202

Filing 131, 161; essential records 15; slide and photo 117; correspondence 81; slides and photos 117; drawings 118, 161, 162; job sheets 118; record photographs 118; slides 118; samples 118, 161; typesettings 118, 161; artwork 161; copy negatives 161; reference material 161; specimens 162

Film setting design: fee letter structure for 41

Film graphics: fee letter structure for 41

Final accounts: checking and certifying 40, 50, 92; from contractors and suppliers 102

Final designs: preparation and submission of 39

Finished work: 156; submission of 85; identified 85; specification notes with 85; delivering 85; specimens of 110

Finishes 188, 191

Fire Officers 186

Fire proofing 186

First aid box 131, 137

First batch/runs: checking 37, 42, 49, 85

First year budget 135, 165

Fixed (or lump sum) fees 52, 63, 66; quoted between brackets 64; to assess 65; non-chargeable costs allowed for in 65; for adaptations 66; for textile design 69; invoicing 105

Floor coverings: linoleum and plastic 69; fee estimate for design of 69; for design office 137

Floor loading 186

Foreign language settings 217

Free-lance: working as 170

Furniture design: fee letter structure for 37; fixed fees for 64; fees as royalties for 73

Getting paid 200

Graphic design: fee letter structure for 42; adaptations for 48; checking proofs or samples of 49; supervision of production 49; restricted copyright of 51; special costs for 57; production costs of 58; fixed fees for 63

Greeting cards: fees for 70

Guess estimating 194, 196, 216, 217, 218

Guide to expenditure 218

Handling charges 75, 99, 102; percentage 102, 166, 198, 209

Heating 124, 137, 139

Hire or sale: clause in exhibition specifications 188, 189

Hour of time: selling cost of 63

Hourly rate fees 52, 55, 56, 63, 65; monthly invoices for 65, 85; for implementation of corporate identity programme 67; current rate of 66; assistants' 67; subject to review 67; increased to allow for increased costs and overheads 67; for textile design 69; time sheets essential for 78; for development work 85; invoicing 106; how to calculate your own 170, 173; twice yearly check on 174

Hours of work: for staff 167

House marks (see Trade marks)

House styles 45; essential components of 45; applied to various items 45; survey and report for 46; logotype for 45; colour scheme for 45; rationalisation and condensation 46; stage one formula for 45; extra work 55; application of, at hourly rate fees 66; your own 184 (see also Corporate identity programmes)

Household linens: fee estimating for design of 69

Illustration/s: fee letter structure for 43; rough sketches for 46; technical 46, 70; commercial 48; in design reports 183
Income Tax 141, 167, 221; deduction for, from staff salaries: 167
Industrial property 222, 225
Injury to persons and property 191
Inscape 39
Installation: supervising 40, 48
Institute of Contemporary Arts (ICA) 245
Instructions: receiving client's 40; verbal 59, 84; recording in writing 84
Insurance broker 126, 214
Insurances 139, 186, 187, 191, 220
Interiors: preliminary designs for 46; final designs for 46; approximate estimate of cost for 46; tenders and estimates for 48; supervising production and installation of 48; costs in production budget for 58; measured survey for 61; low budget for 67; selection of furniture for 67; clients' own materials and labour for 68; date schedules for 77; contracting procedure for 91; specification for 190
Interior design; briefing 33; fee letter structure for 39; changes to brief 55; lettering and signs for 58; percentage fees for 67; lump sum or hourly rate fees for 63; fees in budget 166; invoicing 204
International Council of Graphic Design Associations (ICOGRADA): 247
International Council of Societies of Industrial Designers (ICSID): 245
Inventions 223
Introductions: personal 19; following up 150
Invoices 15, 104, 200; fees 56; monthly 56; formula for hourly rates 65; when to invoice 104; costs and expenses 104, 106; setting out 105; carbon copies of 105, 164; purchase 200, 209; sales 200.
Invoicing 104, 200; lump sum (fixed) fees 105; costs 106; hourly rates 106; chargeable expenses 107; percentage fees 107; fee instalments 107, 202; regularity of 200; retainers and consultancies 202; for interiors 204;

for exhibitions 210

Jewellery design: fee letter structure for 37
Job: applying for 16
Job files 81
Job histories 118
Job numbers 76; on job sheets 79; on orders 79; in budgets 165
Job sheets 78, 79, 80

Knitted textile design: fee letter structure for 38

Labels: house style applied to 45; corporate identity applied to 45; to rationalise and condense ranges of 46; adaptations of 48
Laminates design: fee letter structure for 38; fee estmating for 69
Late information (TV): 41, 54
Layouts: finished 42
Legal expenses 136, 214
Letterheads 16; essential ingredients of 17; postal code for 17; typed 16; house style applied to 45; corporate identity applied to 45; estimating fee for designing 64; designing your own 127; printed 137
Lettering: fee letter structure for 41; for interior design and exhibitions 58
Lettering and numbering: business letters 20; simple reports 89; survey reports 179
Lighting 139
Lighting consultants 57
Limited company 133, 221
Liquidation 133
Local activities 153
Lump sum fees (see Fixed fees)

Magazine typography: fee letter structure for 41
Magazines: trade and technical 113
Magazine illustration 70
Maintenance: supervising 40, 48, 49, 50; office 168; in specifications 188, 189
Making good: exhibition sites 49
Marine goods design: fee letter structure for 37
Market research 61
Measured surveys: additional fees for 40, 61, 72; interior design 61; exhibition design 61; detailed 61; plans and elevations for 61; hourly rate fees 72; set of dimensioned drawings for 72;

travelling time for 72; photography for 110; invoicing fee for 209

Medical goods design: fee letter structure for 37

Meetings: fees for attendance at 71; diary notes of 84; (see also Committees and panels)

Models 45, 57; scale 45; chargeable 58; cost of, allowed for in fixed fees 65

Modifications: permitted 37, 38, 40, 41, 42, 43, 53; keeping record of 47

Nameplate 127, 136

National insurance 141, 220; deduction from staff salaries 168; employees' contribution to 168; card 168; stamps 168, 220; sick benefits under 168

New address notices 137

Newspaper illustration: fees for 70

Newspaper typography: fee letter structure for 41

Non-completion: damages for 193

Notice to staff 167

Office running expenses (see Overheads)

Offices, Shops and Railway Premises Act 1963 132, 220

Orders: carbon copy of 16; placing on client's behalf 40; placing 49; job numbers on 76; legal rules about placing 91

Order books 79, 80

Ordering procedure 81

Organisations concerned with design 145, 146, 147

Overheads 171; increased 67, 135, 138, 147

Overlays: production costs chargeable 58

Overtime 167, 187, 191

Ownership of designs 51

Packs: adaptations for 48

Package design: fee letter structure for 41

Parcels: maximum weight and dimensions for 86; by train 86

Partnership 132, 170

Patent Acts 1949 222, 223

Patent Agents 126, 222, 224, 225; Chartered Institute of 222

Patent Office 222, 223, 225

Patents Bill 1976/77 222

Paying bills 221; for your client 102; for small orders 102; small items 102, 163

Paying-in book 164; slips 164

Payment/s: of fees 56; stage, progress,

interim 56, 198; on delivery of book illustration 69

Percentage fees: fee letter structure for 39, 40, 63; for abandoned work 52; instalments 56; progress or interim payments of 56; final balance of 56; retention of 56; based on estimated costs 56, 67; based on firm contract price 56; based on lowest tender 56; stage payments of 56; flat rate quarterly instalments of 56; for interior, exhibition, shops and shop-fitting design 67; sliding scale for 52; increased out of scale 67; reduced for selection of stock furniture 40, 67; on client's own materials 68; invoicing 107

Periodical: work commissioned by 70

Personal budget 63, 135, 136, 170

Perspectives 57; coloured 45; black and white 45; allowed for in fixed fees 64;

Petty cash: expenditure 58; job numbers on chits 76; 160

Photo albums 117

Photo copier 130

Photo files 110, 117

Photograph/s: cost of allowed for in fixed fees 65; to the press 113; client's permission to send out 113

Photographic equipment 130, 138

Photography: fee letter structure for 41; record 112, 141

Photographs: copyright of 226

Plagiarism 227

Point of sale design: fee letter structure for 41

Point paper: transferring design to 38

Post Office: messenger service 86, 140; 'Railex' service 86

Postage: chargeable 58, 140; post book for 160; Recorded Delivery parcels 160

Poster design: fee letter structure for 41; restricted copyright of 51

Preliminary designs: preparation of 15, 37, 38, 39, 42; submission of 15, 37, 38, 42, 82; agreed amendments to 39; quantity of 44; alternative 45; for house styles 45; copyright of 51; breaking clause on 52; special costs 57; on colour slides 57; on film 57; production costs not chargeable 58; acceptance of first stage only 59; research as part of 60

Premises: suitability of 41, 60; tenancy of 220

Presentation of design proposals 57
Press: sending material to 116; cuttings 116; list 113, 116
Price: increases 196, 218; lists 216
Prime cost (pc) 188, 190, 192
Principal: acting as 91, 99, 102, 198, 210, 221
Print: contracting procedure for 91; specification for 93; run-on prices for 94; estimate on approximate specification 216
Printers: discussions with 42; specifications for 42
Product design: briefing on 31; engineering 37; fee letter structure for 37; development work on 47; record of modifications 47; adaptations for 48; supervision of production 49; conveyance of full copyright 51; models or prototypes chargeable 58; fixed fees for 64
Production: supervision of 15, 37, 40, 42, 48, 66, 92; advising during production 37, 42, 48, 66; completion of 38, 40, 49; first runs of 38
Production costs: budget for 58; of reports 60; schedule of final 206, 207, 208, 209; guess estimating 216
Professional advisers 126
Profit and loss account 164
Profit/s: margins 63, 173
Progress charts 76
Progressing: the job 15; work 76
Projection equipment 130, 138
Promoting your services 147
Prototypes: preparing drawings for 47; fees due for 53; chargeable 58; special 93; of display units 95 (see also Checking prototypes)
Provisional sums (see Prime cost)
Public holidays 171
Publicity 110, 112, 113, 116
Publicity agents: discussions with 42
Publicity design: fee letter structure for 42
Publicity literature 156
Publicizing: the job 15; your appointments 155 (see also Client's permission)
Punctuation 17

Quantity surveyor 57, 193, 199, 218
Quantum meruit 53, 202

Rate cards 153
Rates: increased 66, 138

Receipts 213
Recorded delivery 86, 161
Redecoration: reserve for 141; office 168
Re-design: copyright position of 52
References: colour and material 85; duplicate set of 85; about financial status
Registered designs 222, 223
Registered Designs Act 1949 222
Registered Office 134
Registering a name 127, 220
Rehearsals (TV): collaborating with producer at 41
Remedial work: supervision of 50, 209
Rent: increased 67; facilities included in 124; standing order for payment of 163
Repeat: putting design into 38, 69
Repetitive work: for interior jobs 70; for shop fitting 73
Replacements: reserve for 141
Report writing: simple 87; survey 179
Reports: (see Design reports and Survey reports)
Reproduction fee 115, 226
Reproduction rights: 51; first British 51, 69; foreign 51
Research 15; special 36, 60; on traditional design 61; fixed fees for 63, 72; report based on 87, 88 (see also Design reports)
Retainer contract: exclusivity clause in 34
Retainers: 37, 117; starting date 202; invoicing 202; renewals of and increases to 203
Retaining fees 63, 72, 74, 174; instalments of 56; exclusive services clause in 74, 174; design programme for 174; assessing 176
Retention: of final fees 49, 56, 109, 199; of percentage of contractors' bills 50, 199; of full copyright 51; of letters and drawings 162, 221
Revenue 143; gross estimated 164
Revenue and expenditure budget 164
Royal Society of Arts (RSA) 231
Royalties 38, 39, 41, 61, 63; importance of copyright position 51, 73; fees as 61, 73; irrecoverable advance of 61; fee letter about 61, 73; legal agreement for 62, 73; percentage based on wholesale price 62, 73; VAT excluded from 62, 73; for book illustration 69; Licenses granted 73
Rugs and carpets design: fee letter

structure for 38; adaptations for 48; fee estimating for 69

Rules and regulations: exhibition organisers' 186

Running the office 63, 172

Safety regulations 186, 221

Sailing equipment design: fee letter structure for 37

Salaried appointment: designer in 170

Salaries: increases to assistant's 67; payment of staff 167; deductions of Income Tax and National Insurance from 167

Salary: increase to own 67; own basic 170

Sale outright: clause in exhibition specifications 189

Scale drawings 41

Samples 216

Secrecy 81

Secretary: taking on 167

Services provided: in fee letter 37, 38, 39, 41, 42, 43, 71; amended 37

Shop drawings: for engineering product design 48; in client's own drawing office 48; designer not responsible for checking 49

Shop fittings design: fee letter structure for 39; percentage fees for 67

SIAD (see Society of Industrial Artists and Designers)

Sick leave 171

Sign/s: exterior 45; house style applied to 45; corporate identity applied to 45; for interior design 58

Signed work 39, 43, 54

Silver design: fee letter structure for 37

Site: suitability of 60; supervision 177

Sketch design proposals: 39; rough 43

Slides 57; colour 110; to Design Council Slide Library 113; files 117

Society of Industrial Artists and Designers: 35, 53, 145, 152, 233; designer's professional society 14; development work 47; modifications 53; late information 54; travelling time 55; repetitive work 70; 'Designer' Magazine 146; Designers' Register 146; Visible Record of Designers' Work 146; Staff Vacancy Register 146; Competitions 155 (see also Code of Professional Conduct; Categories of Practice)

Sole trader 132

Solicitors 62, 83, 126, 133, 134, 176, 214, 220, 223, 227

Souvenir design: fee letter structure for 37

Special clauses in fee letters 52; to cover increases in hourly rates 67

Specialist contractors 188, 189, 191

Specialists and technicians 38, 44

Specifications 38, 40, 42, 47, 93, 94, 95; checking materials and services included in 68; writing 91; variations to 92; general clauses 93; administrative instructions 94, 95; for exhibitions 186; standard clauses 187, 191

Specimens: free 37, 39, 42, 43, 53; of work in production 111; master set of 112

Sports goods design: fee letter structure for 37

'Sprats to catch mackerel' 74

Square metre costs 195, 217

Staff: amenities for 132, 220; confirming appointment of 167; agreed salaries 167; deductions for Income Tax and National Insurance 167; hours of work 167; annual holiday 167; overtime 167; notice to be given 167; written acceptance of job by 167 (see also Disabled staff)

Stamps design: fee letter structure for 41

Standing orders 163

Statements: job numbers used on 76, 105, 200, 201, 211

Stationery: adaptations for departmental use 42; to rationalize ranges of 46; office 140; printed 140

Stationery design; fee letter structure for 41

Storage space 125, 137

Strike-offs of colour: inspecting 38, 69

Sub-contractors 186, 188, 191

Subscriptions 140, 154; standings orders for payment of 163

Supervising: work in workshops and studios 40; construction and erection (TV) 41; production and maintenance 48

Supplanting another designer 75, 149

Survey (see Measured survey)

Survey reports: initial 38, 42, 60; number of copies of 60, 184; in depth 179; production costs of 60, 184; fixed fees for 64, 72; programme for 179; illustrations in 183; framework for 180; binding of 184

Symbols (see Trade marks and symbols)

Synthetic fabrics design: fee letter structure for 38; fee estimating for 69

Teaching: slides 110; part time 123
Technical illustration (see Illustration)
Telephone: number 17; long distance calls chargeable 58; British Telecom Plan 107; 124; answering services 124; getting installed 126; installation costs 136; charges 139
Television setting design 41; copyright 41; fee for repeats 52; daily (day) rate fees for 67
Television graphics: fee letter structure for 41
Tendering procedure 189
Tenders: inviting 40, 91, 95; obtaining and submitting 41, 92; fees for cancellation after obtaining 53; amendments to 92; summarizing 92; competitive not appropriate 93; how long to prepare 97; single 97: collated 97; competitive and single 193
Tenders and estimates: obtaining 48; collating 194
Textile design: fee letter structure for 38; printed and woven 38; adaptations for 48; supervision of production 48; restricted copyright for printed 51; research on traditional 61; fixed fees for 64, 69; collection of 69; commissioned 69; hourly rate fees for 69; development work on 69; putting design into repeat 68; additional colourways for 69; first strike off of colours 69; finished artwork 69; fees as royalties for 73; mounting for submission 82; finding clients for 152
Textile designers 39; commissioned 39; collections prepared by 39
Theatre setting design 39, 42; fee letter structure for 42
Time 64; selling value of 64, 65, 171, 172; on development 65; assistant's 72, 170; basic cost 78, 170; off 171; unsaleable 171, 172 (see also Travelling time)
Time sheets 78, 202; job numbers used on 76

Time table 39
Toy design: fee letter structure for 37
Trade Marks Act 1938 222
Trade marks and symbols: fee letter structure for 41; alternative preliminary designs for 45; as industrial property 222, 224; registration of 223; search for registration 224
Trade union labour 187, 189
Transport: clause in exhibition specification 188, 189
Travel 136, 141
Travel goods design: fee letter structure for 37
Travelling time 37, 39, 40, 41, 42, 55, 177
Type face design: fee letter structure for 41
Typesetting/s: as production costs 58, 217; allowed for in fixed fees 65
Typewriter 129, 137; serviced 169
Typing 140
Typography: fee letter structure for 41

Vanside: house style applied to 45
Variations: agreed 92; in writing 92; in specifications 188, 192
VAT 62, 142
Visits: agreed number of 37, 38, 39, 44, 71; extra 37, 39, 40, 42, 44, 55, 71; to factories, showrooms, branch offices 44; hourly rate fees for 44; to contractors and suppliers 49; travelling time for 55

Wage awards 218
Wallpaper design: fee letter structure for 38; adaptations for 48; fee estimating for 69
Working drawings: finished 15; finished working drawings 38, 40, 41, 42, 47, 49; fees due after completion of 53; production costs chargeable 58; at hourly rate fees 65; completion of 91 (see also Shop drawings)
Working for nothing 35, 52
Working on spec 35, 152